America in World Politics

America in World Politics

Foreign Policy and Policy-Makers Since 1898

PETER A. POOLE

PRAEGER PUBLISHERS
New York

Published in the United States of America in 1975
by Praeger Publishers, Inc.
111 Fourth Avenue, New York, N.Y. 10003

© 1975 by Praeger Publishers, Inc.

Library of Congress Cataloging in Publication Data

Poole, Peter A
  America in world politics.

  Bibliography: p.
  Includes index.
  1. United States—Foreign relations—20th century.
2. World politics—20th century. I. Title.
E744.P65   327.73   74-31390
ISBN 0-275-51090-5
ISBN 0-275-85190-7 (pbk.)

Printed in the United States of America

To Rosemary Poole

Contents

	Preface	ix
1	From Continentalism to Imperialism	3
2	Theodore Roosevelt and the New Internationalism	21
3	Wilson and the Collapse of World Order	39
4	Wilson and the Postwar World	54
5	The Rise and Fall of the Rule of Law	71
6	The Road to War, 1935–41	86
7	World War II: Summitry and Strategy	105
8	Origins of the Cold War	120
9	Containment and Reconstruction	139
10	Confrontation in Asia	160
11	The Eisenhower-Dulles Era	180
12	Kennedy and Khrushchev	201
13	Indochina: From Truman to Johnson	219
14	Kissinger and Nixon: The Policy of Détente	235
15	Foreign Policy Problems Today	252
	Index	258

Preface

America emerged from a half-century of continental isolation in 1898 with the physical attributes of a great power. But most Americans still had little contact with the outside world; they were quite confident that all virtue had been concentrated on their side of the Atlantic. As a result, both Theodore Roosevelt and Woodrow Wilson found it easier to persuade their fellow countrymen that the world was in a mess than to get them to pursue any long-term efforts to improve the situation, particularly if it meant entering into "entangling alliances."

In 1940, after Hitler defeated France, the liberal internationalists came into their own. These were men like Henry Stimson, who could see the strengths of Teddy Roosevelt's amateur *Realpolitik* and Wilson's lofty idealism. In the crucible of World War II was forged the first generation of Americans who were willing to assume major, long-term responsibilities for world peace and order. Some would say they greatly overdid it—far exceeding the bounds of what America could and should undertake as a nation. It has become fashionable for historians of American foreign policy to blame the leaders of the Truman administration for both the cold war and a quarter-century of tragic blunders in Indochina. But I believe that their central creative concept—the reconstruction of Western Europe and Japan—weighs far more heavily in the scales of history than the mistakes they made during the incredibly fast-paced years between Potsdam and the Korean War.

No one would claim infallibility for the makers of American foreign policy. But it seems equally wide of the mark to posit a tragic flaw in the American character that forces the United States to be a constant danger to humanity. American policy in this century has generally been conceived by men who worked within a loose framework of shared values; while seldom dictating an exact course, it left them enough latitude to fashion their own responses to novel events.

To illustrate this point, I can cite such random events as Dean Acheson's realization that there could be "only one decision" on the question of aid to Greece and Turkey, Robert Kennedy's plea for no surprise attack on the Russian missile sites in Cuba, and Henry Kissinger's belief that America had a duty not to let Israel be destroyed in 1973—and not to let it advance into Egypt.

My preparation for this book began when I was a student in Samuel Flagg Bemis's seminar on American diplomatic history at Yale. For the following five and a half years (1959–64), I was a foreign service officer, serving first in Cambodia and then in the Bureau of African Affairs. Those assignments allowed me a glimpse of the real world of foreign affairs. During those years, and later when I began to teach, I was privileged to interview some of the authors of American postwar policy: Dean Acheson, John M. Allison, McGeorge Bundy, William P. Bundy, Marshall Green, Averell Harriman, Roger Hilsman, George F. Kennan, Dean Rusk, and John Carter Vincent. Other debts are noted in the footnotes and in the short reading lists at the end of each chapter.

I am grateful to my students at Howard University, the Naval War College, and George Washington University for their reactions to material contained in these chapters.

I appreciate the help of Denise Rathbun of Praeger; she has been a patient and constructive editor. My thanks also to Gladys Shimasaki and Mary Swinyer for their friendly encouragement while typing the manuscript.

PETER A. POOLE

Sugar Hill, N.H., and
Washington, D.C.
November 1974

America in World Politics

1

From Continentalism to Imperialism

Eighteen ninety-eight was an astonishing year in the history of American foreign policy. Within a few months, America abandoned its comfortable habit of isolation, seized what was left of the Spanish Empire, and proclaimed itself a new world power. Then, just as swiftly, Americans began to doubt the wisdom of what they had done. The initial burst of imperialism seemed to blaze an intensely clear path into the twentieth century. Yet the clarity lasted only an instant—long enough, however, to spark the first great revolution in American foreign policy.

In fact, the events of 1898 marked a revival, not the beginning, of America's conscious involvement in world affairs. George Washington had admonished his countrymen to avoid foreign entanglements; he had not told them to forgo foreign relations. For half a century, his successors made skillful use of diplomacy to secure their weak foothold east of the Alleghenies and enlarge it into a vast continental domain, while avoiding foreign alliances and commitments. *Manifest Destiny*

By mid-century, some Americans began to look overseas and covet territories in the Caribbean and Pacific. In 1853, Commodore Perry was sent to "open" Japan to American commerce. In dispatches sent home, he proposed that he be allowed to declare an American protectorate over Formosa and seize one of the Ryukyus (the island group that includes Okinawa) as a naval base. His government told him, however, that it would be embarrassing to raise the American flag over these islands only to have to lower it at the first foreign challenge, because Congress would never pay to defend such distant outposts. (Either Perry was a century ahead of his time or MacArthur and Dulles were a century too late!)

Continentalism: The Inward-looking Policy

Perry's scheme and others like it met with no success in the 1850s. America was deeply absorbed in the problems of developing the continent and was also approaching its greatest domestic convulsion of the century. The original issue was whether to allow the westward extension of slave territory. No one doubted that this great debate took precedence over the question of overseas expansion. In some instances, however, the two subjects became linked. A movement to annex Hawaii in this period collapsed over the question of whether those racially diverse islands could ever claim statehood. And Northerners killed the movement to annex Cuba, because they feared that Southern Democrats wanted to absorb Cuba as a new slave territory.

During the 1860s and 1870s, therefore, America was far too preoccupied with civil war and reconstruction to engage in the luxury of competing with the European powers for overseas colonies. The 1880s were a decade of intensive development, much of it financed by loans from England and France.

Unwilling to enter into alliances or to divert scarce dollars to military programs, America tacitly relied on the British fleet and Foreign Office to shield it from world politics. A century later Japan followed a parallel course, relying on the United States for external defense while devoting all of its own resources to rapid economic growth. In both cases, that of America in the nineteenth century and that of Japan after World War II, the "protected" power seemed at first to have very little choice in the foreign policy it adopted. But the range of options quickly increased as the nation's economic base—and war-making potential—expanded.

Americans in the second half of the nineteenth century were

certain that theirs was the greatest civilization the world had ever known. On the whole, they also believed that it was enough to set an example for other nations, which they could follow if they wanted to. However, there were a few Americans who felt that a more active approach was called for. They had absorbed the message of social Darwinism, which posited a world divided into strong and weak societies, with only the former able to survive. In order for America to prove itself worthy of surviving, it would have to plunge into profitable competition with other great powers to save the world's colored races from their backwardness. While bringing them the Christian gospel and all the benefits of science and technology, the United States would also transform them into willing buyers of the surplus products of American farms and factories. *Markets*

Mahan and Mercantilist Imperialism

The most influential writer on this subject was an American naval officer, Alfred Thayer Mahan. His concept of mercantilist imperialism became the bible of American expansionists and made an even deeper impression on political and military leaders abroad. In essence, Mahan argued that a nation's strength depended on maintaining a favorable balance of trade and that this in turn required the acquisition of colonies to serve as markets, a merchant marine to carry the goods, a navy capable of defending the nation's commerce, and bases and coaling stations to allow the navy to operate far from its home waters.

Mahan was a gifted and energetic scholar-publicist, although he spent his early career in routine shore duty or at sea in full-rigged frigates and paddle steamers—the major vessels of the fleet until the 1880s. Mahan's most enlightening experience in this period was a tour he made of British imperial outposts from China west through the Indian Ocean. He was assigned in 1886 to the U.S. Naval War College, where he lectured on the rise of the British imperial system and the need for the United States to follow the same principles.

In 1890, Mahan published his lectures as *The Influence of Sea Power upon History*, which brought him instant fame. His book was translated into the main European languages and Japanese. The kaiser made it required reading for German naval officers. British leaders hailed Mahan for explaining to them the secrets of their own imperial success.

At home, Mahan provided the rationale for a navy-building program that accelerated during the 1890s and early years of the twentieth century. He also strongly influenced the advocates of Hawaiian annexation, who failed in 1892 but triumphed in 1898. Mahan continued to press his views for many years in articles and as a member of the Naval Policy Board. During President Cleveland's second administration (1893–97),[1] Mahan was the mentor and frequent dinner guest of a circle of progressive Republicans who were destined soon to carry out great changes in American foreign policy.

The Hay-Adams Group

During the Democratic interregnum of Cleveland's presidency, a small group of wealthy, well-educated, progressive Republicans met regularly at the adjoining homes of John Hay and Henry Adams, across Lafayette Square from the White House. The group included Theodore Roosevelt, Henry Cabot Lodge, and various like-minded senators, journalists, and State Department officials. Cecil Spring-Rice of the British embassy was another regular member of the group (and was in later years to become Theodore Roosevelt's main private channel of communication with the British government).

Lodge, the cool, somewhat arrogant senator from Massachusetts, had been Henry Adams's student at Harvard; there were many links of friendship and marriage between the two families. Henry Adams was temperamentally unable to carry on the Adams family tradition of public service; a "stableman to statesmen,"

---

[1] President Cleveland, the only Democrat to occupy the White House from Buchanan to Wilson and the last true believer in "no foreign entanglements," stubbornly fought against the rising tide of native jingoism during his second term. Yet, ironically, Cleveland's forceful assertion of the Monroe Doctrine in the Anglo-Venezuelan dispute of 1895 released the public's pent-up chauvinism and helped make war with Spain a popular cause three years later.

in his own cynical phrase, he thrived on being close to the center of power and well informed of its mood and gossip. Yet he was also one of America's most original thinkers on foreign policy problems, and was perhaps the first American to articulate the view that his country's security was linked to the balance of power in Europe.

Theodore Roosevelt came to Washington as a Civil Service commissioner when he was still an impressionable young lawyer in his early thirties; he held that post from 1889 to 1895. Bright and extremely energetic, he became a protégé of Lodge, who was beginning to play an important role in the Senate.

John Hay, Adams's close friend and neighbor, had once been at the center of Washington politics as Lincoln's private secretary. He then spent a long period lobbying ineffectively for a high diplomatic post, during which time he also occupied himself with writing, foreign travel, and the cultivation of a wide social circle. Brilliant, charming, comfort-loving Hay was a realist in foreign affairs but not a convinced expansionist. Fate would place him in high office when the winds of empire would seem irresistible.

Thus, for almost the first time since the days of John Quincy Adams, there was a talented group in Washington whose main interest in life was foreign affairs. They had the imagination to realize that America would soon burst the bonds of continentalism and become a great world power—perhaps the main force in shaping human progress in the twentieth century. In their domestic views, the members of the Hay-Adams group were mainly "progressive" Republicans in that they wanted to use the machinery of government to right the worst socio-economic wrongs of the industrial revolution. The common thread of their views on domestic and foreign affairs was their advocacy of a much more powerful and active executive branch of government. The conservative wing of the Republican party was dominated by newly rich industrialists whom the progressives regarded as selfish reactionaries in domestic affairs and timid isolationists in their foreign policy views.

Both progressive and reactionary Republicans backed McKinley in 1896 because he seemed a pliable and persuasive front man for a divided party. McKinley ran on a moderately expansionist platform. (Even the conservatives felt the American people could use some diversion from their economic troubles at home.) McKinley's victory and Lodge's growing influence in the party made John Hay minister in London and Theodore Roosevelt assistant secretary of the Navy. Henry Adams bemoaned the end of leisurely after-dinner seminars on foreign policy. But the other members of his circle were delighted with their chance to translate words into action. Two months after McKinley's inauguration, Roosevelt wrote Mahan, "All I can do toward pressing our ideas into effect will be done."

Cuba offered the obvious opportunity to implement an expansionist policy. Since 1895, an insurrection against Spain's repressive rule had provoked increasingly cruel reprisals by the Spanish forces. A growing number of Americans, reacting to press reports of torture, starvation, and concentration camps, began to regard their country's failure to intervene as a national disgrace.

President Cleveland had resisted these pressures. But McKinley proved to be a man of no fixed views, although he doubtless hoped to avoid responsibility for declaring war on Spain. Throughout his first year in office, the attention of informed Americans focused on Cuba and the desperate efforts of Spanish leaders to find a solution that would be acceptable to the Cubans, to their own public, and to the United States.

The Spanish-American War

By the latter part of 1897, Roosevelt, along with most of the Hay-Adams group, regarded war as a certainty, and he began to think ahead to prizes that could be won in the Pacific. In September, he briefed McKinley on the need to attack the Philippines in the event of war. And in February 1898, he sent his famous cable ordering Commodore Dewey to begin "offensive operations in the Philippines" as soon as he should learn that war had been declared. The cable was sent along with a sheaf of similar orders to other commanders on a day when Secretary of the Navy Long left Roosevelt in charge of the Navy Department. When Long learned of the order, he angrily reminded Roosevelt that his instructions had been only "to look after the routine of the office while I got a quiet day off."

In fact, war was by now fast approaching. Ten days earlier, the U.S. battleship *Maine*, which was paying a "courtesy call" at Havana following some rioting there, exploded at her anchorage. Two hundred and sixty U.S. sailors died as a result. American newspapers fanned the flames of public indignation. A U.S. Navy investigation concluded that the explosion had probably been caused by a submarine mine. On March 27, McKinley yielded to Congressional pressure and sent Spain a virtual ultimatum offering to mediate the current struggle in Cuba but demanding independence for the insurgents.

No European power was willing to take the lead at this point in supporting Spain against the United States; therefore, the Spanish government was forced to seek a compromise that would avoid a clash with the United States and not provoke unrest at home. The reply, sent March 31, declined McKinley's offer of mediation and seemed to stop short of granting Cuba full independence. The American minister in Madrid considered this response conciliatory, but McKinley abandoned all caution. He asked Congress for the right to use American land and naval forces to "secure a full and final termination" of hostilities between the government of Spain and the people of Cuba.

A week later, Congress passed a resolution that recognized Cuba's independence, demanded that Spain withdraw its forces from Cuba and Cuban waters, and authorized McKinley to back this demand with land and naval power. In addition, Congress passed the Teller amendment, disclaiming any intention of retaining control of Cuba "except for the pacification thereof," and asserting its determination to return the government to the Cuban people as soon as the island was pacified.[2] Spain then

[2] Senator Teller of Colorado explained when he offered his amendment that his aim was to make it impossible for European governments to say the United States had gone to war to gain Cuba, "whatever we may do as to some other islands."

had little choice but to declare war on the United States. It did so on April 24, 1898, and the U.S. Congress responded in kind, making its declaration effective April 21.

As Lodge, Roosevelt, and all other proponents of war with Spain had hoped, the war itself was mercifully brief. Dewey proceeded as swiftly as possible to Manila Bay and defeated the Spanish squadron on May 1, 1898. The other major battle, for control of Cuba, was delayed by gross inefficiency and misman-agement in the War Department. But an expeditionary force of 18,000 men finally disembarked from Tampa on June 15. These troops, including the Rough Riders under Colonel Leonard Wood (with Roosevelt assuming command when they landed), stormed and captured the well-defended heights around Santiago by July 1. On July 3, an American blockading squadron destroyed what remained of the Spanish fleet when the latter made a desperate attempt to break out of Santiago harbor to continue the war on the open sea.

Meanwhile, a group of American ships en route to the Philippines stopped at Guam on May 25 and fired a warning shot at the Spanish fortress there. Spanish officials on Guam had not heard of the outbreak of war; they also lacked any ammunition for their guns, and in great embarrassment they rowed out to the Americans ships to apologize for being unable to return what they assumed was a friendly salute. They were astonished to learn that their surrender was being demanded; the American flag was run up over the fortress later in the day.

On July 7, 1898, Hawaii was finally annexed by the United States. American annexationists, including a group of wealthy planters in Honolulu, achieved their long-awaited aim by argu-ing that Hawaii was essential to the war effort against Spain and that the Hawaiians should be protected from Spanish re-prisals and rewarded for assisting the American Navy.

On July 18, the Spanish government asked France to obtain President McKinley's terms for peace. The United States delayed responding until after Puerto Rico was taken on July 25. By this time, McKinley's cabinet was about evenly divided between those who wanted to take only a naval base in the Philippines and those who wanted the whole archipelago. McKinley himself was moving toward the latter position, but he wanted to be sure the American public was with him. Thus, his armistice terms stated only that the United States would continue to hold Manila pending disposition of the rest of the Philippines. The war with Spain ended after only three months of fighting. The United States suffered minimal casualties in the naval engagements and only moderate losses in land combat with the Spaniards. However, yellow fever, dysentery, and other diseases made heavy inroads before the U.S. expeditionary force was brought home from Cuba in mid-August. And the war with Spain turned out to be only a preliminary skirmish. A much more costly and demoralizing campaign remained to be fought against Filipinos who wanted their islands to become an independent nation. This struggle ended only in 1902 after General Arthur MacArthur (father of General Douglas MacArthur) employed draconian tactics to end the nationalist struggle.

Annexing the Philippines

President McKinley made the most important decision of his administration—to substitute American for Spanish rule in the Philippines—sometime between Dewey's victory at Manila on May 1 and the appointment of the American delegation to the peace conference held in September 1898. During his first year in office, McKinley's cautious handling of the Cuban issue reflected the views of the conservative wing of his party, which feared that expansionism might upset the U.S. economy. After the sinking of the *Maine*, however, McKinley catered to the public's new mood and adopted an uncompromising stance toward Spain that made war inevitable.

Like many other American politicians of his day, McKinley thought about the war almost exclusively in terms of its impact on U.S. domestic politics, although he spoke a good deal in public about "duty" and "destiny" and other vague but high-sounding concepts. A short, victorious campaign would keep people's minds off unpleasant economic realities at home; this could be helpful in the off-year 1898 election and in the 1900 presidential race as well. Thus, when Dewey sank the Spanish squadron at Manila, McKinley had not yet made any decisions about the Philippines; he stated, quite plausibly, that he did not even know where to find them on the map.

However, by the time the war was less than two months old, businessmen who had been nervous about its economic impact were discovering that their fears were greatly exaggerated. And in the euphoria produced by a string of military victories newspaper editors began proclaiming that it made sense to "seize this never-to-be-repeated chance," that Americans should "never lower their flag where once it has been raised," and that the islands of the Pacific were vital to American interests in China.

By the end of June, leading spokesmen for business and missionary groups were beginning to talk openly of the need to keep the whole Philippine archipelago. McKinley himself was inclined not to make up his mind on important issues until he saw how the wind was blowing; he certainly was not given to deep thinking about the national interest.[3] If he believed that the public would probably reach a consensus on keeping the islands, he was content to let the pressure for imperial conquest build its own momentum.

In September, McKinley appointed a peace commission with a three-to-two majority of expansionists. He issued confidential instructions to them on September 16, stating that the United

[3] McKinley told a group of clergymen, a year later, about his struggle to decide what to do with the Philippines. This classic account was recorded by one of the visiting ministers:

I walked the floor of the White House night after night until mid-night; and I am not ashamed to tell you, gentlemen, that I went down on my knees and prayed Almighty God for light and guidance more than one night. And one night late it came to me this way—I don't know how it was, but it came: (1) That we could not give them back to Spain—that would be cowardly and dishonorable; (2) that we could not turn them over to France or Germany—our commercial rivals in the Orient—that would be bad business and discreditable; (3) that we could not leave them to themselves—they were unfit for self-government—and they would soon have anarchy and misrule over there worse than Spain's was; and (4) that there was nothing left for us to do but to take them all, and to educate the Filipinos, and uplift and civilize and Christianize them, and by God's grace do the very best we could by them, as our fellow men for whom Christ also died. And then I went to bed and went to sleep and slept soundly.

States should not accept less than the whole island of Luzon and rationalized this as a necessary step to maintain the "open-door" in China.[4] He then embarked on a whistle-stop tour across the country that enabled him to test the public mood. His standard speech promised that the war would bring "blessings that are now beyond calculation," predicted that the "American people will never shirk a responsibility," and concluded somewhat inscrutably that "duty determines destiny."

The crowds that McKinley addressed were enthusiastic and probably helped convince him that the country wanted a bold policy of imperialism. The press supported this view also. A *Literary Digest* survey of 192 newspapers, completed just before McKinley's speaking tour, showed that the only real issue was whether the United States should keep a naval base in the Philippines or take the whole archipelago. Yet public support for imperialism, which had erupted so suddenly a few months before, may have reached its peak and begun to taper off during September 1898. At the end of the month, a survey of Democratic and Republican state convention platforms showed that almost half of the conventions ignored the Philippines; six (all Democratic) favored *no* acquisition of overseas territory, while only sixteen (less than half of the state conventions) favored keeping some of the Philippine islands.

Nevertheless, the President had already decided that he would at least keep Luzon, and this was as great a departure from past U.S. policy as taking the whole archipelago. Strong Spanish resistance to giving up the Philippines caused some of the U.S. peace commissioners in Paris to suggest compromise, but the attitude of the Spaniards seems to have stiffened McKinley's position. On October 26, Secretary Hay (newly arrived in Washington from London) cabled the commission that the President had decided it must be "the whole archipelago or none." Hay made it clear that only the former course was acceptable. The only concession allowed to Spain was the American payment of

---

[4] Although this concept was already established as traditional American policy, McKinley's instruction to the peace commission may have been the first official U.S. document in which the term "open door" appeared. The first "open door notes" were sent a year later.

$20 million in return for the archipelago. In the treaty signed December 10, 1898, Spain also turned over Puerto Rico and Guam to the United States and relinquished its claims to Cuba.

The debate over ratification of the peace treaty focused on the unprecedented idea of annexing territory without issuing a promise of eventual statehood. Senator Lodge led the fight for the treaty. (His role was therefore the reverse of the role he played in regard to the Versailles Treaty in 1919.) Lodge's colleague from Massachusetts, Senator Hoar, led the opposition. Neither side based its case on realistic grounds of national security or tangible economic factors.

Senator Hoar argued that it was both unconstitutional and immoral to subject an alien people to American rule against their will. Lodge responded by claiming a higher morality for the "large policy" in Asia which annexation would make possible. On February 4, 1899, two days before the Senate voted to ratify the peace treaty, Filipino nationalists launched their rebellion against U.S. occupation. Ironically, this fact seems to have benefited Lodge's side more than Hoar's. Many senators were indignant that the Filipinos should reject the blessings of American rule.

Lodge probably also gained support for the treaty by his assertion that the Philippines were the key to American commercial expansion in Asia—that the United States should maintain an open door to the commerce of all nations in China by the contradictory means of gaining an exclusive U.S. sphere of influence in Asia. One senator pointed out that American trade with Asia was only a tiny fraction of total U.S. world trade and was likely to remain so whatever happened to the Philippines. But most of the senators seem to have been captivated by the myth of a limitless China trade. To many Americans, China was the great meeting ground of U.S. commercial interests and humanitarianism.

The Open Door Policy in China

During the first century of its existence, the United States routinely sought commercial rights equal to those of the "most favored nation" in every corner of the globe, including China.

Great Britain, a vastly greater trading power than the United States, followed the same principle and dubbed it the "open door" policy.[5] By 1898, trade with China represented only two percent of total U.S. trade; all indicators suggested that the industrialized countries of Europe (and Japan) would continue to be America's main trading partners for the foreseeable future. Nevertheless, Americans looked to China as a potentially limitless field of activity for U.S. businessmen—and Christian missionaries. Thus, the open door policy was seen by many Americans as the key to their country's future prosperity and influence in the world.

While serving in London in the late 1890s, John Hay, more Anglophile than expansionist, had been convinced by his British friends that something had to be done to stop the division of China into tightly controlled spheres of foreign influence. The chief obstacle to any action by the United States government, besides its relative weakness, was the traditional American phobia against "foreign entanglements" (especially those that could be claimed to serve British rather than American interests).

By the summer of 1899, however, that obstacle had been greatly reduced if not removed. Anglophobia remained strong in the United States, but the British government was no longer actively seeking to promote the open door in China. This made it much easier, politically, for the McKinley administration to take the lead. Moreover, a commission that McKinley sent to survey the situation in the Philippines returned and threw its weight behind the view that America should do something to maintain an open door in China. In effect, having seized the Philippines without any plan for their use, the expansionists now had to rationalize so great a departure from America's traditional anticolonialism. They proved equal to the task. Manila would become America's Hong Kong, they said, a commercial *entrepôt* and naval base from which to promote the open door policy for the benefit of all mankind.

[5] Because of the Manchu dynasty's sometimes harsh treatment of foreign missionaries and merchants in China, the Western powers also demanded the privilege of extraterritoriality—in effect, immunity from Chinese laws for Western visitors and residents.

Thus, by August 1899, domestic political factors favored some kind of an American gesture in support of the open door principle. It could not be a very bold gesture, however; the existing spheres of foreign influence in China would have to be recognized as facts of life. Mining and railway concessions could not be disturbed without creating great resentment. Nor could there be any attempt to secure free access for capital investment in the spheres of influence. But the U.S. government could go so far as to send diplomatic notes to the other powers seeking formal assurances that Americans would enjoy free commercial access throughout China. Having balanced the political pros and cons at his vacation retreat in New Hampshire, Secretary Hay penned a languid note to his friend and chief State Department adviser on China, William Rockhill:

> . . . I agree with you that some more formal engagement of that sort would be desirable. If you have time between now and Wednesday to set down your views on this question—in the form of a draft instruction [to the American Ministers in the capitals of the great powers] I would be greatly obliged. . . .
>
> I am taking a good deal for granted—your presence in Washington, your leisure, and your inclination to give us a *coup d'épaule.*

Rockhill, who had been pressing Hay to adopt such a course for months, needed no further prompting. He and his close friend Alfred Hippisley, a British official of the Chinese Customs Service, had worked out together what the diplomatic notes on the open door principle should contain. Hippisley collaborated with Rockhill on this matter in an entirely personal capacity, without instructions from the British government, which had begun to show much less interest in the subject. However, no one in the McKinley administration publicized Hippisley's role for fear of producing a sharp reaction among Anglophobe elements in Congress and the public.

The first round of "open door notes" asked Britain, France, Germany, Italy, Japan, and Russia to respect the principle of free commercial access in their spheres of influence in China, and to cooperate with the United States in gaining similar assurances from the other powers. The first point was standard

American policy, well known to all the powers. The second point probably caused some raised eyebrows among leaders of foreign governments, because it was one of the first U.S. efforts to influence the political situation outside the Western Hemisphere. It showed that Washington was not pulling back from the bold new posture in world affairs which it had begun to assume in 1898.

Five out of six replies to Hay's notes agreed to act according to the open door principle if all the other powers would do the same. Since the sixth reply, Russia's, was full of loopholes, it became the lowest common denominator of agreement among the powers. Hay and Rockhill realized this fact, but Hay decided to try and salvage as much national and personal dignity as he could by announcing, in March 1900, that he had received satisfactory assurances from all the powers, and he considered these to be "final and definitive."

American newspaper editors across the country hailed the exchange of open door notes as the greatest diplomatic triumph of all time. The dominant reaction was one of pride that the United States was asserting its influence on the world stage, mingled with relief that their country was trying to halt the imperialist scramble for spheres of influence rather than taking part in the race.

Support for China's Territorial Integrity

There was danger in exaggerating the importance to America of the open door—and of Hay's diplomatic ploy to halt the dismemberment of the Chinese Empire. The danger was that someone might call the U.S. government's bluff. Unexpectedly, the power that deflated American pretensions was not Russia, Germany, or any of the great powers; it was the Chinese people themselves.

The Boxer Rebellion, which erupted in the spring of 1900, was a peasant uprising against the intrusion of foreign technology and religion. It took its name from the fact that one of the groups involved was known as the "Fists of Righteous Harmony." At first, the target of the Boxers' wrath was the Chinese Christian community in country villages of northern China, but they soon began to converge on the major cities amidst reports that they were backed by the reactionary old Empress Dowager, Tzu Hsi, in their aim of driving all foreign influence from China.

Boxer bands overran Peking, the capital, in June 1900 and besieged the legation quarter. Just before cable links with the outside world were cut, the American minister requested U.S. military support and gained Hay's permission to coordinate the defense of his little community with those of other foreigners in the city. The Americans took refuge in the British legation, and for a month no word reached the outside world from Peking. Western newspapers made up for this by providing totally imaginary reports of a bloody massacre.

Meanwhile, small military contingents of several nations, including a U.S. infantry regiment from Manila, were assembled at Tientsin, the port nearest Peking. Of the 19,000 troops, 2,500 were Americans, the rest mainly Japanese and Russians. As they advanced toward Peking in early August, the Empress Dowager wavered, then lost her nerve and fled the capital disguised as a peasant. Deprived of her support, the Boxers melted into the countryside. When the siege ended on August 14, the foreign community of nearly a thousand counted 73 dead and 179 wounded.

Hoping to prevent other powers from using the rebellion as a pretext to complete China's dismemberment, Hay issued a second round of notes while the siege was still in progress. This time Hay indicated that the United States hoped to find a solution to the crisis which would preserve China's territorial integrity as well as the right of free commercial access. He did not specifically ask the other powers to support this new position, but he made it clear in which direction American influence would be used.

China was forced to pay a staggering $333 million indemnity for lives and property lost during the Boxer Rebellion. The United States tried to set an example by accepting the relatively modest share of $25 million (most of which was remitted) out of the total indemnity. The foreign powers also gained the right to station troops in Peking and Tientsin and to keep communications open from the capital to the sea. (Japan was one that gained this right, and therefore had a nucleus of forces in northern China in the 1930s when Sino-Japanese tensions reached the flash point.) Although the foreign powers did not actually increase their spheres of influence in China at this stage, Hay's diplomacy had very little to do with this outcome. The main factor was the intensive rivalry on the continent of Europe, which was projected into Asia and held everyone temporarily in check.

Expansionism Loses Its Savor

Americans who had played leading roles in implementing the country's expansionist policy soon began to realize that world politics was a complex and vicious game. The newly acquired possessions of the United States could be threatened at any moment by obscure shiftings of the worldwide balance of power. Hay commented that "the talk of the papers about 'our pre-eminent moral position giving us the power to dictate to the world' is mere flap-doodle." Rockhill, Hay's China specialist, became profoundly disillusioned about American efforts to prevent China's dismemberment:

> England has her agreement with Germany. Russia has her alliance with France, the Triple Alliance comes in here, and every other combination you know of is working here just as it is in Europe. I trust it may be a long time before the United States gets into another muddle of this description.

President McKinley, seeking re-election in 1900, wanted to bring U.S. troops back from China and the Philippines as quickly as possible. He knew the American people's enthusiasm for overseas expansion had disappeared. The country's normal preoccupation with internal affairs had swiftly reasserted itself.

What was far more surprising, though, was the speed with which key figures in the expansionist movement—men like Roosevelt, Mahan, and Lodge—abandoned the quest for overseas bases and colonies. They remained convinced that the

Spanish-American War had served a useful purpose by ending America's isolation. They still believed as strongly as ever that the United States must play a role worthy of its national power and ideals. But they began to realize that expansionism had more disadvantages than advantages. They found that it involved the United States in dangerous entanglements. These great prophets of a new internationalism found they shared a basic instinct with their isolationist countrymen: They insisted on maximum freedom of action for the United States in the conduct of foreign affairs.

Suggested Reading

DENNETT, TYLER. *John Hay: From Poetry to Politics*. New York: Dodd, Mead, 1933.

DULLES, FOSTER RHEA. *The Imperial Years*. New York: Crowell, 1966.

GOLAY, FRANK H. (ed.). *The United States and the Philippines*. Englewood Cliffs, N.J.: Prentice-Hall, 1966.

GRISWOLD, A. WHITNEY. *The Far Eastern Policy of the United States*. New York: Harcourt Brace Jovanovich, 1938.

LEECH, MARGARET. *In the Days of McKinley*. New York: Harper & Row, 1959.

MAHAN, ALFRED THAYER. *The Influence of Sea Power upon History, 1660–1783*. Boston: Little, Brown, 1898.

MAY, E. R. *American Imperialism: A Speculative Essay*. New York: Atheneum, 1968.

MORGAN, H. WAYNE. *America's Road to Empire: The War with Spain and Overseas Expansion*. New York: John Wiley, 1965.

PRATT, J. W. *Expansionists of 1898*. Chicago: Quadrangle, 1964.

SPROUT, HAROLD, and MARGARET SPROUT. *The Rise of American Naval Power, 1776–1918*. Princeton, N.J.: Princeton University Press, 1939.

WEINBERG, ALBERT K. *Manifest Destiny: A Study of Nationalist Expansionism in American History*. Baltimore: Johns Hopkins Press, 1935.

YOUNG, MARILYN B. *The Rhetoric of Empire: American China Policy, 1895–1901*. Cambridge, Mass.: Harvard University Press, 1968.

2

Theodore Roosevelt and the New Internationalism

After achieving nationwide fame with his Rough Riders in Cuba, Roosevelt served briefly as a reform police commissioner in New York City and then was elected governor of New York. It is sometimes forgotten that domestic problems interested him almost as much as foreign policy; they were also more challenging politically. As a tribute to his qualities of leadership and integrity (but above all to get him out of their state), conservative New York Republican bosses sought his nomination as McKinley's running mate in 1900.

Despite Roosevelt's status as popular hero, vigorous campaigner, and proven vote-getter, his nomination for the vice-presidency was resisted by many right-wing Republicans at the national convention. "Don't any of you realize," Mark Hannah bluntly asked his colleagues, "that there's only one life left between this madman and the White House?" GOP conservatives had warned McKinley against naming Roosevelt assistant secretary of the Navy in 1897—and felt the result had proved them right. The man seemed, to conservatives in his own party, hell-bent on destroying the country one way or another, either by war-mongering abroad or by sticking his nose into all sorts of economic and social matters at home, which they considered no business of his—in fact, no business of government at any level.

On September 14, 1901, McKinley was assassinated and Theodore Roosevelt was sworn in to replace him. Seeking to calm the fears of business leaders and to reassure the public generally, the young president promised to "continue, absolutely unbroken, the policy of President McKinley, for the peace and prosperity and honor of our beloved country." Yet Roosevelt proved to have far more definite and constructive plans than his predecessor had for coping with the twentieth-century issues he inherited. Always a whirlwind of activity, he threw himself into the regulation of trusts, labor relations, conservation of natural resources, and other vexing national problems brought on by the industrial and urban revolutions of the late nineteenth century.

Yet Roosevelt was also one of the first American presidents to employ his skill in foreign affairs deliberately to tip the balance of power from Congress to the executive branch. "While President I have *been* President, emphatically," he wrote to a friend in 1908.

> I have used every ounce of power there was in the office . . . and wherever I could establish a precedent for strength in the executive, as I did for instance in regards external affairs in the case of sending the fleet around the world, taking Panama, settling affairs of Santo Domingo and Cuba . . . why in these cases I have felt not merely that my action was right in itself, but that in showing the strength of, or in giving strength to, the executive, I was establishing a precedent of value.

The twentieth-century presidents who have earned the greatest respect from the American people have tended to follow this pattern. Woodrow Wilson published a book in 1885 that described the American system as "Congressional government." But by 1907, he would write:

> Our President must always, henceforth, be one of the great powers of the world, whether he act greatly and wisely or not. . . . We have but begun to see the presidential office in this light; but it is the light which will more and more beat upon it, and more and more determine its character and its effect upon the politics of the nation.

No doubt one of the reasons Theodore Roosevelt so enjoyed foreign affairs was that he could freely indulge his taste for personal power. He could negotiate directly and secretly with foreign ambassadors, correspond with emperors, draft the instructions to his own ambassadors, manage the press, appeal to the American public over the heads of Congress, and choose the best moment to submit treaties for the Senate's approval.

Frequently, Roosevelt acted as his own secretary of state, although John Hay and Elihu Root (who served him in this capacity) were both extremely capable. Also typical of Roosevelt's personal diplomatic style was his tacit assumption that close friends who happened to represent foreign powers—in particular, Speck von Sternberg of Germany ("Specky") and Cecil Spring-Rice of Great Britain ("Springy")—bore him their primary loyalty.

In spite of these and other eccentricities, Theodore Roosevelt was one of the most able diplomatists ever to occupy the White House. Such skill did not come easily and without some early blunders. But like the best presidents of this century, he grew in office. During his first term, Theodore Roosevelt concentrated mainly on domestic problems, leaving foreign affairs largely in the hands of Hay, Root, and William H. Taft. Roosevelt's main foreign policy concerns in this period were the Panama Canal and the Caribbean area. During his second term, he engaged in two major and simultaneous mediation efforts in Europe and Asia. In this period he also worked out his own concept of American interest in the Far East (which his successor unfortunately failed to follow).

The Panama Canal

Before Roosevelt entered the White House, Secretary of State Hay took the first step toward realizing Mahan's vision of an American-controlled canal across Panama. Hay persuaded the British government that it could gain American good will on larger matters if it abandoned certain rights that it had acquired under the 1850 Clayton-Bulwer treaty. (In this document, America and Great Britain had agreed not to seek exclusive control over an isthmian canal.) The new treaty, signed by Hay in 1900, allowed the United States to build and operate a canal by itself, but the canal could not be fortified, and it had to be open to warships of all nations in time of war. Theodore Roosevelt (who was governor of New York in 1900) argued against these restrictions:

> If the canal is open to the war ships of an enemy it is a menace for us in time of war. . . . If fortified by us, it becomes one of the most potent sources of our possible sea strength. Unless it is fortified it strengthens against us every nation whose fleet is larger than ours. . . .
>
> To my mind, we should consistently refuse to all European powers the right to control, in any shape, any territory in the Western Hemisphere which they do not already hold.[1]

Henry Cabot Lodge expressed similar views in the Senate. He and Roosevelt had played a leading part in ending America's isolation, but they wanted to combine internationalism with maximum freedom of action. In 1901, Hay negotiated a new treaty in which Great Britain tacitly conceded the United States an exclusive right to build and fortify a canal through the isthmus. No explicit *quid pro quo* was demanded. British statesmen could see a storm brewing in Europe, and they were looking for friends and allies. The new treaty was approved by the U.S. Senate in December 1901.

Six months later, Congress ended a long dispute over where to build the canal, by choosing to build it through Panama (at the time a province of Colombia) rather than through Nicaragua. Lobbyists for the Panama route were aided by the timely eruption of Mount Momotombo, lending credence to their charge that the Nicaraguan route was unsafe.

With the choice of route decided, President Roosevelt pressed

---

[1] This letter from Roosevelt to Hay is quoted in A. L. P. Dennis, *Adventures in American Diplomacy, 1896–1906* (New York: Dutton, 1928), pp. 160–161. In the same letter, Roosevelt urged the McKinley administration to "drop the treaty and push through a bill to build *and fortify* our own canal!" (Italics in the original.)

forward negotiations with Colombia for a treaty granting the United States broad powers to build and fortify the canal and to administer a zone on either side of it. The United States agreed to pay Colombia $10 million for these rights in a treaty signed in January 1903 by the Colombian representative in Washington. However, the president of Colombia, fearing political attack for "selling out" to Yankee imperialism, submitted the treaty without recommendation to the Colombian Senate. That body rejected it, hoping to raise the price to $25 million and perhaps impose some limits on U.S. rights in Panama.

At this stage, Roosevelt could have chosen to renegotiate the treaty or revive the concept of a Nicaraguan canal. Instead, he allowed his irritation with the Colombian Senate to get the better of him. To lobbyists for the Panama route he seems to have discreetly let it be known that the United States would be glad to see Panama gain its independence from Colombia. And in November 1903, when an independence movement (subsidized by these lobbyists) broke out in Panama, U.S. warships were on hand with orders to prevent Colombian forces from landing within fifty miles of Panama City.

Almost immediately, the chief lobbyist for the canal became acting minister of the Panamanian Republic in Washington and signed a treaty granting the United States perpetual rights of a sovereign in the canal zone; in return, the new state of Panama got $10 million. The canal zone was to stretch for five miles on either side of the canal. The United States also assumed a protectorate over the new republic and gained the right to maintain public order and sanitation services in the two cities of Colón and Panama.

Although this high-handed action quite unnecessarily poisoned U.S. relations with Latin America, Roosevelt proved unable to see when he was wrong. "I took the canal zone and let Congress debate," he boasted shortly after leaving office, and in his autobiography he called his handling of the affair his most important foreign policy action. (Many historians would disagree, although it was certainly his most notorious action.)

The Panama canal was formally opened to the world's commerce on August 15, 1914, two weeks after the outbreak of

World War I. Since the major naval battles of this war were fought in the Atlantic, the canal did not play a strategic role. In World War II, however, the canal was vital to the U.S. government's coordination of operations in the Atlantic and the Pacific.

TR and the Monroe Doctrine

In 1902, Congress was still debating whether the canal should go through Panama or Nicaragua when Germany and Great Britain set up a joint blockade of Venezuela's coast (having exhausted other means of collecting a defaulted debt). They assured the U.S. government that they planned no territorial acquisitions, and Roosevelt at first saw no challenge to the Monroe Doctrine. He even wrote the German diplomat "Specky" von Sternberg at this time, saying that "If any South American state misbehaves toward any European country, let the European country spank it." But when Germany next proceeded to sink two Venezuelan warships, the American press reacted hotly, and Roosevelt himself began to see the whole Caribbean situation in a different light.

Historians have been unable to find proof of TR's later assertion that he gave Germany an ultimatum: Accept arbitration of the dispute with Venezuela or the U.S. fleet would sail for the Caribbean. Whether or not his views were actually phrased this strongly, they were not, in any case, the decisive factor in ending the blockade. Venezuela's military dictator had already bowed to Anglo-German pressure and agreed to submit the dispute to arbitration. The American press claimed a U.S. diplomatic victory, but Roosevelt took no personal credit at the time. (He modestly wrote former President Cleveland congratulating him on this "rounding out" of his policy in the 1895 dispute between England and Venezuela.)

The American public's sharp indignation over European intervention in Venezuela surprised Roosevelt. In a letter to "Specky" in March 1903, he stated that another such move by the European powers would "simply not be tolerated here." But when Santo Domingo became the next Caribbean state to lapse into political chaos and default on a large foreign debt, Roosevelt said he had about as much desire to annex that country "as a gorged boa constrictor might have to swallow a porcupine wrong-end to."

Roosevelt was undoubtedly sincere in wanting to do the absolute minimum about the crisis in Santo Domingo to ward off the possibility of European intervention. Yet he established a precedent for U.S. intervention which would last for nearly three decades. In May 1904, he informed a public gathering in New York that the conditions prevailing in Santo Domingo may "require intervention by some civilized nation, and in the Western Hemisphere the United States cannot ignore this duty."

This first formulation of the Roosevelt "corollary" of the Monroe Doctrine was applauded by most Republican newspapers and attacked by most of the anti-imperialist press, which tended to be Democratic. Roosevelt stuck to his guns and in a December 1904 message to Congress developed the concept that "adherence of the United States to the Monroe Doctrine may force the United States, however reluctantly, in flagrant cases of such wrongdoing or impotence, to the exercise of an international police power."

Action soon followed words. In the next month, the president of Santo Domingo was persuaded to sign an agreement allowing the United States to take control of his country's customs houses and to collect import duties. U.S. officials would allocate 55 percent of customs receipts to pay foreign debts. The remainder would go into Santo Domingo's treasury. This agreement produced a great hue and cry among anti-imperialist newspapers and public groups in the United States, and Roosevelt was forced to submit the accord to the U.S. Senate in the form of a treaty. But when the Senate balked at approving the treaty, Roosevelt moved ahead with his original plan on the basis of an interim agreement with Santo Domingo. (Finally, in 1907, he gained Senate approval for a program which had long been in effect.)

Meanwhile, Roosevelt's thesis that the United States must police the Western Hemisphere was gaining broader public acceptance at home. Thus, when Cuba's 1905 election led to virtual warfare between rival factions, Roosevelt first tried to mediate the dispute, then dispatched U.S. troops to occupy key points and restore order. Under the Platt amendment to the Cuban constitution (which had been accepted by Cuban leaders under strong pressure from Washington), the United States had a legal basis for intervening to keep order.

At the time, these episodes of U.S. imperialism brought only a mild reaction in Latin American countries. This was due partly to the public relations skill of Secretary of State Root, who made an extended tour of South America in 1906. However, Roosevelt's corollary would be used many times to justify U.S. intervention during the next two decades, and this provoked an increasingly bitter outcry against the northern colossus. Finally, in 1928, the State Department produced the Clark memorandum which declared that the Monroe Doctrine could not legitimately be stretched to justify U.S. intervention in the hemisphere, because it "states a case of United States vs. Europe, not the United States vs. Latin America."

Mediating the Russo-Japanese War

The first great test of Roosevelt's Far Eastern diplomacy as president came in 1904, when Japan set out to prove to Russia and the world that it deserved to be the dominant power in southern Manchuria. Nine years earlier Japan, according to the imperialist rules of the day, had won a sphere of influence in that province by its military victory over China. However, Russia had rallied the European powers to prevent Japan from keeping Manchuria and then had turned it into a Russian colony. The United States showed itself a friend of Japan by providing timely warning of the other powers' aims.

By the early years of this century, Anglo-German rivalry was beginning to dominate the international scene. Each power sought to tip the European balance in its own favor. British leaders first eliminated all sources of friction with the United States, then made an alliance with Japan,[2] and finally reached

[2] The Anglo-Japanese alliance was signed in 1902 and remained in effect until 1922, when it was dissolved as a result of U.S. pressure. (See Chapter 5.) Under the terms of the alliance, each power agreed to stay neutral if the other went to war with a third power. If one power were attacked by two or more enemies, the other power would support its ally.

an *entente* (understanding) with France and Russia. Germany, meanwhile, developed its industrial and military power, tried to keep the opposing coalition off balance, and reached out in a belated effort to grab Asian and African colonies. Because none of the European nations was primarily interested in maintaining the open door or China's territorial integrity, the United States often found that it could muster little support for its position on these issues.

In 1903, Japan and Russia began negotiations on their respective claims in Korea and Manchuria. Finding agreement impossible, Japan attacked the Russian fleet near Port Arthur in February 1904. It soon developed that Japan's strength was greater, both on land and sea, because its lines of supply were shorter. The war lasted a year and a half; Japan's greatest victories were at Port Arthur (taken after a long siege), Mukden, and the Tsushima straits, where Admiral Togo destroyed the Russian Baltic fleet after it had sailed halfway around the world.

British and American bankers financed the Japanese war effort; France provided large loans to its Russian ally. The German kaiser also helped to embroil Russia in the war. The motives of each of these powers were different. The British wanted Russia pinned down as far from India as possible; they had no objection to Japan gaining a foothold in Manchuria, because this would tend to keep it well away from British interests in the Yangtze valley.

Theodore Roosevelt adopted a position of "benevolent neutrality" toward Japan, in part because he admired the self-reliance of the Japanese people and despised Russian autocracy. On the whole, the American public seemed to share these attitudes. More important, perhaps, Roosevelt regarded Russia as a greater threat than Japan to the open door policy and China's territorial integrity. As Japan's military supremacy emerged, however, Roosevelt began to fear that the Asian balance of power was being tipped too far in one direction. His mediation efforts were designed to end the struggle with Japan controlling enough of Manchuria to balance Russia in that region. If the war had been allowed to continue, Japan might have plunged deep into Siberia. But Russia's superior resources would probably have given it eventual victory. Roosevelt wanted to leave both powers in positions in which they would be strong enough to check each other.

France supported its ally, Russia, out of loyalty and to protect the French public's substantial direct investments in Russian railroads and other projects. The German kaiser, on the other hand, had characteristically devious reasons for urging the tzar to fight Japan. First, he felt less threatened on his eastern flank with Russian armies fighting in Manchuria. Second, he expected Russia to win the war and he hoped to join with it in the final carving up of North China.[3] Yet when the mounting evidence of civil and military incompetence on the part of the tzarist government brought Russia to the brink of revolution, the kaiser changed his tune. One antimonarchist revolt could spark another.

Japan's first peace feelers coincided with the defeat of the main Russian army at Mukden, in February and March 1905. In April, the French foreign minister (already embroiled in the Moroccan crisis, to be discussed later) relayed Russian interest in peace to Japan. After a month of hints and soundings, Japan asked Roosevelt to serve as mediator. Three days later, Kaiser Wilhelm urged the tzar to accept Roosevelt in this role.

The peace conference was convened at Portsmouth, New Hampshire (away from sweltering Washington), in August 1905. Once again, the Japanese sought a free hand in Korea and southern Manchuria, and this time their opponents agreed in a businesslike fashion. Meanwhile, Foreign Minister Witte of Russia had skillfully won over the American press to his side. This, coupled with Japan's error in pressing somewhat unrealistic demands, improved the Russian bargaining position during the second month of negotiation. The Japanese threatened to resume the war unless they received an indemnity and Sakhalin island. Realizing that Japan was not strong enough

---

[3] To this end, the kaiser falsely accused France of plotting to partition China and then urged Roosevelt to issue a new round of open door notes seeking guarantees for China's integrity, *except* certain parts of North China. Roosevelt and Hay were puzzled by the kaiser's motives, but the notes they issued did not contain any exception for North China.

economically or militarily to make good its threat, Witte refused to budge. President Roosevelt personally intervened to help arrange a compromise in which Japan received no indemnity and only the southern half of Sakhalin.

The terms of the settlement produced angry mob rioting in Japanese cities; government buildings and Christian churches were attacked, and President Roosevelt was burned in effigy. Many Japanese believed their military sacrifices and victory entitled them to an indemnity. Roosevelt professed to be un-ruffled by the Japanese reaction. But he and others realized that it marked the end of a half-century of good feeling in U.S.-Japanese relations, which began when Townsend Harris was posted as consul in 1856. Henceforth, the Philippines would seem a very vulnerable hostage, and American leaders would have to calculate every move they made in support of the open door policy and China's territorial integrity.

TR and European Power Politics

It was noted earlier that the kaiser wanted Russia at war with Japan because he felt he was being hemmed in by the Anglo-French-Russian *entente*. Germany was a late starter in the race for Asian and African colonies. Its leaders feared their country's economic growth would be strangled unless the open door principle could be made to prevail worldwide. As the Russo-Japanese War was drawing to a close, Kaiser Wilhelm II created a new world crisis in the French protectorate of Morocco, taking advantage of the temporary weakness of France's Russian ally.

In March 1905, the kaiser visited the city of Tangier and made a speech denouncing the French government's policy of closing the door to non-French commerce in its North African protectorate. Typical of what Roosevelt often referred to as the kaiser's "instability and jumpiness," his speech set off alarm signals all over Europe. This challenge to the newly proclaimed solidarity of France and England showed how easily the European network of military alliances could magnify small issues into a threat of major war. Surprised by the strong reactions of other powers, but hoping to gain U.S. support for an enlarged open door policy, the kaiser sought Roosevelt's aid in convening a conference to define Morocco's status.

If he complied, Roosevelt knew he would be attacked in Congress for getting involved in European power politics. However, he had just received a strong electoral mandate from the American people.[4] He was, in any case, hardly a man to duck a fight over a principle in which he believed. It was plain that Russia's defeat had disrupted the European balance of power; only the United States could take Russia's place temporarily in the scales.

In June 1905, French leaders agreed to attend the proposed conference, preferring to regard Roosevelt's "meddling" as a lesser evil than a military clash with Germany. After a suitable cooling off period, the conference opened in January 1906 in the little Spanish town of Algeciras. Roosevelt rationalized his decision to send two American delegates on the basis of an old commercial treaty with Morocco, which presumably gave the United States a certain interest in maintaining the open door there.

However, Roosevelt had larger ambitions than increasing North African trade. The reason he sent his ablest diplomat, Henry White, to Algeciras was to help the other powers compose their differences over Morocco and restore the European balance of power. White played a useful role, and the conference ended by affirming support for the open door in Morocco and allowing Germany to share in a new international bank to manage Morocco's finances. But France and Spain gained exclusive control over the police in their respective spheres of Morocco. Elihu Root, who succeeded Hay as secretary of state, remarked that America helped to "preserve world peace because of the power of our detachment."

---

[4] The 1904 Republican nominating convention was enlivened by the news that a supposed American citizen, Ion Perdicarus, was captured by a Moroccan chieftain named Raisuli. On TR's instructions, Secretary Hay sent a cable demanding "Perdicarus alive or Raisuli dead." Roosevelt was popularly applauded for this application of the "big stick."

TR on U.S.-Japanese Relations

With the Portsmouth and Algeciras conferences behind him, Roosevelt's prestige as a diplomatist was at an all-time high. He received the Nobel Peace Prize in 1906. But he still had to face the greatest foreign policy challenge of his presidency—the problem of resolving U.S.-Japanese tensions before they led to a Pacific war. We have noted that Roosevelt's mediation of the Russo-Japanese war was partly motivated by concern that Japan's impressive victories might transform its leaders into reckless expansionists. By the same token, Roosevelt had begun to realize as early as 1903 that Japan must be allowed a reasonable amount of scope in East Asia, if only because the Philippines were so vulnerable to attack.

Accordingly, Roosevelt sent William H. Taft, his secretary of war, to Tokyo a few weeks before the Portsmouth conference to meet with Prime Minister Katsura and trade assurances of respect for Japanese interests in Korea and U.S. interests in the Philippines. As already noted, however, the first anti-American demonstrations in Japan's history followed the Portsmouth agreement, because it failed to include an indemnity for Japan. Before long, Roosevelt would also have to react to Japan's tendency to exclude American commerce from southern Manchuria.

However, the most immediate problem was mounting anti-Japanese prejudice in California. Various trade unions and other interest groups feared Japanese economic competition and were beginning to exert a powerful influence at the state and local levels. Although the U.S. government had, for some years, excluded Chinese immigrants, the Japanese government hoped to avoid the racial slur implied by such a ban against its own people. Thus, Japanese authorities adopted the practice of refusing ordinary laborers passports for travel to the continental United States. Nevertheless, by 1906 Japanese immigrants (arriving via Mexico, Hawaii, and Canada) were entering the United States at a rate of about a thousand per month. In October of that year, the San Francisco school board ruled that the ninety-three Japanese students attending city schools with white students must move to special Oriental schools, along with Korean and Chinese children.

Without power to overrule the school board, Roosevelt had to rely on persuasion. He invited the mayor of San Francisco, the superintendent of schools, and the school board to Washington, lectured them on the danger of war with Japan, and promised action to limit Japanese immigration. The school board, duly impressed, rescinded its segregation order. Roosevelt then worked out with Japanese leaders a formal "Gentlemen's Agreement," by which Tokyo would continue to refuse passports to Japanese laborers to come to the continental United States. Not only did Japan not protest American efforts to bar the entry of Japanese laborers via Mexico, Hawaii, or Canada, it even did its best to prevent them from entering by these routes.[5]

The Gentlemen's Agreement provided only the most fragile and uneasy solution to the problem of anti-Japanese prejudice in the United States. Roosevelt came to believe that it was essential, for the sake of Pacific peace, to prevent new immigration of Japanese laborers into America and at the same time for the people of the United States to behave "with scrupulous courtesy to Japan as a nation and to the Japanese who are here." As the president well knew, discriminatory bills were piling up in the legislatures of several western states; recurring tension over the issue of racial discrimination was predictable.

Nor was this the only problem area in U.S.-Japanese relations. Roosevelt saw clearly that Japan's vital interest was in Manchuria and Korea. "It is therefore peculiarly our interest," he reminded his successor in 1910, "not to take any steps as regards Manchuria which will give the Japanese cause to feel, with or without reason, that we are hostile to them, or a menace—in however slight degree—to their interests." To this end, a memorandum was signed by Secretary Root and Japan's Ambassador Takahira in November 1908; in return for Japan's promise to

---

[5] In 1908, the U.S. government interpreted the Gentlemen's Agreement as permitting the immigration of Japanese who were nonlaborers as well as the following three classes of laborers: former residents of the United States; parents, wives, or children of residents; and settled agriculturalists.

respect the status quo in the Philippines, the United States gave Japan a free hand in Manchuria. The new agreement was therefore more advantageous to Japan than the Taft-Katsura agreement of 1905, which merely recognized its position in Korea.

Meanwhile, the president, in his own words, had "become uncomfortably conscious of a very, very slight undertone of veiled truculence" in Japanese communications. He decided that "they thought I was afraid of them," and that it was "time for a showdown." The device he chose for this purpose could hardly have been more Rooseveltian: a world cruise for the American battleship fleet. This cruise occupied the last two years of his presidency; the fleet's visit to Japan (at the emperor's invitation) was a resounding public relations success on both sides and seemed to improve the atmosphere of U.S.-Japanese relations. The world tour also advertised the fact that the U.S. Navy was extremely efficient and second only to the British Royal Navy in size. Roosevelt was inordinately proud of the fact that, in spite of opposition from many quarters, sixteen of the twenty-five battleships in this fleet had been built during his administration.

Taft and Dollar Diplomacy

William Howard Taft had been Roosevelt's secretary of war and a trusted diplomatic trouble-shooter. When he entered the White House in 1909 as TR's hand-picked successor, he was expected (not least by Roosevelt) to continue the previous administration's foreign policy. Instead, Taft and Secretary of State Philander Knox, a corporation lawyer, developed a new concept, which was aptly described as "dollar diplomacy." In part, its aim was similar to that of the Truman administration's post-World War II foreign aid program: to help produce political stability and economic growth in developing countries. Taft's program differed from Truman's in placing much heavier emphasis on developing opportunities for U.S. trade.[6]

However, there was no question of President Taft seeking (or of Congress providing) public funds for this purpose. Hence, the

[6] For a discussion of various interpretations of the Truman administration's foreign policy, see Chapter 9.

chief instrument of Taft's "dollar diplomacy" was private capital. His administration played an active role in identifying major investment opportunities abroad (such as railroad construction and mining ventures) and encouraging American capitalists to participate by securing favorable terms of investment or, in some cases, guarantees against loss due to political turmoil. It is hardly surprising that this led to charges, both in the United States and abroad, that American prestige was being used to exploit poor countries for the benefit of a small group of rich capitalists. Few writers have given Taft the credit he deserves for at least conceiving his policy in more generous and constructive terms than this.

Dollar diplomacy was perhaps an obvious foreign policy for the Taft administration to adopt, given its small, highly conservative political base and its rather grandiose idea of the role American capital could play in remaking the world. However, before long it became evident that this concept was not very realistic. To begin with, the United States did not, in the early years of this century, have a large surplus of capital seeking outlets abroad. Nor did the building of railroads in China and port facilities in Latin America necessarily offer the most attractive prospects for the capital Americans had. Often, the Taft administration found itself in the position of trying to persuade leading American bankers to float loans in Europe in order to invest in a country where U.S. "influence" seemed in danger of being excluded by the European powers. A basic assumption of dollar diplomacy was that influence accrues to the lender. Yet Taft and his colleagues were increasing America's dependence on the very powers with whom they hoped to compete for commercial and political influence.[7]

[7] With the advantage of hindsight, we should not be surprised that dollar diplomacy failed in its primary aim of producing rapid socio-economic development in Asia and Latin America. We have learned that, almost by definition, an underdeveloped society usually needs many other things besides capital in order to move toward self-sustaining growth. However, Americans even today find it difficult to believe that dollars alone cannot produce foreign policy miracles and that socio-economic change in developing countries tends to be measured in generations rather than years.

Dollar diplomacy not only failed to achieve its aims, it also did considerable harm to the U.S. position abroad because of the way in which it was carried out. The condescending manner adopted by Taft and Knox provided a focus for Latin American resentment of the northern colossus. In Asia, the administration's aggressive efforts to enhance U.S. influence in Manchuria produced exactly what Roosevelt had been so careful to avoid throughout his second term—an unnecessary challenge to Japan at a time when no other power was available to balance Japan's strength in the western Pacific. Roosevelt's historic falling out with Taft involved substantive matters such as these as well as purely personal considerations.

In any event, Roosevelt's decision to bolt the Republican party and seek election on a progressive platform gave the 1912 election to Woodrow Wilson. One of Wilson's first moves as president was to repudiate the concept of dollar diplomacy; he withdrew U.S. government support for participation by American bankers in an international consortium investing in China. However, there was an important distinction between Roosevelt's and Wilson's reasons for rejecting dollar diplomacy. Roosevelt considered it an *unrealistic* concept, while Wilson believed it *immoral* to conduct foreign policy in a way that further enriched a few already wealthy men.

During Wilson's administration, Roosevelt became one of his sharpest and most vocal critics, particularly before America's entry into the First World War. As in the Taft-Roosevelt dispute, personalities were involved as well as issues. Roosevelt and Wilson were, among other things, extremely vain; each doubtless considered his own viewpoint a superior blend of realism and idealism. But Roosevelt was certainly more pragmatic, Wilson more inclined to pursue ideal solutions. Both men played major roles in burying isolationism and in shaping twentieth-century American internationalism. Their successors have usually been at their best when they managed to combine the Roosevelt and Wilson traditions—and at their worst when they leaned toward extremes of pure idealism or pragmatism.

Suggested Reading

BEALE, HOWARD K. *Theodore Roosevelt and the Rise of America to World Power*. Baltimore: Johns Hopkins Press, 1956.

CLINE, H. F. *The United States and Mexico*. Rev. ed. Cambridge, Mass.: Harvard University Press, 1963.

DENNETT, TYLER. *Roosevelt and the Russo-Japanese War*. Garden City, N.Y.: Doubleday, 1925.

DULLES, FOSTER RHEA. *Forty Years of American-Japanese Relations*. New York: Appleton-Century-Crofts, 1937.

ESTHUS, R. A. *Theodore Roosevelt and Japan*. Seattle: University of Washington Press, 1966.

GRISWOLD, A. W. *The Far Eastern Policy of the United States*. New York: Harcourt Brace Jovanovich, 1938.

IRIYE, AKIRA. *Pacific Estrangement: Japanese and American Expansion, 1897–1911*. Cambridge, Mass.: Harvard University Press, 1972.

JESSUP, P. C. *Elihu Root*. 2 vols. New York: Dodd, Mead, 1938.

MINER, DWIGHT C. *The Fight for the Panama Route*. New York: Columbia University Press, 1940.

MUNRO, D. G. *Intervention and Dollar Diplomacy in the Caribbean, 1900–1921*. Princeton, N.J.: Princeton University Press, 1964.

PERKINS, BRADFORD. *The Great Rapprochement: England and the United States, 1895–1914*. New York: Atheneum, 1968.

PRATT, J. W. *Challenge and Rejection: The United States and World Leadership, 1900–1921*. New York: Macmillan, 1967.

3

Wilson and the Collapse of World Order

The second decade of the twentieth century, when Woodrow Wilson came to power, was a desperate period. The world's most advanced and powerful nations were poised to begin a war of unprecedented slaughter. Weaker countries that had been held in bondage for decades or centuries were beginning to grope for some means of freeing themselves. America's vast economic strength and military potential gave Wilson the power to become mankind's spokesman, and he tried to turn one of history's darkest hours into a new beginning. Few American presidents in this century have come closer to giving the world a blueprint for a just and lasting peace; few have known the bitterness of such a sharp political defeat as Wilson suffered, and for which he himself was in part to blame.

"It would be the irony of fate," Wilson told a friend a few days before his inauguration, "if my administration had to deal chiefly with foreign affairs." Supreme confidence in his ability to cope with domestic problems—a self-confidence often bordering on arrogance—is reflected in this chance comment, rather than humility about his failure to school himself in world politics. However, the remark also suggests that, when he entered the White House in 1913, Wilson was aware that distant crises might be building toward the first world war of the century.

Since the Moroccan dispute of 1905–6,[1] European rivalries

[1] See Chapter 2.

had centered on the Balkan peninsula. Germany and Austria-Hungary sought access to the Middle East through the Balkans and Turkey; the Berlin-to-Baghdad Railway symbolized this thrust. However, Russia, claiming the leadership of the Pan-Slav movement, had begun to champion the rights of fellow Slavs in the Balkans. Of these groups, the Serbs were the most vigorous in seeking revenge against Austria for annexing nearby Slavic regions.

A series of wars were fought in 1912–13 by the Serbs and their neighbors to liberate what remained of Turkey's European empire; afterwards, the liberators fought over the spoils. Intervening against Serbia, Austria collided with Russia and raised the level of tensions throughout much of Europe. Germany and France became involved, being allied with Austria and Russia respectively. Great Britain was linked by its formal understanding with France and Russia. Each nation's efforts to prepare for possible war made war the most likely outcome. The Continental powers extended the period of military service in their armies during 1913; Britain raised its naval budget; Germany and Russia built strategic railways.

In Washington, meanwhile, neither President Wilson nor most other American officials had much time to brood over European problems during 1913. Wilson deluged Congress with a series of major bills designed to reduce the autonomy of the great U.S. industrial barons and move America closer to the ideal of social and political democracy. The graduated income tax, the Federal Reserve system, tariff reduction, a trade commission, and procedures for arbitrating labor disputes were all instituted early in his first administration.

As a political scientist, former president of Princeton University, and reform governor of New Jersey, Wilson was admirably equipped to carry on Roosevelt's quest for economic and social justice in the United States. Yet for a man of his intellectual range and depth it is astonishing how little interest Wilson took in foreign affairs before entering the White House.

Wilson's books and articles before the Spanish-American War reflected the country's preoccupation with continental development; foreign affairs were ignored or treated as an activity of minor importance. Wilson's writings in this period also document the degree to which Congress had made itself the dominant branch of government. While initially somewhat dubious about the 1898 war, the tone of Wilson's articles in the *Atlantic* and other journals soon turned to solid support for McKinley's decision to keep the Philippines. In terms close to those used by Captain Mahan and Senator Lodge, Wilson applauded the emergence of the United States as a world power. By 1907, he recognized that this had "changed the balance of parts" between Congress and the executive branch of government; he saw the chief result of the Spanish-American War as "the greatly increased power and opportunity for constructive statesmanship given the President, by the plunge into international politics and into the administration of distant dependencies."

Wilson's Foreign Policy Advisers

As only the second Democrat to occupy the White House in fifty-three years, Wilson had an enormous task cut out for him in transforming his badly fragmented, faction-ridden party into an instrument for national leadership. Having been denied national office so long, the Democrats were woefully lacking in experienced leaders. Thus, for example, Wilson was forced out of sheer political expediency to appoint James W. Gerard, a wealthy Tammany Hall politician from New York, to the crucial post of ambassador in Berlin. For the same reason, William Jennings Bryan was named secretary of state, although the Great Commoner had no background in this field and spent much of his incumbency on the lecture circuit. Even when Wilson managed to find a man of first-rate natural ability, such as Walter Hines Page, whom he sent to London, Wilson's own lack of experience and his insistence on total loyalty made him refuse to accept unwelcome advice or criticism from Page.

Bryan was succeeded as secretary of state in 1915 by Robert Lansing, the State Department's counselor, who was a highly skilled international lawyer and diplomat. But Wilson, a subjective idealist, was often irritated by Lansing's cool, objective approach to problems, and he often failed to make the most effective use of Lansing's abilities, which were considerable. Instead, he relied on the astute Texas politician Colonel Edward M. House for substantive advice and frequently sent House abroad to conduct delicate negotiations behind the back of the State Department.

America did not have a career Foreign Service until 1924 (and presidents continue as late as the 1970s to nominate generous contributors of party funds and other noncareer men to serve as ambassadors in a large number of countries). Before 1924, all would-be members of the diplomatic corps had to pull political strings to obtain their assignments, and most of them supplemented meager salaries from private means. Not surprisingly, Wilson assumed that most of the men who had been appointed by Roosevelt and Taft were Republicans, and he doubted that they shared his zeal for social and economic reform. Many of them tried to remain as inconspicuous as possible for fear of being replaced on political grounds. Because of Wilson's lack of rapport with the men he appointed secretary of state, as well as many of his ministers and diplomatic secretaries abroad, he made little substantive use of the State Department or of the overseas missions. When it came time to prepare U.S. policy papers for the Versailles peace conference, Wilson asked Colonel House to organize a new bureaucracy for this purpose; known as "The Inquiry," it was composed mainly of nongovernment specialists in such fields as history, economics, geography, and banking.

Mexico and the Caribbean

Before the outbreak of war in Europe in 1914, Wilson faced the first foreign policy challenge of his administration in the Western Hemisphere. Wilson's intervention in Mexico—like his later dispatch of troops to Russia [2]—revealed his worst qualities as a diplomatist. He assumed that American values were universally accepted, that an alien people would be grateful for U.S. meddling in their affairs, and that his own intuition was a better guide for policy than the knowledge of trained

[2] See Chapter 4, page 58.

specialists or established diplomatic precedent (as in the recognition of foreign governments).

In Mexico, a reformist government had been overthrown and its president shot by one General Victoriano Huerta a few weeks before Wilson's inauguration. Shortly after taking office, Wilson issued an announcement that strongly hinted at a novel position he would soon adopt on diplomatic recognition. The normal practice was to recognize any government that was in de facto control of the national territory and capable of honoring its international obligations. Wilson established a new criterion: He would recognize only governments that had gained power by constitutional means and refuse to deal with any that had come into being by force and violence.

Ignoring the State Department's specialists on Mexico, Wilson sent his personal agents to investigate the situation in that country and report to him directly. On the basis of their findings, he then proceeded to mount a campaign to drive Huerta from office. This included withholding recognition, allowing Huerta's opponents to buy arms in the United States, and occupying Veracruz with U.S. troops to deny Huerta the European arms which he had been receiving through that port. All of this meddling Wilson justified on the ground that he had come to feel a "passion . . . for the submerged eighty-five percent of the people of that Republic who are now struggling toward liberty."

After Huerta resigned and went abroad in 1914, Mexico remained in a state of civil war between various factions. Wilson and Bryan considered backing Francisco Villa, an illiterate ex-bandit with a following in northern Mexico. However, when Lansing became secretary of state in 1915, he sought the advice of a conference of Latin American leaders, and the U.S. government followed their recommendation in granting de facto (informal) recognition to Carranza, the head of the strongest Mexican faction.

Francisco Villa then tried to involve the United States in a war with Carranza by shooting a group of American engineers. In March 1916, Villa's forces invaded the town of Columbus, New Mexico. General Pershing led an expedition into Mexico but failed to catch Villa. After a clash between the forces of Carranza and Pershing, Wilson sent the National Guard to the Mexican border in June 1916. Carranza suggested and Wilson agreed to a joint commission to study and defuse this charged situation. In February 1917 (when war between Germany and the United States was imminent), the United States withdrew its troops from Mexico and granted full diplomatic recognition to Carranza, thus ending one of the most dangerous fiascos in the history of U.S. relations with Latin America.

However, Mexico was not the only scene of Wilsonian intervention in the Western Hemisphere. In July 1915, the Haitian president, Guillaume Sam, massacred 170 political prisoners and was then assassinated by a mob. The U.S. government had been worried for some time about the growing chaos in Haitian politics, and the possibility of European intervention to collect defaulted debts. On the day of Guillaume Sam's assassination, the U.S. Navy landed marines and occupied Port au Prince. The United States then proceeded to dictate the choice of a new Haitian president and to force him to agree to a treaty giving the United States full control over the republic's government.

In 1916, a very similar American takeover occurred in the Dominican Republic, which shares the island of Dominica with Haiti. It proved easier for the mediocre officials sent by Wilson to these islands to insure the regular payment of the Haitian and Dominican foreign debts (eliminating any excuse for European intervention) than to implant the seeds of democracy. In fact, no serious effort was made to prepare either of these two republics for democratic self-government—work which was significantly advanced during the Wilson administration in the Philippines and Puerto Rico.

Wilson's Concept of Neutrality

The murder of Archduke Ferdinand of Austria-Hungary in June 1914 quickly activated Europe's competing alliances and dragged all the Continental powers into war. President Wilson proclaimed U.S. neutrality on August 4, 1914, the same day that

Germany attacked neutral Belgium and Great Britain declared war on Germany. Two weeks later, Wilson made his first great wartime speech, calling on the American people to "be neutral in fact as well as name." This policy had the overwhelming support of the American people, but Wilson encountered various difficulties in pursuing his chosen course during the thirty-three months that America remained neutral.

Most Americans, including most leading members of the Wilson administration, identified with Great Britain and France from the early days of the struggle because they felt linked with the great democracies by ties of blood and affection. However, only a relatively small group of Americans, at any stage in the war, believed that a German victory would pose a strategic threat to their country's security. Some members of the large German and Irish minorities in the United States hoped for a German victory or a British defeat (the Irish particularly after Britain suppressed the 1916 Easter uprising). The British press and propaganda services were generally far more effective in reaching the U.S. public than German propaganda. And ruthless German actions, such as the invasion of neutral Belgium and the torpedoing of passenger liners, were convincing proof to many Americans that the Allies were fighting a barbaric enemy.

Within the top level of the Wilson administration, Secretary of State Bryan was the leading spokesman for noninvolvement and pacifism. To prevent American intervention in the war, he tried to impose a ban on American loans to any of the belligerent powers, knowing that this would deny them the means of buying any substantial amounts of arms or supplies in the United States. With great difficulty, the French ambassador eventually managed to persuade Bryan that denying loans or refusing to trade with either side would be unneutral; in this, the ambassador was on solid legal ground.

Robert Lansing, counselor of the State Department, was one of the first members of the Wilson administration to reach the conclusion that "Germany must not be permitted to win this war or break even, though to prevent it this country is forced to take an active part." In these sentiments Lansing was warmly seconded by Ambassador Walter Hines Page in London. Colonel Edward

House, Wilson's personal adviser on foreign policy, reached the
same conclusion and tried to persuade Wilson to declare war
long before he was ready to do so.

The President himself stated privately during the first year of
the war that "England is fighting our fight." But he seems
to have meant by this only that the United States shared a set
of common values with England and not with the existing
government of Germany. He may have underestimated the
chances of France and England being defeated while the United
States remained neutral. Certainly, he had little or no sense of
Germany posing a strategic threat to the United States in the
event of an Allied defeat. Thus, he was reluctant to declare war
if he could avoid doing so. He considered neutrality to be in
the best interests of the nation, and he knew it to be the clear
desire of the American people. As he became preoccupied with
the quest for a stable postwar world, Wilson sought to play
the role of mediator and tried to persuade both sides to accept
"peace without victory." Not until early 1917 did Wilson
conclude that his influence as a mediator would be maximized
if America entered the war.

It was through no fault or design of the United States's that
its merchants could trade with only one side, since the British
fleet prevented access to German ports. Wilson had little interest
in the niceties of international law. But he was certainly astute
enough to realize that his policy of neutrality was bringing
windfall profits to American business as the United States became
the arsenal and granary of the Allied powers. America's wartime prosperity benefited the Democratic party and particularly
Wilson's own chances of re-election in 1916.

Wilson considered the German U-boat threat as a violation
of "human rights," hence far more serious than Allied violations of "property rights." However, there were times when the
president regarded both sides in the struggle as almost equally
menacing to America's position as a neutral. Britain was determined to make up for the Allies' relative weakness on land by
pressing home its superiority at sea. In March 1915, Britain
announced its intention of preventing goods of any sort from
being shipped to the Central Powers either directly or indirectly

via neutral nations. Washington protested this order as being in direct conflict with America's concept of its rights as a neutral—as were other British practices such as interfering with the mails and imposing long delays while ships were searched for "contraband." (The term was eventually stretched to include anything that could be used to sustain the civilian as well as military component of the opposing side.) Until 1916, however, the Wilson administration's protests over British affronts tended to be "for the record," to satisfy angry American businessmen and to give the impression of treating England and Germany impartially. As Lansing himself later wrote:

> The notes that were sent [to Great Britain] were long and exhaustive treatises which opened up new subjects of discussion rather than closing those in controversy. Short and emphatic notes were dangerous. Everything was submerged in verbosity. It was done with deliberate purpose. It insured continuance of the controversies and left the questions unsettled, which was necessary in order to leave this country free to act and even to act illegally when it entered the war.

The Submarine Issue

In February 1915, the German government declared that its submarines would sink any Allied merchant ships venturing into the waters. immediately surrounding the British Isles. Berlin also announced that neutral vessels might be sunk if they ventured into the same area because of the British practice of flying neutral flags from their ships. The United States promptly replied that it would take any necessary steps to "safeguard American lives and property and to secure to American citizens the full enjoyment of their acknowledged rights on the high seas." At the same time the United States indicated that it would hold the German government to a "strict accountability" for its actions.

According to existing international law, the Germans should have seized merchant ships suspected of carrying armaments and taken them to a German port or, since this was impossible, destroyed them at sea after making provision for the safety of the crew and passengers. This, too, was an impossible condition for a submarine commander to meet. If his vessel surfaced during its attack, it was likely to be destroyed by the guns with which all Allied merchant ships were then armed. Besides, there was no space in the cramped hull of a submarine for large numbers of additional passengers. Therefore, the German government claimed that the old rules of international law on commerce destruction no longer applied, particularly when the Allies violated accepted practice by arming their merchant ships and disguising them with neutral flags.

Secretary Bryan, in the hope of avoiding a confrontation with Germany, recommended giving in to Berlin's threats; he favored advising all American citizens not to travel on the ships of any belligerent power, unless they wished to do so at their own risk. His position accorded with international law. However, Wilson chose to follow Lansing's advice and adopted the position that Americans had a right to travel on any ship they wanted, whether it was armed or unarmed, and they could look to the United States for protection while doing so. This position ignored the fact that international law did not require a neutral government to protect its citizens while traveling on a belligerent ship. Nor did international law provide *armed* merchants ships with immunity from attack.

Within a very short time, the U.S. government's stand was put to the test when a German submarine sank the British liner *Lusitania;* 1,198 people lost their lives, including 128 Americans. The German embassy in Washington had published warnings to American citizens not to travel on the *Lusitania*. The ship was not armed, but it carried several thousand cases of rifle cartridges.

President Wilson's position in this crisis was attuned to the American public's outrage as well as the general desire not to go to war. Disregarding the truculent views of Lansing and others in his administration as well as the appeasing instinct of Bryan, the president demanded that Germany disown the sinking, pay reparations, and take "immediate steps to prevent the recurrence" of similar incidents. Bryan's resignation and his replacement by Lansing was closely linked to Wilson's rejection of Bryan's advice in this matter.

To German military leaders, Wilson's repeated demands seemed tantamount to denying them the only weapon they could use to break Britain's mastery of the sea and cut its lifeline of vital imports from abroad. However, the Germans would not risk American belligerency at this stage, and they secretly ordered their U-boat commanders not to attack passenger ships without some semblance of warning required by international law.

In March 1916, Berlin seemed briefly to be abandoning its policy of caution when a German U-boat torpedoed the steamer *Sussex* in the English Channel. The little ship made port, and although some Americans were injured, none died as a result of the attack. Wilson disregarded the advice of Lansing and House that he break diplomatic relations with Germany; instead he threatened a break unless Germany would "immediately declare and effect an abandonment of its present methods of submarine warfare against passenger and freight-carrying vessels."

Perhaps hoping to make the most of existing ill will between England and the United States, Berlin responded much more promptly and favorably than in the *Lusitania* case. It said that merchant ships would "not be sunk without warning and without saving human lives, unless these ships attempt to escape or offer resistance." In return for these concessions, the German government indicated it expected the United States to compel England to live up to the letter of international law. The German response ended with a warning that if Britain continued its allegedly illegal practices, Berlin would reserve to itself "complete liberty of action."

Wilson as Neutral Mediator

On of the slogans of Wilson's re-election campaign was "He kept us out of war." Throughout 1916, the overwhelming majority of the American people probably still wanted to avoid direct involvement, if possible. Wilson's anger at British maritime

practice was undoubtedly genuine, but it also served to reassure
the public that he was doing everything in his power to remain
neutral.

Wilson approved plans for expanding the U.S. Army and
Navy in this period, but the emphasis in the naval construction program was on battleships. These would have no use in
antisubmarine warfare but would help to remind Britain of
the rights of neutrals. In September, Wilson made an un-
characteristically anti-British remark to House: "Let us build
a navy bigger than hers and do as we please." [3]

Although Wilson considered his own re-election vitally important, he would never have modified his stand on anything
as serious as the submarine issue for the sake of winning votes.
In a September 1916 speech he stressed the distinction between
"property rights," which the British were abusing, and "human
rights," which were violated by the German submarines. The
former could be arbitrated after the war, he said, but "the
loss of life is irreparable."

By declaring the U-boat an absolute evil, he knowingly gave
Germany the initiative; its leaders could turn the United States
into a belligerent whenever they decided to resort to all-out
submarine warfare. Hoping to avert this danger, Wilson sought
the role of neutral mediator with increasing urgency throughout
1916. German leaders tried to end the war while they were
ahead; they therefore urged Wilson to adopt this role and
call a peace conference. The Allies, wanting no peace talks
until the United States had tipped the balance to their side,
side-stepped Wilson's first overtures as mediator.

Wilson's mediation efforts occurred in early 1916, when
Colonel House told Sir Edward Grey, the British foreign
secretary, that Wilson was prepared to call a peace conference
when the Allies secretly signaled him they were ready for one.
If Germany refused to attend—as House and Grey seem to have
expected—the United States would enter the war on the side of

[3] After America entered the war on the side of the Allies, this ship-
building program was redirected toward submarine warfare. With the return of peace, however, competition with Britain (and Japan) in the building of battleships resumed.

the Allies. The United States would do the same if Germany agreed to attend a peace conference and then refused to accept "reasonable" terms (to be agreed upon in advance by Wilson and the Allies). After House and Grey signed a memorandum to this effect, Wilson modified it by saying the United States would "probably" enter the war, since Congressional approval would be necessary.

The Allied governments never decided it was in their interest to ask Wilson to call a peace conference. The most obvious explanation for this was that the plan, as conceived by Wilson, was a device to end the war without U.S. intervention; and throughout 1916, the Allies came increasingly to regard U.S. intervention as essential to their success, if not their actual survival.

There were moderate elements in the German government who advocated defeating the Allies one at a time while avoiding the type of submarine warfare that would provoke U.S. belligerency. However, German military leaders wanted either an immediate and favorable peace or all-out use of the submarine to starve the British into submission. Wilson delayed calling a peace conference, as the Germans urged him to, all through the fall of 1916. House advised against such a move without Allied approval; neither Lloyd George (the new British prime minister) nor Clemenceau of France was willing.

When the Germans announced, in December 1916, that they were ready to talk peace, the Allies rejected the offer. Wilson, still hoping to avoid entering the war, asked both sides to state their peace terms. Germany replied that this could best be done at a formal peace conference, while the Allies presented terms they knew their enemies would reject. This failure to open peace talks made it likely that the United States would soon face a showdown with Germany over the submarine issue.

President Wilson therefore decided to play the last card he held as a neutral mediator. He offered to recommend that the United States help underwrite the postwar world order by joining a "League for Peace," provided the belligerent powers would agree to certain basic principles that must govern such a system. These principles were: peace without victory (a conciliatory peace settlement to avoid planting the seeds of future wars); equal rights for all nations; government by the consent of the governed; access to the sea for "every great people"; freedom of the seas; and a general reduction of armaments.

These principles were not as easy for all powers to subscribe to as might appear at first glance. Germany's acceptance would entail severe limits on its use of submarines against neutral shipping. British acceptance would concede the U.S. position on neutral rights and perhaps encourage other powers to meddle in British Empire affairs. Moreover, Wilson's principles would deny both groups of belligerents the territorial gains for which they were fighting. Wilson already knew, at least generally, that both sides harbored territorial ambitions, which made acceptance of his principles highly doubtful. Yet he was grimly determined to help shape the peace, whether the United States remained neutral or joined the war.

In fact, the German government had already decided on a desperate gamble: to try to defeat Great Britain through unrestricted submarine warfare before this strategy brought American reinforcements to the western front. The fact that Russia was on the brink of collapse slightly improved the chances of this basically reckless policy. Germany's decision to resume unrestricted submarine warfare was relayed to the German ambassador in Washington on January 19, 1917, three days before Wilson's speech. On January 31, the ambassador informed Secretary Lansing, as he had been instructed to do. The United States promptly severed relations with Germany, and war followed inexorably as soon as Germany put its new policy into practice.

Suggested Reading

BAKER, R. S. *Woodrow Wilson: Life and Letters.* 8 vols. Garden City, N.Y.: Doubleday, 1927–39.

COLETTA, P. E. *William Jennings Bryan.* 3 vols. Lincoln: University of Nebraska Press, 1964–70.

CURRY, R. W. *Woodrow Wilson and Far Eastern Policy, 1913–1921.* New York: Twayne, Bookman, 1957.

FISCHER, FRITZ. *Germany's Aims in the First World War.* New York: Norton, 1967.

GEORGE, A. L., and J. L. GEORGE. *Woodrow Wilson and Colonel House: A Personality Study.* New York: John Day, 1956.

GRAEBNER, NORMAN A. (ed.). *An Uncertain Tradition: American Secretaries of State in the Twentieth Century.* New York: McGraw-Hill, 1961.

HENDRICK, B. J. *The Life and Letters of Walter Hines Page.* 3 vols. Garden City, N.Y.: Doubleday, 1923–27.

LANSING, ROBERT. *The War Memoirs of Robert Lansing.* Indianapolis: Bobbs-Merrill, 1935.

LINK, ARTHUR S. *Wilson.* 5 vols (to date). Princeton, N.J.: Princeton University Press, 1947–
———. *Wilson the Diplomatist: A Look at His Major Foreign Policies.* Baltimore: Johns Hopkins Press, 1957.

MAY, E. R. *The World War and American Isolation, 1914–1917.* Cambridge, Mass.: Harvard University Press, 1959.

SEYMOUR, CHARLES (ed.). *The Intimate Papers of Colonel House.* 4 vols. Boston: Houghton, Mifflin, 1926–28.

SMITH, DANIEL M. *The Great Departure: The United States and World War I, 1914–1920.* New York: John Wiley, 1965.

TUCHMAN, BARBARA W. *The Zimmermann Telegram.* New York: Viking, 1958.

4

Wilson and the Postwar World

Begin Paper

Calling on Congress to "accept the status of belligerency that has been thrust upon us," Wilson announced in his April 1917 war message that America would lead a crusade "to vindicate the principles of peace and justice . . . and to set up amongst the really free and self-governed peoples of the world such a concert of purpose and of action as will henceforth insure the observance of those principles."

This address echoed Wilson's speech of the previous January in which he had listed the conditions for American entry into a postwar "League for Peace": There must be general disarmament and no harsh treatment of the vanquished; the peace settlement must be based on equal rights for all nations, government by the consent of the governed, freedom of the seas, and access to the sea for "every great people."

During the remainder of 1917, Wilson concentrated with single-minded drive on the task of rallying public support and turning the United States into an efficient military power. Americans found the experience exhilarating. Never before in U.S. history had the nation's energies been so completely focused on a common purpose. Wilson found that he could carry out almost any program he wished as long as it could be linked to the war effort.[1] A War Industries Board was given

---

[1] Nowhere in Wilson's wartime speeches did he suggest, however, that U.S. national security interests might require preventing German domination of

far-reaching powers to control and manage the economy. The Navy's capital ship-building program was suspended in favor of destroyers and other antisubmarine vessels. Publishers of major newspapers agreed not to print news that might undermine the solidarity of the Alliance. Congress virtually suspended partisan debate for the duration of the war. And four million men were drafted or enlisted into the armed forces: of these, two million were in Europe before the armistice.

By late 1917, Wilson had placed America on a war footing but new foreign policy problems demanded his attention. The Bolshevik revolution brought a swift end to Russia's vast, crumbling military effort, allowing Germany to transfer scores of divisions to the western front. At the same time, Soviet publication of secret Allied treaties made it impossible to ignore the diverse national aims for which the Western powers were fighting. Therefore, Wilson and his advisers began planning a simple, dramatic statement of American aims that might serve as a rallying point for the Western powers, perhaps hold Russia in the war, and weaken the German people's support for their leaders.

The Fourteen Points

Wilson unveiled his "Fourteen Points" in an address before Congress on January 8, 1918. Although it would take weeks, even months, for the message to reach some parts of the world, Wilson was speaking to war-weary people everywhere. The essentially passive presence of Congress added dignity to the occasion, but Wilson did not ask Congress or the Allies to endorse his principles. He simply assumed the role of spokesman not just for the United States and the Allies but for people everywhere who might choose to associate themselves with his message. The Fourteen Points were:

Europe. Realists such as Theodore Roosevelt knew that such thoughts were incomprehensible to most Americans, who still believed that their country's isolated position behind two great ocean "barriers" provided security from all potential aggressors.

1. An end to secret diplomacy and secret agreements
2. Freedom of the seas, unless restricted by League of Nations sanctions against an aggressor
3. Removal of all possible economic barriers between League of Nations members
4. Disarmament to the "lowest point consistent with domestic safety"
5. Colonized and colonizing peoples to share in adjusting the status of colonies
6–13. The most pressing territorial issues in Europe and the former Turkish Empire to be dealt with according to two basic principles: evacuation and restoration of territory occupied by Germany and self-determination in adjusting national boundaries
14. Establishment of a "general association of nations . . . for the purposes of affording mutual guarantees of political independence and integrity of great and small states alike"

These ideas were not invented by Wilson. Some had been debated by political philosophers for centuries. Many of them had recently been expressed by men like Lodge in Washington, Lloyd George in London, and Trotsky in Moscow. What made Wilson's formulation so powerful was the fact that American armies were at last on their way to France to help repel Germany's knockout blow with one of their own. The fact that Allied leaders did not take exception to Wilson's principles made it seem that they endorsed them. In fact, Lloyd George and Clemenceau disagreed with certain points, but they knew their silence would help undermine the German people's will to fight.

During the remaining months of the war, Wilson added some thirteen additional points, which were mainly elaborations of the original fourteen. He also began to learn how difficult it would be to find just and practical solutions to the world's most urgent problems. One of the many great issues that Wilson wrestled with during 1918 (and after) was the task of reconciling Allied aims toward revolutionary Russia.

Intervention in Russia

When Tzar Nicholas Romanov was overthrown in early 1917, Wilson's instinct was to try to make common cause with Russia's new middle-class rulers. Having been forced to renounce his intervention in the affairs of Mexico, he transferred his sympathies to the emerging Russian people. He wanted to keep Russia in the war against Germany, but he hoped even more to influence the revolution along the path of Western-style democracy. What he (and the leaders of France and England) failed to perceive was that trying to keep an utterly spent Russia at war was the surest way to promote chaos and Communist takeover.

Following Lenin's bold tactics, the numerically insignificant Bolsheviks instigated rebellion in the Russian Army and Navy and finally seized control of the country on November 6, 1917. One of their first moves after ousting Kerensky's Provisional Government was to renounce the war and begin peace negotiations with Germany, while urging working-class people of all belligerent powers to cease supporting their governments. Finding Germany's peace terms too harsh, Trotsky broke off negotiations. Germany then launched an offensive that threatened Saint Petersburg, and in March 1918, the Bolsheviks accepted the treaty of Brest-Litovsk, in which they surrendered Finland, the Baltic states, Russian-occupied areas of Poland, and the vast Ukraine.

As already noted, Wilson's Fourteen Points speech was partly aimed at influencing these developments. However, his words had little meaning for the Russian people or their self-appointed leaders. What Wilson overlooked was that most Russians were preoccupied with the immediate struggle to survive amid revoluntionary upheaval and incipient civil war.

British and French leaders, who were equally ill-informed about developments in Russia, were planning a series of small invasions to counteract the Bolshevik takeover. Their strategy depended on American and Japanese troops and a variety of anti-Communist Russian leaders, who generally lacked any real support from the people. Wilson was never happy about these plans for counterrevolution. But, as a full-fledged member of the Alliance, he found he could not hold out indefinitely against the Anglo-French view that intervention might revive Russian belligerency.

In the summer of 1918, Wilson finally agreed to send U.S. troops to Arckhangelsk and Siberia, partly to prevent Japan from seizing the latter territory. Those who went to Arkhangelsk soon became involved in skirmishes with troops of the Soviet Red Army, despite Wilson's instructions. They survived two subzero winters and were withdrawn in 1920.

In Siberia, some 9,000 U.S. troops "chaperoned" a much larger Japanese force. Here again, their planned role of linking up with Czech and anti-Communist Russian forces and helping to reopen an eastern front against Germany proved totally unrealistic. The American force scrupulously avoided becoming involved in the murky power situation of eastern Russia and were withdrawn in 1919; their Japanese cohorts saw them off with a band that played "Hard Times Ain't Here No More!" [2] As might have been foreseen, the net result of these two fiascos was to greatly assist the Bolsheviks in consolidating their position. The Allied intervention undoubtedly confirmed the view, which seems to have been shared by most Russian rulers through history, that foreigners are not to be trusted. Years later, during World War II, Lenin's heirs skillfully played on the Roosevelt administration's sense of guilt for Wilson's role in the Allied intervention.

The Pre-Armistice Agreement

One of the reasons Wilson mismanaged the subject of intervention in Russia so completely was that his attention was focused on the much larger task of ending the war and organizing the postwar world. The first trickle of American troops began to arrive in France in the spring of 1918; by summer, the trickle turned into a flow and helped contain a final German offensive

[2] The Japanese troops were withdrawn after the Washington Naval Conference, as related in Chapter 5.

against the exhausted armies of Britain and France. In July, an Allied counteroffensive began forcing the Germans to retreat slowly toward their own border.

In the first week of October, Germany and Austria-Hungary sought peace on the terms that Wilson had publicly proposed. There followed a month of negotiations between the Central Powers and Western Allies in which Wilson played the pivotal role. He told the government of Austria-Hungary that it would have to accept the fact that the United States had already gone far toward recognizing the independence of Czechoslovakia and Yugoslavia, which were still officially part of the Austro-Hungarian Empire.

To Germany, Wilson announced that the Allies required full acceptance of the Fourteen Points, evacuation of Allied territory, abandonment of "illegal" practices (such as submarine warfare), and establishment of a representative German government. Although German forces occupied unbroken lines on Allied territory, they had lost the will to fight. The German kaiser abdicated on November 9, 1918, and was replaced by a self-styled German People's Government, which accepted Wilson's conditions.

Meanwhile, Wilson and House were having no small difficulty negotiating with their own major allies. Each of them now came forward with important objections to the Fourteen Points. In order to obtain Allied support for these principles, House even went so far as to threaten to make a separate peace with Germany. The Allies finally endorsed the Fourteen Points, but with two major qualifications: Britain reserved its position on freedom of the seas, and France insisted on the right to claim reparations from Germany. The latter demand—which Wilson accepted in order to get peace talks started—became the basis for a long and bitter controversy, to which we will later return.

The allied and associated powers' military terms for an armistice were set forth by Marshal Foch, the Supreme Commander. They were frankly designed to cripple the German war machine and make it possible for the Allies to dictate peace terms. German forces were required to move east of the Rhine and surrender all German-held territory west of that river.

Germany was also to surrender its fleet, a large percentage of its railway cars and locomotives, and its heavy artillery. These terms were accepted by the German government, and the armistice was signed on November 11.

The Politics of Peace-Making

As soon as the guns fell silent on the western front, Wilson's influence began to shrink on both sides of the Atlantic. The Allies were no longer dependent on America either militarily or economically. Moreover, the off-year Congressional elections of November 1918 were being watched by all the statesmen of Europe for signs of Wilson's waxing or waning support by the American people. Wilson must have known that he was in real danger of losing his majorities in both houses of Congress; democracies tend to clip the wings of their wartime leaders the moment victory is won. Yet he quite unnecessarily made the off-year election (which was being fought, as usual, on a wide range of issues) appear as a simple vote of confidence in his own leadership. He asked the voters to elect a Democratic Congress in order that he might "continue to be your un-embarrassed spokesman in affairs at home and abroad."

The appeal backfired. Republicans, who were enraged by the slur on their loyal support of the war effort, gained control of both houses of Congress. In the Senate, where the peace treaty would have to be ratified by a two-thirds majority, the Republicans gained an advantage of forty-nine to forty-seven. Theodore Roosevelt proclaimed that Wilson had lost the right to speak for the United States. To European heads of government, who would have had to resign under similar circumstances, Wilson's prestige suffered a major blow.

It would have been prudent for Wilson to follow the example set by McKinley in his peace negotiations with Spain and appoint influential senators of both parties to the peace commission. However, Wilson decided before the election that he personally must head the U.S. peace commission, and this decision seems to have governed his choice of the other members: House, Lansing, General Tasker Bliss, and the career diplomat Henry

White. All were able and trusted subordinates (and Democrats, except for White), with whom Wilson knew he could work smoothly and efficiently.

By contrast, if he chose Senator Lodge, who was due to become chairman of the Foreign Relations Committee, the peace commission would have had at least two power centers. In Wilson's view, this was unthinkable.[3] To have appointed some other prominent Republican, either a senator or someone like former President Taft, Elihu Root, or Charles Evans Hughes, would also have reduced Wilson's dominance of the commission while quite possibly failing to placate Lodge, who would play the key role in the ratification process. Wilson's decision to lead the U.S. peace commission and take only trusted subordinates to Versailles meant that he was staking everything on getting the best possible peace agreement—one that would be so right in the eyes of the American people that Congress would not dare to reject or amend it.

Undoubtedly Wilson erred in asking for a vote of confidence and in failing to name leading Republican senators to the peace commission. With the advantage of hindsight, we can also point to tactical advantages he might have enjoyed, in his dealings with Allied leaders and with the Senate, if he had stayed in Washington; there he would have been able to keep in touch with the U.S. political climate and communicate with the delegates at Versailles by transatlantic cable. However, the theory that he should not have attended the peace conference in person tends to break down when we analyze the role he played there.

The Versailles Conference

Wilson and the other U.S. peace commissioners sailed for France on the *George Washington*, accompanied by a large and distinguished group of academic and government specialists

[3] It was a tragic irony that Wilson and Lodge, both brilliant and high-minded men, should have come to view each other as little more than vain and fanatical partisans. Each firmly believed the other had no better motive than to insure that he and his party received the lion's share of credit for the peace settlement.

on the subjects they would face at the peace conference. This group, known as "The Inquiry," had been assembled by House in the latter part of 1917 at Wilson's request. Its members tended to replace regular State Department officers in substantive roles at the conference. Wilson's colleagues thought he seemed more than usually tense and aloof during the voyage. However, when they arrived in Paris on December 13, the president was given a magnificent welcome by the French people, which seemed to augur well for the success of his mission.

Wilson's two overriding objectives at Versailles were a just peace and a worldwide mutual security organization. Having gained general acceptance of his Fourteen Points in the pre-armistice negotiations, Wilson turned his attention to the League of Nations Covenant when the conference opened in January. As chairman of the commission in charge of drafting the Covenant, he and his British colleagues rejected a French plan for a league of victors and adopted Wilson's concept of a universal alliance of all nations, both victors and vanquished. As conceived by Wilson, this organization would depend on the cooperation and leadership of the major powers, the responsible participation of smaller nations, and continual pressure from world public opinion.

Wilson not only designed the League to his own standards, he also made it an integral part of the peace treaty, thus increasing its chances of acceptance by most governments. However, the other delegates did not adopt Wilson's draft of the Covenant when he first presented it to a plenary session in February. They bargained for concessions on specific issues as their price for accepting his draft. Wilson also himself found strong Senate opposition to his mutual security concept when he returned briefly to the United States in February, and he was forced to seek modifications of his own draft Covenant when he went back to Versailles. Under these circumstances, he obviously could not hope to gain his maximum aim on all aspects of the peace settlement.[4]

[4] The fact that the Versailles treaty, including many punitive measures, was presented to the Germans as a *fait accompli* was obviously at variance with Wilson's basic concept of a "peace without victory." It was generally

The first and most important issue of the settlement was the problem of protecting France from future German aggression. Having twice been overrun by their stronger neighbors during the past fifty years, the French believed their security required the creation of one or more buffer states along the Rhine under French control. Wilson stubbornly fought this plan, which he believed would violate the pre-armistice agreement with Germany and serve to provoke future wars.

When Premier Clemenceau, in the heat of debate, accused Wilson of being pro-German, Wilson threatened to leave the conference. Finally, Clemenceau yielded on the creation of a buffer state and permanent French occupation of the Rhineland. Wilson and Lloyd George agreed to a fifteen-year French occupation of the Rhineland and signed a treaty promising Anglo-American support if France were attacked. Germany was also required to demilitarize both banks of the Rhine, and severe limits were placed on the size of its armed forces.

The second most divisive issue that the Allied leaders faced was reparations. The pre-armistice agreement stated that Germany must pay civilian damages; Lloyd George and Clemenceau, driven by strong domestic political pressures, insisted on making Germany pay the entire costs of the war. Wilson conceded many of their specific demands (for example, German payment of disability pensions to veterans and their families). However, he fought hard for the creation of a Reparations Commission that would adjust the actual burden on Germany to what it could afford to pay, rather than insist on a flat sum acceptable to the Allies. In April, Colonel House (acting for Wilson, who was ill) conceded that the Reparations Commission could enforce full payment by Germany of the Allies' demands. This concession greatly reduced Wilson's confidence in House.[5]

Another highly sensitive question that the Allied leaders dealt

---

assumed, until several months after the conference began, that the defeated powers would attend and that they would be allowed to negotiate with the Allies over the peace terms. The unexpectedly bitter disagreements that arose among the Allies probably account for their decision not to invite the defeated powers.

[5] In fact, however, reparations were finally based on the principle of what Germany could afford, after several years of trial and error. See Chapter 5.

with, somewhat more successfully, was the disposition of former German colonies. Wilson wanted the League to assume title to these territories and supervise their administration by smaller nations until they were ready for self-government. However, Britain had promised its dominions and Japan that control of the former colonies would pass to them. Wilson had little choice but to yield on the question of mandating most of the former colonies to small nations. They were given to the British dominions to administer under League mandate and supervision. In the case of Shantung, Japan had gained a no less legal claim to Germany's concession on the peninsula. Wilson created much ill will in Tokyo by strenuously contesting this claim only to lose face with liberals in America when he failed to budge the Japanese. They did promise verbally to restore Shantung to China, however, and the promise was kept a few years later.

Another great controversy centered on Italian efforts to gain control of both shores of the Adriatic Sea. Wilson did not dispute Italy's claims, based on a 1915 treaty with the Allies, but he stubbornly resisted Premier Orlando's effort to gain Fiume, the only good seaport for the new state of Yugoslavia. Once again, Wilson refused to haggle with men whom he considered basically unreasonable. He made a direct appeal to the Italian people over Orlando's head, whereupon Orlando and his foreign minister left the conference. They returned a few weeks later, but no basis for compromise could be found, and the issue was left for direct Italian-Yugoslav negotiations.

The Allied leaders grappled with many other important questions which produced less spectacular debate. For example, one of Japan's major aims at the conference was to obtain a general declaration on the equality of races by the major powers. The effort failed, at least partly because Wilson (for domestic political reasons) did not support it.

On the question of disarmament, Wilson proposed that the Allies accept the same types of arms limitation they were imposing on Germany. He gained only vague promises, but a fresh start was made with naval limitations at the Washington conference three years later. On the subject of how to deal with the Soviet regime in Russia, Wilson stood firmly against taking part in any further joint military intervention with the Allies. However, he also applied to the Soviet Union his novel policy of refusing diplomatic recognition to a regime that he believed had come to power by force.

On the more positive side, the Allied leaders managed to redeem their wartime promise to establish an independent Poland. Wilson and Lloyd George worked together to obtain the internationalization of the port of Danzig and a plebiscite to decide the fate of the ethnically German province of Upper Silesia. Wilson also played a major role in creating the new states of Central Europe from the old Austro-Hungarian Empire. His main contribution, made possible by the expertise of his staff, was to try to preserve some economic unity in the region while drawing the new boundary lines as nearly as possible according to ethnic distribution.

The Germans regarded the treaty of Versailles as a dictated and punitive peace settlement. As noted, it failed in some important respects to square with the pre-armistice agreement. However, in his chosen role of mediator or arbitrator, Wilson probably steered the straightest course he could through the many special interests of the Allied powers. It was an amazing feat of negotiation, given his rapidly diminishing influence over the situation. In his own view, the League of Nations, in which he confidently expected the United States to play the leading role, provided the means of righting whatever wrongs the peace conference had failed to right—or whatever new ones it had created.

The Light on the Path

As Wilson sailed for home with his precious treaty containing the League Covenant, he was exhausted from the strain of months of negotiation under crushing pressures. He still faced a fight to get the treaty ratified by the Senate, but he was about as willing to engage in partisan give-and-take as Moses when he descended with the Ten Commandments. If the Republican senators failed to see how important the stakes were, he would go to the country and start such a groundswell of public support for the treaty that there would be no alternative to passing it intact. As usual, he made no effort to hide his intentions. For example, the French ambassador pointed out that it would be politic to accept some changes of language, mainly to protect the right of Congress to declare war. Wilson said gruffly that he would accept no changes: "The Senate must take its medicine."

When Wilson presented the treaty to the Senate on July 10, he did not even pay lip service (as he had in the past) to the idea that the senators were reasonable men who must decide the matter on its merits. There was only one choice to make, he told them:

> The stage is set, the destiny is disclosed. It has come about by no plan of our conceiving, but by the hand of God who led us into this way. We cannot turn back. We can only go forward, with lifted eyes and freshened spirit, to follow the vision. It was of this that we dreamed at our birth. America shall in truth show the way. The light streams upon the path ahead, and nowhere else.

Where in fact did the various senators stand on the central issue—U.S. membership in the League of Nations? Since Wilson's tactics were based on the assumption of party loyalty, they tended to polarize the Senate on party lines. Some Democrats had doubts about the League, but they were afraid of what might happen to their careers if they opposed the president. At least thirty-eight of the forty-seven Democratic senators were prepared to vote the way Wilson asked them to, and only three were strongly opposed to the League.

Republicans, who controlled the Senate by a majority of two votes, tended to oppose the treaty, because Wilson had identified it far too clearly as a monument to himself and his Democratic administration. Of the forty-nine Republican senators, fifteen would vote against the treaty under any circumstances; they became known as the "irreconcilables." The rest were prepared to accept it with strong, moderate, or mild changes, which were referred to as "reservations." There were eighteen Republican "strong reservationists," six "moderate reservationists," and about ten "mild reservationists."

Since ratification required two-thirds of the Senate vote, it could be achieved only by winning the support of some of the strong reservationists. Senator Lodge placed himself at the head of this group, because he considered it his duty as chairman of the Foreign Relations Committee to take a position acceptable to most Republican senators. Thus, the crucial issue was the attitude of Lodge and the strong reservationists toward a worldwide mutual security system designed to pit the strength of its members against any nation that embarked on a course of aggression.

Lodge believed such a system would not work because the major powers would not accept such sweeping limits on their sovereignty. He argued that no nation would go to war unless it felt compelled to protect its vital interests; thus, the League Covenant's guarantees of all national borders were worse than no guarantees because they were illusory. To these arguments, proponents of the League replied that the most vital interest of all nations was to prevent a repetition of the great war and that statesmen must be forced by world public opinion to accept this new reality.

More basically, the strong reservationists questioned the value of trying to preserve for all time the borders and distribution of power which had resulted from the war and the Versailles peace conference. They pointed out that change and growth are the rules of history, and they asked if the American people would ever dream of going to war to protect Japan's hold on Shantung or Britain's position in India or Ireland. To this, League proponents answered that no power, including the United States, would be asked by the League to assume the risks of war except in situations in which that country's vital interests were clearly involved.

Membership in the League, according to strong reservationists, would raise grave dangers to the U.S. constitutional system by increasing the president's powers at the expense of Congress, by making necessary a large peacetime army, and by reducing the government's autonomy in immigration and tariff matters. League supporters answered that the powers of Congress in foreign affairs would be little affected by League membership and that far larger armed forces would be needed by nonmembers than by members of the League. Furthermore, a partial loss of autonomy in tariff and immigration matters would be more than compensated by easier access to foreign markets and a healthier functioning of the world economic system.

The strong reservationists were prepared to ratify most aspects of the Versailles treaty that were unrelated to the League. They would even accept U.S. membership in the League of Nations, provided Congress retained the right to evaluate each situation requiring possible use of American forces as it arose. They were determined to issue no blank checks for future U.S. participation in collective security measures.

This was how the debate stood in early September 1919, when President Wilson decided to take his case to the country. He had met several times in July and August with selected groups of senators for extended discussion of the treaty, but he had failed to make any converts to his position. Meanwhile, as Lodge expected, the normal caution and isolationism of the American people were being reasserted with each passing day. As the comfortable ways of peace returned, Wilson would find it harder to demand the disciplined sacrifice of a nation on a wartime footing.

In spite of being in poor health and under great nervous strain, Wilson set out on a nationwide speaking tour. He traveled eight thousand miles in three weeks, often delivering two major speeches a day and conducting endless meetings and press conferences while his unairconditioned train rocked through the sweltering heat. In Pueblo, Colorado, he suffered a partial nervous breakdown and was rushed back to Washington; there, a paralytic stroke almost completely incapacitated him for the next few months. During this period, Mrs. Wilson shielded him from virtually everything, including the sound advice of his closest associates. By January 1920, his body had partially recovered, but his mind never seemed to regain its full grasp on reality.

Meanwhile, a series of votes in November showed that the Democrats had enough votes to defeat the treaty with Lodge's reservations, while Lodge had the votes to defeat it with only minor changes or none at all. The Senate minority leader had waited until this late date to make known certain changes that Wilson had decided to accept if necessary before his illness. These were similar to Lodge's reservations in many respects and almost identical with the original position of the Republican mild reservationists. Thus, it appeared that a compromise could easily have been reached if Wilson had shown some flexibility in July or August before positions began to harden. Even in November, there was still room for compromise, but Wilson wrote from his sickbed advising his supporters to vote against the Lodge reservations.

During the next few months, liberal pressure groups and prestigious individuals brought strong influence to bear on moderate senators of both parties to compromise their differences and save the treaty. Lodge himself took part in discussions with his opponents, but he gave little ground on his main reservations, which concerned the collective security aspect of the League.

As Wilson regained some of his strength, he sought to rally Democratic senators against any significant compromise. Nevertheless, when the final vote took place in March 1920, twenty-one Democrats broke ranks and voted for the treaty with Lodge's reservations. Twelve Republicans voted against Lodge and the treaty. Thus, neither Lodge nor Wilson commanded a two-thirds majority. Yet even if the Lodge version had received the necessary votes, the United States might still not have joined the League. Wilson could have refused to ratify the treaty in this form, on the ground that Lodge's reservations amounted to nullification; his statements at the time suggested that he would do so.

The March 1920 vote ended all hope of American participation in the League, but some of Wilson's principles were embodied in the treaty system that his successors built during the decade of the 1920s. As we shall see in the next chapter, when their frail system of international law came under attack in the 1930s, the United States took the lead in trying to make the concept of collective security work.

Suggested Reading

BAILEY, THOMAS A. *Woodrow Wilson and the Great Betrayal.* New York: Macmillan, 1945.
————. *Woodrow Wilson and the Lost Peace.* New York: Macmillan, 1944.
FIFIELD, RUSSELL H. *Woodrow Wilson and the Far East: The Diplomacy of the Shantung Question.* New York: Crowell, 1952.
GARRATY, J. A. *Henry Cabot Lodge: A Biography.* New York: Knopf, 1953.
GELFAND, L. E. *The Inquiry: American Preparation for Peace, 1917–1919.* New Haven, Conn.: Yale University Press, 1963.
JOHNSON, C. O. *Borah of Idaho.* New York: Longman, Green, 1936.
KENNAN, GEORGE F. *Russia and the West Under Lenin and Stalin.* Boston: Little, Brown, 1960.
————. *Soviet-American Relations, 1917–1920.* 2 vols. Princeton, N.J.: Princeton University Press, 1956, 1958.
LODGE, HENRY CABOT. *The Senate and the League of Nations.* New York: Scribners, 1925.
MAYER, ARNO J. *Politics and Diplomacy of Peace-Making: Containment and Counterrevolution at Versailles, 1918–1919.* New York: Knopf, 1968.
TEMPERLEY, H. W. V. *A History of the Peace Conference at Paris.* 6 vols. London: Frowde, Hodder, & Stoughton, 1920–1924.
THOMPSON, JOHN M. *Russia, Bolshevism, and the Versailles Peace.* Princeton, N.J.: Princeton University Press, 1966.

5

The Rise and Fall
of the Rule of Law

The Republican secretaries of state in the 1920s tried to steer a moderate course between Wilsonian universalism and pure isolation. Their views resembled those of the "strong reservationists" summarized in the previous chapter. Charles Evans Hughes (who served from 1921 to 1925) was the dominant figure at the Washington Naval Conference, which produced a decade of naval disarmament and reduced tensions in the western Pacific. Hughes also took the lead in revising the Versailles treaty system for assessing German reparations payments.

Frank B. Kellogg (1925–29) is often ridiculed for his grandiose and illusory "treaty to outlaw war." But by other and less spectacular means he too pursued the goal of an international system based on law. Henry L. Stimson (1929–33) fought hard to defend the treaty system when worldwide depression gave birth to lawless, expansionist regimes in Europe and Asia. In order to understand the aims of the treaties that gained acceptance in the 1920s, we must go back and trace some problems that developed before and during World War I.

Policy Toward Asia

The Japanese had grown extremely sensitive to alleged American interference in Japan's relations with China since the Taft administration tried to neutralize Japanese gains in Manchuria.

In 1913, the California legislature passed a law forbidding Japanese to own land in the state. This served to revive Japanese bitterness about racial discrimination in the American West, which had been only partially laid to rest by the Gentlemen's Agreement. On both sides of the Pacific, there was no lack of demagogic politicians and journalists and representatives of special interests who began to spread the word that a Pacific war was inevitable. However, Secretary Bryan made every effort to conciliate Japan on the issue of California's discriminatory land law.

With the outbreak of war in Europe, Japan laid claim to Germany's Asian possessions. The embattled Allies, unable to restrain Japanese ambitions in the Pacific, chose to legitimize them by secret treaties. In so doing, they hoped to moderate Japan's aims and prevent Tokyo from signing a separate peace with Berlin. Although these Allied treaties remained unknown in the United States until it entered the war, a segment of U.S. opinion reacted strongly to Japan's expansionist moves in Asia and to the purely imaginary threat of a Japanese attack against the United States itself.

In early 1915, Japan presented the Chinese with its notorious twenty-one demands, aimed at reducing China to a protectorate. Chinese leaders astutely made the demands known abroad, and the world press condemned the Japanese demands. In the United States, they were viewed as a direct challenge to the open door policy and to American interests in China. However, President Wilson's government was not prepared to risk war with Japan. Bryan responded to the Japanese move with a relatively mild note stating that the United States could not recognize any transfers of territory brought about by force (thus originating the nonrecognition doctrine that would play a key role in later U.S.-Japanese relations).

America's entry into the war made this country the ally of Japan, which forced the Wilson administration to focus some of its attention, however briefly, on Far Eastern affairs. The administration's basic attitude toward that region had been summed up already by Lansing before he succeeded Bryan as secretary of state. Lansing remarked that it would be "quixotic in the extreme to allow the question of China's territorial integrity to entangle the United States in international difficulties."

The approach adopted by Lansing with Wilson's blessing was not unlike the method followed by other U.S. administrations before and after them. They minimized the danger of a collision with Japan over the issue of China by temporarily and conditionally recognizing Japan's special interests on the mainland, but continued to stress the open door and China's territorial integrity as basic U.S. aims—while making it clear that America had no intention of fighting for these principles.

Since the United States had no forces to spare to defend the Philippines or the Hawaiian Islands, the best course seemed to be to persuade Japan that it was in its interest to respect the status quo. Japanese leaders, for their part, realized that America's mood of self-righteous exaltation upon entering the war provided an ideal atmosphere in which to settle all outstanding issues.

Secretary Lansing and Viscount Ishii negotiated for several months over the precise wording of a joint declaration of policy. Ishii sought American recognition of past and future Japanese expansion on the mainland. Lansing tried to limit the statement as nearly as possible to the open door concept. The result was a deliberately ambiguous document in which each side could point to language that supported its aims. Lansing had refused to recognize Japan's "paramount interest" in China. However, he did trade public recognition of Japan's "special interests" in China for a reaffirmation of the open door policy by Japan. This latter pledge was made in somewhat general terms in the public agreement and in more specific terms in a secret memorandum signed by the two statesmen.

Tension had been building in the western Pacific for many years. The Lansing-Ishii agreement had merely papered over the perennial conflict between American and Japanese aims in China. Japan remained ensconced in Shantung, and the United States continued verbally to support the open door and China's territorial integrity. Racial slights suffered at Versailles made the

Japanese grimly determined to resist Western "bullying." For their part, U.S. leaders disliked seeing Japan fall heir to the German island groups that lay between Hawaii and the Philippines and surrounded Guam.

Issues such as these began to stimulate naval rivalry among the former Allies in the early 1920s. America sent most of its fleet to the Pacific; Japan countered by launching a vast program of naval building. Since England and Japan were allies, the chances of Britain being drawn into a Japanese-American clash could not be totally ignored. The threat of a naval building race between England and the United States finally brought all concerned to the negotiating table.

The Quest for Worldwide Stability Through Disarmament

The first and most successful of three disarmament conferences held in the 1920s was convened in Washington on November 11, 1921. Secretary of State Hughes delivered an opening speech in which he told the other delegates precisely what he hoped they would accept. Hughes captured headlines all over the world by proposing that capital ships already built or under construction by the major powers be limited to 500,000 tons each for Britain and the United States and 300,000 for Japan.

The fact that his terms were clear, public, and very simple gave Hughes a great advantage over the other delegates; millions of people supported his terms before anyone else had even been heard from, and this made it extremely awkward for other powers to debate the issues. The British would have enjoyed a clear advantage if the unit of measure had been completed ships alone. Japan would have almost equaled the United States if the unit had been all ships completed, under construction, and planned. Although the Japanese delegates fought hard for a more favorable 10:10:7 ratio, they finally accepted 5:5:3 with two provisos. They insisted on not scrapping their huge new battleship _Mutsu_, and they demanded a British and American pledge not to strengthen their fortifications in the western Pacific or build new ones there. These conditions were accepted, and the total capital ship tonnage figures finally worked out were 525,000 for the United States and Britain, 315,000 for Japan.[1]

The conference also produced a series of interrelated agreements, mostly initiated by Secretary Hughes, intended to resolve the main political conflicts in the Pacific area and reduce the danger of war between the great powers. This was hardly an isolationist approach to foreign policy, and Hughes realized that conservative senators would examine his work carefully to be sure there were no "entangling alliances" or open-ended military commitments. Given the economizing spirit of Congress, he knew he was far less likely to be attacked for "abandoning" America's Far Eastern interests.

In addition to the five-power treaty limiting capital ships, all nations represented at the conference (except China) agreed to maintain the open door principle and to respect China's sovereignty, independence, and territorial integrity. There was also a four-power treaty, signed by America, Britain, Japan, and France, which ended the Anglo-Japanese alliance and pledged all four states to respect each other's territorial rights and possessions and to consult together if a controversy arose between any two of them.[2]

The United States recognized Japan's League of Nations mandate over the Caroline, Marshall, and Mariana islands; in return, it gained free access to the cable station at Yap and the right to trade and carry on missionary activity in these islands. The wartime Lansing-Ishii agreement was canceled, and Japan renounced the "twenty-one demands" it had made to the Peking government. Finally, Japan and China signed a treaty restoring Chinese sovereignty over the Shantung peninsula, and Japan indicated that it would withdraw its troops from Siberia and Sakhalin (which it did in 1922 and 1925 respectively).

Of the major powers, the country with the greatest economic

---

[1] France and Italy accepted capital ship tonnage limits of 175,000 each, but France refused to reach an agreement covering cruisers, destroyers, or submarines. The limits set on total tonnage of aircraft carriers were 135,000 each for Great Britain and the United States, 81,000 for Japan, and 60,000 each for France and Italy.

[2] This treaty was attacked as an "alliance" by certain senators, but Lodge, as majority leader, successfully steered it through the Senate.

and strategic stake in the western Pacific was Japan, which emerged from the Washington conference the dominant naval power in that region. The 5:5:3 ratio did not allow the British or American governments a large enough margin of strength to challenge Japan in the western Pacific. Although Japan issued new promises to respect American territorial rights in the region, the Philippines remained a hostage.

Since the United States had great potential strength and the least clearly defined aims in the Pacific region generally, it was imperative for Japan and the United States to understand each other better if they were to avoid war. A tacit meeting of minds was achieved between Hughes and Baron Shidehara (Japanese delegate to the conference and foreign minister during much of the 1920s). Japan would avoid direct challenge to the open door and China's territorial integrity. In return, the United States would avoid racial discrimination against Japanese living in America or attempting to immigrate there. In addition, both sides probably assumed that the United States would regard with favor Japan's claim to most favored nation trading privileges and other perquisites of a major world power.

Unfortunately, this unwritten understanding began to erode as early as 1924, when Congress passed a frankly racist ban on immigration by any Asians (including Japanese) on the grounds that they were ineligible for citizenship. The racial slight was far more deeply felt in Japan than most Americans realized. And Japanese leaders' closely related fears of being denied access to vital overseas markets were heightened by the rise of Chinese nationalism and the worldwide depression of the late 1920s.

In 1927, President Coolidge invited Britain, France, Japan, and Italy to a second naval conference at Geneva to try to limit cruiser strength. This had not been covered by the Washington agreements, and Britain and Japan were busy adding to their fleets, while the economy-minded United States stood still. France and Italy refused even to attend the 1927 conference because strong elements in their governments resented the inferior status they had accepted at Washington.

Anglo-American differences provided the crucial reason for the failure of this conference. Britain wanted a sufficiently large number of lightly armed small cruisers to protect its far-flung empire and commerce. The United States wanted a smaller number of heavy, long-range cruisers that would require a minimum of overseas bases. Although the Japanese tried to mediate the dispute, no formula could be found that would meet everyone's needs.

The 1928 Kellogg-Briand pact originated as a plan by which the United States and France would renounce war as a means of settling disputes with each other. A Columbia University professor suggested the idea to French Foreign Minister Aristide Briand, who was evidently prepared to take seriously any scheme that might link the United States a little closer to his country. Briand proposed the idea in an open letter to the American people.

Secretary Kellogg at first liked neither the substance of the plan nor the way in which it was presented; he disregarded Briand's overtures for the better part of a year. Yet when he finally discussed it with the Foreign Relations Committee, he found the senators receptive to a multilateral treaty to outlaw war, though cool to a bilateral pact with France (as being too close to an "alliance"). Perhaps because it was so rare to find this committee in favor of anything, Kellogg himself began to wax enthusiastic. In the end, it was he who overcame Briand's reluctance to open the treaty to signature by all nations. Fifteen signed in August 1928, and most other nations eventually followed suit.

With one dissenting vote, the U.S. Senate ratified the treaty in early 1929—and then promptly voted funds to build fifteen new cruisers, as proposed by Coolidge. Few senators seem to have been bothered by the inconsistency. They had voted for the Kellogg-Briand pact precisely because it committed the United States to nothing. They supported naval appropriations because Coolidge had allowed Anglo-American relations to degenerate into renewed rivalry and suspicion.

President Hoover and Secretary of State Stimson took office in March 1929 and immediately set to work to improve the climate of transatlantic relations. Hoover met with Ramsay MacDonald, newly elected Labour prime minister, and the two statesmen reached a full understanding on naval matters. In 1930, Stimson led the American delegation to a third naval conference in London, which produced a comprehensive agreement acceptable to both Britain and the United States.

The chief dissenter at this conference was Japan, whose military leaders were demanding full naval parity. Civilian members of the Japanese delegation took the risky step of accepting unequal ratios during the temporary absence of the Japanese naval minister from the conference. This challenged the power of Japan's military leaders in an area where they traditionally enjoyed the final word. So great was the resulting crisis that it led within a few years to full control of the government by the military. This, in turn, made it much more difficult for Japan and the United States to reach any understanding on China, the basic issue that divided them. To understand this sequence of events we must first turn our attention to the economic factors that produced the 1929 depression.

Crisis in World Economic Relations

The United States emerged from World War I in the strongest financial position of any nation. Former Allies owed America more than $10 billion; Americans proceeded to invest abroad an equal sum over the next ten years. However, since the United States had always been a net borrower of foreign capital (paid for by commodity exports) before 1914, its leaders were unused to the responsibilities that accompany power. This is one reason why they showed so little concern for preserving a healthy world economic system during the 1920s and 1930s.

High tariff walls, aggressive export expansion, and a grim determination to collect all debts the day they fell due—regardless of the debtor's ability to pay—were the hallmarks of America's interwar economic policy. There can be little doubt that such attitudes caused great harm and that the United States would have been wiser to write off its Allies' debts as part of America's contribution to the common cause. During the 1920s Great Britain, also a net lender to other Allied powers, twice suggested canceling all war debts; the proposal was sternly rebuffed by

Congress and the administrations of Wilson and his successors. After all, as Coolidge put it, "they hired the money."

Nevertheless, the United States conducted lengthy negotiations with its former allies, gradually scaling down the sums it claimed from them and softening the terms of payment. Although Washington rejected the debtor nations' position that they would pay only what they could collect from Germany in reparations, this was, in fact, all that most nations paid.

Germany had agreed (under threat of occupation) to pay the equivalent of some $33 billion. When Germany first defaulted on its payments in 1923, the European Reparations Commission authorized France to occupy the Ruhr industrial zone. German output was slow to recover under these conditions, and the government resorted to printing paper money. The resulting inflation devoured the savings and self-respect of Germany's middle class and fueled a bitter desire for revenge. American financiers helped negotiate two successive agreements to scale down German reparations payments. These agreements, named for their authors, were the Dawes plan of 1924 and the Young plan of 1930. The latter scheme finally recognized the fact that the only way the Allies could—or would—service their war debts to the United States was from German reparations payments.

Meanwhile, Americans with surplus capital invested about $2.25 billion in German government and industrial securities during the decade of the 1920s. Over the same period, Germany paid the Allied powers some $2 billion in reparations, and the Allies paid the United States $2 billion in war debts. In effect, American investors were paying the war debts which the U.S. government claimed from its former Allies. Americans poured large sums into other countries as well, raising the total invested abroad to about $13.5 billion by 1928. This steady flow of capital was needed to stave off a worldwide economic disaster, because the United States kept raising its tariffs on foreign goods. As a result, other countries found it extremely difficult to earn money to service their debts and pay for needed imports.

The stock market crash of October 1929 wiped out much of the American public's surplus capital. With dollars no longer finding their way abroad, foreign governments had no way to pay their debts to the United States; foreign consumers had no money with which to buy U.S. exports. Under these conditions, it would have been sound economic policy for the United States to lower its tariffs and give foreign producers a chance to compete in U.S. markets. Instead, Congress shortsightedly raised tariffs and helped reduce world trade to disastrously low levels.

In 1931, Germany and Austria formed a customs union, in violation of the peace treaties. France reacted by demanding payment of its short-term loans to Austrian and German banks, bringing both countries close to bankruptcy. This was the final blow needed to topple Europe's shaky economic system. President Hoover proposed, and the other powers agreed to, a one-year moratorium on reparations and war-debt payments. The countries that claimed reparations from Germany sharply reduced their demands on condition that the United States would do the same with its war-debt claims. Unfortunately, Congress not only refused, it even voted new penalties against nations that failed to service their debts on time, thus gaining the United States widespread ill will.

During 1932 and 1933, intensive studies of the causes of depression were made in preparation for a World Economic Conference, which would seek to enact remedies. Among the chief problems identified were high tariffs, war debts, the drying up of investment capital, and the abandonment of the gold standard by certain powers, notably England. Shortly after taking office, President Franklin D. Roosevelt indicated that his policy was to support stabilization of the major currencies (including the dollar) by keeping them pegged at a fixed rate in terms of gold. However, before the conference began, Roosevelt took the United States off the gold standard to help raise the price of U.S. commodities. This important national priority was partially achieved, but only at the expense of a major international effort to restore stable exchange rates among currencies—a necessary step toward reviving world trade. Other nations acted equally selfishly during the depression years, but few had the power of the United States to influence the world economy for better or worse.

Conflict over Manchuria

The occupation of Manchuria by Japanese troops during 1931–32 marked the start of a new era. In the next decade, radically expansionist forces would rise to challenge the concepts of international law and order that had been fostered by the United States, Britain, and France (the so-called status quo or "satisfied" powers) in the 1920s. That the first round of this epic struggle should involve a clash between Japan, China, and the United States in remote Manchuria deserves some explanation.

We have seen that Japan won important rights in Manchuria by its victory in the Russo-Japanese war (1904–5). These and later gains were achieved by tactics learned from Western imperialist powers; they were sanctioned by perfectly legal treaties. Each U.S. administration since Theodore Roosevelt's had wavered between recognizing a Japanese sphere in Manchuria and contesting it (verbally) as a violation of the open door and China's integrity. Each had also announced it would never back its stand with force.

In the 1920s, Chinese Nationalist forces began a long struggle to reunify China and erase all privileges enjoyed by foreigners (including Americans) that violated its sovereignty. By the late 1920s, military and political clashes between the Nationalists and Japanese troops guarding the South Manchurian Railway became common. The young Chinese warlord of Manchuria leaned toward the Nationalists. Perhaps even more disturbing to Japanese commanders were signs that Foreign Minister Shidehara was willing to compromise with the Chinese Nationalists. In the eyes of the Japanese military, this compounded the earlier encroachment on its prerogatives by civilian leaders who had accepted unequal ratios at the London Naval Conference.

The worldwide economic depression provided new dangers and new opportunities so far as Japanese military leaders were concerned. On the minus side, there was growing pressure on Japanese statesmen to cut the defense budget and to accept inferior status among the major powers and declining access to world markets.[3] On the plus side, a depression, like a world war, tended to occupy the attention of other powers and give Japan a freer hand in East Asia.

Thus, on the night of September 8, 1931, Japanese troops, probably acting without authority from Tokyo, carried out a well-planned coup against Chinese Nationalist strongholds near the South Manchurian Railway, using an alleged Chinese attack as pretext. China's appeal for League of Nations and United States support produced an initially cautious response; Stimson and others believed that, by avoiding public criticism, they might help Japan's civilian leaders assert control over the army in Manchuria. However, by December, it was plain that nothing of the sort would happen.

President Hoover and British Prime Minister Sir John Simon ruled out applying economic sanctions against Japan, which Secretary Stimson favored. Stimson was left with two alternatives: to do nothing or to organize moral and political pressure against Japan. He chose the latter course and, in conjunction with Hoover, revived Bryan's policy of refusing to recognize a situation that had been created by violating U.S. treaty rights. The treaties he cited were the nine-power treaty supporting the open door policy signed at the Washington Naval Conference in 1922 and the Kellogg-Briand pact of 1928.

The British prime minister announced that he saw no need to support the U.S. nonrecognition policy, but he changed his mind after Japan bombarded Shanghai. (The attack was aimed at forcing the Chinese to end their boycott of Japanese goods.) In March 1932, the League of Nations Assembly endorsed the nonrecognition policy; however, Japan proclaimed the independence of Manchukuo, as it called its puppet state in Manchuria.

In February 1934, the League adopted the recommendations of the Lytton Commission, which had been sent to investigate the situation in Manchuria (at Japan's suggestion). These recom-

---

[3] Japanese advocates of radical expansionism usually identified the United States as their chief antagonist because it alone had the power to check Japan, because it had inflicted humiliating racial slights against their people, and because it had begun to resort to economic protectionism, which could have disastrous consequences whether intended by Washington or not.

mendations tried to reconcile Chinese sovereignty over Manchuria with protection of legitimate Japanese economic interests in the province. However, the Japanese Army was far too entrenched in Manchuria to accept this well-meaning interference. Ambassador Matsuoka, a fiery spokesman for the radical expansionists, announced Japan's withdrawal from the League.

Before his inauguration in 1933, Franklin Roosevelt conferred with Stimson and indicated his intention of maintaining the latter's Far Eastern policy. However, Roosevelt and Secretary of State Hull adopted a milder tone in protesting Japan's violations of U.S. treaty rights. At the same time, the new administration refused to recognize Manchukuo and kept the U.S. fleet in the Pacific, announcing that it would be built up to the strength allowed by the London treaty.

Thus, the years from 1933 to 1937 were a period of mild and indirect conflict between Japan and the United States. The Japanese were preparing the way for further expansion in North China. The American ambassador in Tokyo, Joseph Grew, watched for signs of a political swing back to the policies of Baron Shidehara of the 1920s. However, most moderate Japanese politicians had been demoralized by the depression and by the tactics of political violence by which young military extremists seized power.

In fact, President Roosevelt had little time for Asian affairs in the mid-1930s; domestic problems demanded almost all of his attention. The one foreign area he could not ignore because it was too close to home—Latin America—was also the one area in which previous administrations had laid the groundwork for a substantial improvement in relations.

The Good Neighbor Policy

The tide of imperialism receded slowly in the 1920s and early 1930s. Harding began and Coolidge completed the restoration of self-government in the Dominican Republic. Coolidge withdrew the small detachments of U.S. Marines from Nicaragua as well as Santo Domingo, but Coolidge sent the marines back to Nicaragua in 1927, claiming U.S. interests were threatened by a new civil war. He also sent Henry Stimson (secretary of war under Taft and soon to be secretary of state under Hoover). Stimson negotiated the "peace of Tipitapa," in which both sides agreed to let the marines disarm their forces and create a new national army; the marines remained until January 1933.

Therefore, the main thrust of U.S. policy, in the years just before FDR's inauguration, was toward renouncing Theodore Roosevelt's corollary to the Monroe Doctrine. (This, we will recall, was the assertion of an inherent U.S. "right" to keep order in the hemisphere to deny external powers a pretext for intervention.) Latin American statesmen had been demanding for some years that the United States renounce this concept, and Hoover went a long way toward meeting their demand. However, it remained for Secretary Hull finally to renounce the Roosevelt corollary in a solemn inter-American treaty signed at Montevideo in December 1933.

During the summer of 1934, the last marines left Haiti; the issue of armed intervention did not arise again in the hemisphere until the 1960s. In the interim, U.S. officials and corporations continued to exert great influence, often simply by passing the word that a particular politician was "unacceptable." Nevertheless, Washington's abandonment of Theodore Roosevelt's corollary produced an era of unparalelled good will in U.S.-Latin American relations. The tangible rewards for this new "good neighbor policy" included support by Latin American republics for the Allied cause during World War II, in spite of serious Axis efforts at subversion.

In abandoning the practice of armed intervention, the United States returned to its traditional concept of the Monroe Doctrine, a policy of resistance to interference by *external* powers in the Western Hemisphere. However, the traditional American policies toward Europe ("no entangling alliances") and in Asia (the open door and China's territorial integrity) proved far less helpful guides to U.S. interest during the second half of the 1930s.

Suggested Reading

ADLER, SELIG. *The Uncertain Giant: American Foreign Policy Between the Wars, 1921–1941.* New York: Macmillan, 1969.

ELLIS, L. ETHAN. *Republican Foreign Policy, 1921–1933*. New Brunswick, N.J.: Rutgers University Press, 1968.

FEIS, HERBERT. *The Diplomacy of the Dollar: First Era, 1919–1932*. Baltimore: Johns Hopkins Press, 1950.

FERRELL, ROBERT H. *American Diplomacy in the Great Depression: Hoover-Stimson Foreign Policy, 1929–1933*. New Haven, Conn.: Yale University Press, 1957.

————. *Peace in Their Time: The Origins of the Kellogg-Briand Pact*. New Haven, Conn.: Yale University Press, 1952.

FLEMING, D. F. *The United States and World Organization, 1920–1933*. New York: Columbia University Press, 1938.

GRISWOLD, A. W. *The Far Eastern Policy of the United States*. New York: Harcourt Brace Jovanovich, 1938.

HOOVER, HERBERT. *The Memoirs of Herbert Hoover*. Vols. 2 and 3. New York: Macmillan, 1952.

PUSEY, M. J. *Charles Evans Hughes*. 2 vols. New York: Macmillan, 1963.

RAPPAPORT, ARMIN. *Henry L. Stimson and Japan*. Chicago: University of Chicago Press, 1963.

STIMSON, HENRY L., and McGEORGE BUNDY. *On Active Service in Peace and War*. New York: Harper & Row, 1948.

YANAGA, CHITOSHI. *Japan Since Perry*. New York: McGraw-Hill, 1949.

6

The Road to War,
1935-41

From the passage of the first Neutrality Act in
1935 until Pearl Harbor, Congress and President Roosevelt
often worked at cross-purposes. Each tried to avoid mistakes that
they perceived in U.S. policy during the 1914–18 war. For Congress, the lesson was to isolate America from all future European
conflicts; this short-sighted goal made it practically certain that
Hitler's threat to his neighbors would grow into a clear and
present danger to the United States. For Roosevelt, the problem
was to avoid repeating political errors that helped defeat Wilson's
postwar plans and left Germany with a deep sense of injustice.

Franklin Roosevelt combined the energy and charisma of his
great cousin with historic opportunities for leadership that were
very similar to Wilson's. Although perhaps less able in dealing
with the substance of foreign policy than either TR or Wilson,
Franklin Roosevelt was one of the greatest builders and leaders
of coalitions in modern times. His reputation as a liberal internationalist (born of past service as assistant secretary of the Navy)
was something of a political liability in the isolationist climate
of the late 1930s. Therefore, Roosevelt's initial response to the
rising war danger in Europe and Asia was carefully ambiguous
—avoiding moves that could be attacked as interventionist, yet
groping for ways to use American influence to contain the
restless expansionism of Germany, Italy, and Japan.

Only in the Western Hemisphere did Roosevelt feel free to

act decisively during the 1930s. As we have seen, the good
neighbor policy pursued by his administration had already been
sketched out by Hoover and Stimson; it helped to prevent the
possible spread of German and Japanese influence into the
Western Hemisphere.

Hitler Attacks the Treaty System

By 1935, the Roosevelt administration recognized an acute
danger to U.S. interests from the strategy Hitler had announced
and that he seemed to be pursuing. In his book _Mein
Kampf,_ Hitler had stated that he planned to unite all German
peoples (including those in neighboring countries) within an
enlarged German state, conquer additional territory in eastern
Europe, recover the colonies lost in the Great War, and raise
Germany's stature to an all-time high. This clearly meant
trampling on the rights of other nations and nullifying the peace
treaties of 1919.

Mussolini seized power in Italy as early as 1922. Hitler tried
to copy his example the following year and failed miserably.
Ten years later, depression-ridden Germany was ripe for the
combination of fanatic racism, strong-arm tactics, and glowing
promises of national revival that Adolf Hitler had concocted.
Von Hindenberg, senile president of the Weimar Republic,
named him chancellor in January 1933, and the Reichstag
(parliament) gave him power to rule by decree for four years.

Franklin Roosevelt took office in March 1933, only five weeks
after Hitler, and promptly announced the U.S. position for the
forthcoming general disarmament conference. Roosevelt's proposal attracted very wide attention, not only because it departed
from previous U.S. policy, but also because it challenged Hitler
to indicate his own intentions.

Specifically, Roosevelt proposed that the major powers sign a
nonaggression pact and adopt a program of mutual disarmament to include abolition of all offensive weapons and a reduction in defensive arms. If the other powers would agree to this,
Roosevelt indicated that the United States was prepared to take
part, to a limited degree, in the League's collective security

system. Going much farther than any president since Wilson, Roosevelt offered to consult with the League of Nations governments if a case of aggression occurred; moreover, he said the United States would not interfere with League sanctions against an aggressor (if the U.S. view on who had committed aggression coincided with the League's judgment). Although the lower House of Congress approved the plan, the U.S. Senate refused to grant the president such wide discretionary powers. No bill was passed at this time, although the concept of limiting U.S. arms shipments in time of war would be revived in later neutrality laws.

Hitler's initial response was to claim willingness to defer rearming for five years. (The Versailles treaty required that Germany forgo indefinitely all except very small and lightly armed defensive forces.) Hitler also made it clear that he would not be bound by any majority votes at the disarmament conference or sign any document tending to hold Germany in an inferior position. Even so, the climate of international meetings did not prove congenial to the Nazi regime. Germany withdrew from the disarmament conference after the first round of talks and also withdrew from the League of Nations in October 1933.

A year and a half later, Hitler announced the goal of a 500,000-man army, five times what the Versailles treaty allowed; all male Germans would be liable for military service. At the same time, Hitler promised to observe the territorial provisions of the Versailles treaty. In March 1936, he repudiated his promise and sent two hundred thousand troops to occupy the Rhineland. England and France were caught off balance as their attention was focused on Mussolini's invasion of Ethiopia.

Congress and the Neutrality Laws

To what extent did the neutrality laws enacted by Congress in this period influence the policies of other major powers? No one can say for certain, of course. But the sequence of events in the mid-1930s strongly suggests that isolationist sentiment in Congress encouraged the expansionist powers and helped under-

mine whatever firmness British and French leaders might otherwise have shown.

Italian military pressure on Ethiopia in early 1935 led to a
replay of the 1933 debate between Congress and the Roosevelt
administration over the proper type of neutrality law to adopt.[1]
President Roosevelt wanted a neutrality law flexible enough to
allow him to single out one particular side as the aggressor and
impose a punitive embargo on arms shipments. He also wanted
to be able to coordinate this embargo or "sanction" with
similar moves by League of Nations members. In effect, the
United States would be taking part in the League's collective
security program.

Although there was no certainty that collective security would
succeed in preventing a new world war, liberal internationalists
have always tended to believe that it offered the best hope available. By contrast, appeasement or inaction seemed certain to lead
to eventual war (as proved to be the case). However, there were
two aspects of the collective security principle that many
congressmen found deeply disturbing. First, it involved some
loss of America's highly prized freedom to act independently;
second, it could lead to U.S. involvement in a war.

Congress passed the first Neutrality Act in August 1935, making
it mandatory for the president to deny arms to *both* sides in
any foreign struggle. The president was given discretionary power
to warn U.S. citizens that their government would not undertake
to protect them if they chose to travel on belligerent ships. Moreover, the law made it illegal to transport arms to or for belligerent states in U.S. ships, and it set up a system of licensing that
allowed the secretary of state to control the manufacture of
arms and their export from the United States.[2]

When Mussolini invaded Ethiopia in October 1935, Roosevelt
invoked the Neutrality Act. He was not required to do so because

---

[1] This was one of the first skirmishes in the ongoing legislative-executive
feud over the latter's power to involve the United States in wars.

[2] These broad powers to control the manufacture and shipment of arms
were adapted to a program of economic warfare against the Axis powers
during 1941, the final year of American nonbelligerency.

Italy did not declare war, but a ban on arms shipments to both sides would deprive Italy more than landlocked Ethiopia. Roosevelt supplemented the arms embargo by a request that American exporters of oil observe a "moral embargo" on shipments above and beyond Italy's normal peacetime requirements. These guidelines were followed reasonably closely, according to a later account by Hull.

Meanwhile, the League of Nations met and declared Italy an aggressor; it then took the even bolder step of voting to impose economic sanctions. Britain maneuvered its Mediterranean fleet near the Suez Canal (vital to Italy's war effort), and it seemed for a time that the machinery of collective security might be taking hold. However, Hitler seized the occasion to renounce all aspects of the Versailles treaty and occupy the Rhineland. This created a far more dangerous situation, in which French and British leaders had two basic choices: (1) to try to force both Mussolini and Hitler to yield the fruits of aggression, or (2) to appease Mussolini and try to drive wedges between him and Hitler.

The first choice could have led rather swiftly to war, for which the Western democracies were ill prepared; the second choice virtually guaranteed that war would come at a later date. In part because the United States was hamstrung by its neutrality laws and clearly not to be counted on to fight, England and France chose the course of appeasement. This made it quite certain that Mussolini and Hitler would move again—perhaps separately, perhaps together.

While Mussolini was winning his war in East Africa, Congress defeated a move to make the "moral embargo" on oil official, then passed a second Neutrality Act in February 1936. This contained a new feature that served to weaken any possible British and French resistance to aggression, though its aim was simply to isolate the United States. Under the new law, the president was required to embargo arms shipments to each new country that joined the list of belligerents in an existing war. Thus, for example, if British naval pressure had caused Italy or Germany to declare war on Britain, Roosevelt would have had no legal choice except to embargo arms shipments to Britain.

During 1936, President Roosevelt campaigned for re-election for the first time; both he and his opponent, Alfred Landon, confined their speeches almost entirely to domestic issues. Roosevelt not only failed to educate the public about the dangers of the world situation, he even took the lead in urging Americans to withhold support from either side in a civil war which had broken out in Spain.

General Francisco Franco, whose aim was to remold Spain on totalitarian lines, rose up against the Spanish republican government in July 1936. The European powers quickly reached an agreement not to become involved. In practice, this merely reassured Hitler and Mussolini that they need not fear war with England or France if they supported Franco, which they proceeded to do. Russia, meanwhile, provided some aid to Spanish government forces, which included a Communist element. Americans (including some who were Communist or pro-Communist) joined the Lincoln Brigade, an entirely volunteer and unofficial unit, which fought on the side of the Spanish government.

Roosevelt's neutrality in the conflict may have been influenced by the Catholic church, which condemned the anticlericalism of the government side. Because of the liberal character of his domestic program, Roosevelt was also attacked from time to time by partisan opponents as the witting or unwitting dupe of a worldwide Communist conspiracy, which probably reinforced his desire to avoid involvement in the Spanish struggle. At his request, Congress made the "moral embargo" on U.S. support for both sides in the war a legal ban. Thus, it became somewhat easier for General Franco, aided by Hitler and Mussolini, to crush his poorly armed republican opponents.

On May 1, 1937, Roosevelt signed into law a third Neutrality Act, extending the features of the first two acts without time limits. Abandoning its traditional policy of demanding the full enjoyment of neutral rights in time of war, the United States voluntarily surrendered certain rights whose exercise could bring it into collision with one or more belligerents. The traditional approach had left to a potential enemy the timing of acts, such as submarine attacks, that could involve the United

States in war. The main thing to be said for the new approach is that it was aimed at denying this initiative to other powers.

Collision Course in Asia

From the late 1920s, when Chinese Nationalist and Japanese forces began to clash on the Asian mainland, until the late 1930s, when the United States began to rearm, the State Department's Far Eastern division favored a "low posture" toward Japan—though with continued verbal support for the open door and China's territorial integrity. The American embassy in Tokyo favored abandoning the open door policy, on the realistic grounds that it was provocative and Congress would never risk war to support limited U.S. interests in China. The policy of the Far Eastern division prevailed—with the result that the United States and Japan were on a collision course throughout the 1930s.[3]

In July 1937, the smoldering embers of Sino-Japanese war blazed into full-scale conflict. The American response recommended by Ambassador Joseph Grew in Tokyo was : (1) strict neutrality; (2) vigorous efforts to protect the lives, property, and rights of American citizens; and (3) low-key support of the treaty system, while avoiding the provocative diplomacy of protest and condemnation practiced by Secretary Stimson in 1932. Grew believed that if the United States maintained this posture, it might be in a position to shape the future of East Asia (as Theodore Roosevelt had in 1905) once the war reached the point of military victory or stalemate.

However, Franklin Roosevelt seemed to be following the Stimson approach when he publicly suggested "quarantining" nations that had been infected with an "epidemic" of lawlessness. He raised this trial balloon in an October 1939 speech to see how the American people and Congress would react to the idea of applying sanctions against Japan. No one in the Roosevelt administration was clear about what form the sanctions should take, although the president may have been "toying with

---

[3] Naval officers of both powers had been predicting war and planning for it since the first decade of the century.

the idea of cooperative action by neutral nations to ostracize Japan by breaking relations." [4] U.S. public and Congressional opinion proved highly unfavorable, however, and Roosevelt quickly disowned any intention of applying sanctions.

Shortly afterward, Japanese and American diplomats in Tokyo discussed the possibility of the United States serving as impartial mediator of the current war, as Theodore Roosevelt had done in 1905. Washington officials briefly considered this posibility, but they felt restricted by the American public's strong reaction to Japan's aggression in China. Moreover, both the United States and Japan had signed a treaty, at the Washington Naval Conference in 1922, guaranteeing the open door and China's territorial integrity. The Roosevelt administration was unwilling to recommend peace terms which would violate this treaty.

During November 1937, a meeting of the signatories of the 1922 treaty (minus Japan, which refused to attend) was held in Brussels. The meeting took place in an atmosphere of dreary impotence, as Chiang Kai-shek abandoned his capital, Nanking, and the Japanese Army went on a rampage of violence and looting. Conference delegates found it impossible to agree on any form of common action, although most of the powers were on record as regarding Japan as an aggressor. The net result of the meeting was to goad Japan's leaders to set their sights on total victory in China. This reckless Japanese decision ended any further chance of U.S. mediation.

In December 1937, a major crisis developed when Japanese airmen bombed and sank the U.S.S. *Panay*, which had been stationed by treaty right in the Yangtze River near Nanking. The ship was serving as temporary office for the American embassy in China, and there were U.S. newsmen on board as well. A correspondent and two crew members died as a result of the attack; many people were wounded when Japanese air and ground forces machine-gunned the survivors. The ship's

---

[4] For a well-balanced account of U.S.-Japanese relations in this period, see Waldo H. Heinrichs, Jr., *American Ambassador: Joseph C. Grew and the Development of the United States Diplomatic Tradition* (Boston: Little, Brown, 1966), pp. 165–273. Heinrichs's comment, cited above, is on p. 246.

markings had been plainly visible, and the attack was an act of war. For several days, the world watched to see if it would evoke the same groundswell of rage in America as the sinking of the *Maine* in 1898.

It failed to do so, perhaps partly because people were more numbed by violence in the 1930s than they had been four decades earlier. Besides, neither the Japanese nor the U.S. government wanted war, and a settlement of the incident was reached within a few days—before all the details were known to newspaper readers in America. The Japanese foreign minister took the unprecedented step of calling at the American embassy in Tokyo to apologize, as did many ordinary Japanese citizens; reparations were quickly offered and accepted. There was no evidence that the bombing was ordered or condoned by higher authorities. Indeed, it was quite common for hot-headed Japanese officers in China to precipitate crises of this sort.

During 1938 and 1939, there were additional incidents in which American missionaries, businessmen, and others were attacked by Japanese forces plunging deeper and deeper into China. As Japan consolidated its hold on China's coastal cities and closed the door to foreign commerce in these areas, the United States made no effort to conciliate Japan by relinquishing any of its traditional aims or treaty rights. However, the Roosevelt administration recognized a far greater threat in Hitler's increasingly bold efforts to dominate Europe. America's true interest now was to prevent a close alliance between these two expansive powers.

Hitler Polarizes the World

Hitler's annexation of Austria in March 1938 set the stage for a major test of will with the other powers over Czechoslovakia's future. Hitler demanded the Sudeten region, in which ethnic Germans formed a large percentage of the population; since 1932, this area had been the object of intensive Nazi subversion. By September 1938, a showdown was fast approaching between the impatient führer and a grimly determined Czech government, which had a good army of a million and a half men (including reserves), defensible frontiers, and alliances with France and the Soviet Union.

Instead of making a united stand, the other powers followed England's Prime Minister Chamberlain in trying to appease Germany. After Hitler rejected Chamberlain's plan for peaceful transfer of the Sudetenland as too slow, Roosevelt wrote to Hitler urging him to lay the question before an international conference. Roosevelt, Chamberlain, and Premier Daladier of France also sought Mussolini's cooperation in persuading Hitler to accept the Chamberlain plan. A few days later, Hitler reaped the fruits of his audacity, when Chamberlain and Daladier went to Munich and agreed that he should have all he sought without having to fight for it. Czechoslovakia's complete dismemberment followed within six months.

Italy took advantage of the major powers' preoccupation and timidity to seize Albania. Japan proclaimed a "New Order for East Asia," which it began to implement in early 1939 by occupying Hainan and the Spratly Islands off the southern coast of China.

British and French leaders were now preparing to make a stand against Hitler. They served notice in April 1939 that they would support Poland against Nazi pressures. Roosevelt began, at the same time, to harden his policy toward Japan by moving the fleet to the Pacific. In July 1939, he gave the required six months' notice that he was abrogating the commercial treaty with Japan. Meanwhile, in January 1939, he had begun his campaign to revise the neutrality laws which, by barring U.S. aid to aggressors and victims alike, were an open invitation to aggression. Signs everywhere pointed to war's approach, but Congress, especially the Senate Foreign Relations Committee, only buried its head deeper in the sand; the legislators left for their long summer recess without easing the restrictions on aid to belligerents.

For the moment, Moscow held the balance of power in Europe, and frantic competition developed between Britain and France on the one hand and Germany on the other to gain a Russian alliance. In May, Molotov replaced Litvinov (regarded as a friend of the West) as foreign minister, and he bargained with both sides for territorial concessions. Britain and France both refused to force Poland, Rumania, and the Baltic states to accept a Russian "guarantee" of their territory.

But Germany agreed to divide Poland and the Baltic states with Russia in return for the latter's neutrality, if and when Hitler invaded Poland. The Nazi foreign minister von Ribbentrop, signed a nonaggression pact in Moscow on August 23, 1939. With his eastern flank secure, Hitler now pressed his territorial demands on Poland and, failing to gain them without force, launched a ground and air blitz against his neighbor on September 1. Two days later, Britain and France declared war on Germany.

A Warlike Nonbelligerency

Would Hitler conquer all of Europe? How long would Britain and France be able to hold out? Would the American people support a policy of aiding them by "all means short of war"? And if it seemed necessary for America to fight before all its potential allies were defeated, would the country support such a decision?

These were among the major questions President Roosevelt faced between Hitler's invasion of Poland and the Japanese attack on Pearl Harbor. During these twenty-seven months, the United States was neither at peace nor at war. Legally, some experts argued that "neutrality" ceased to have any meaning with the signing of the Kellogg-Briand pact, which had outlawed war. Thus, a new term, "nonbelligerent," was coined to describe America's status. From June 1940 onward, the line separating the United States from actual involvement in the European war became thinner and thinner. America was mobilized on a wartime basis, and its forces engaged in increasingly hostile acts against German forces.

Yet, for all the differences between "nonbelligerency" and the 1914–17 period of American neutrality, there was one important similarity. In both cases, the president of the United States chose to wait for an overt attack from the other side before seeking a declaration of war. Thus, both Wilson and Roosevelt allowed the enemy to time his first great blow, which they knew would unite the American people.

As required by law, Roosevelt proclaimed U.S. neutrality on September 5, 1939, three days after Britain and France declared war on Germany. Less than two weeks later, however, he called a special session of Congress and renewed his plea for amendment of the neutrality laws. After six weeks of debate Congress passed a new act, allowing sale of arms to belligerents on a cash-and-carry basis. This gave an important boost to British and French morale, because only the Allies could buy on this basis (as in World War I).

Of the Asian belligerents, however, Japan was in a far better position than China to purchase needed commodities in America. Hoping to find a way to aid China, Roosevelt took advantage of the fact that there was no declared war in Asia and did not apply the Neutrality Act. (After the bombing of Nanking in 1938, he called for a moral embargo on the sale of airplanes to Japan.) But Japan continued, until late in 1940, to rely on U.S. markets for such vital commodities of war as scrap metal and oil.

In the summer of 1939, Japanese leaders were temporarily stunned by Roosevelt's decision to abrogate the commercial treaty. The shock was followed one month later by Hitler's nonaggression pact with Stalin, which canceled Japan's main political link with Germany, the 1936 anti-Comintern pact. It left Stalin free to interfere in Japan's master plan for Asia if he so desired. Ambassador Grew, taking advantage of the Japanese leaders' temporary confusion, tried to drive home to them the real danger they faced of war with the United States. But the gulf between Washington and Tokyo had already grown too wide to be bridged by diplomacy.

Hitler's series of lightning victories in the spring of 1940 drew from Roosevelt the following promise, hardly neutral in tone:

> In our American unity, we will pursue two obvious and simultaneous courses: we will extend to the opponents of force the material resources of this nation, and at the same time we will harness and speed up the use of those resources in order that we our-

selves in the Americas may have equipment and training equal to the task of any emergency and every defense.

Congress complied with Roosevelt's request for defense-spending authority that shattered all peacetime records: $5 billion for the year beginning July 1, 1940 and $11 billion more in future contracts. Congress also voted the first peacetime draft law in September 1940. In the same month Roosevelt, on his own initiative, gave Britain fifty old destroyers in return for the right to establish eight bases on British territory to guard the approaches to North America.[5]

Nineteen forty was also an election year, and Roosevelt sought an unprecedented third term against Republican internationalist Wendell Wilkie. Both candidates agreed on the importance of preventing Britain's defeat and each spoke out emphatically against direct involvement in the war. More than likely, both men believed these contradictory objectives to be possible in 1940. But Roosevelt had shown that he believed it necessary to be prepared to fight under certain conditions. And he emphasized the point in June 1940 by naming Henry Stimson and Frank Knox to head the War and Navy departments, respectively. These two prominent Republican internationalists made no secret of their belief that America should arm for possible war with Hitler. Their appointments were aimed partly at securing Republican votes, but Roosevelt soon came to rely on Stimson as much as any member of his cabinet.

Thus, there was some deception in Roosevelt's promise, during the election campaign, that "Your boys are not going to be sent into any foreign wars." But his actions during 1940 and 1941 left little doubt about his basic aim: to prevent Britain's defeat and make possible the defeat of Nazi Germany—without getting too far ahead of American public opinion and endangering the country's basic unity of purpose.

The tempo of U.S. support for Britain increased rapidly after Roosevelt's re-election in November. The Lend-Lease Act, which Congress passed in March 1941, allowed the president to transfer

---

[5] These bases were in Newfoundland, Bermuda, the Bahamas, Jamaica, Antigua, Trinidad, St. Lucia, and British Guiana.

any article, service, or piece of information he chose to the government of any country he considered "vital to the defense of the United States." This virtually eliminated the problem of Allied war debts, which had created so much trouble after the 1914–18 war.[6] While Congress was debating the lend-lease plan, secret talks were begun between British and American staff officers to coordinate strategy on the basis of either continued U.S. nonbelligerency or active American involvement in the war. These talks, held in the first three months of 1941, produced the basic strategic decision to concentrate on the defeat of Germany before Japan.

Pacific Count-down Continues

Meanwhile, Japan had occupied northern Indochina; and in September 1940, it signed the Tripartite Pact with Germany and Italy. Roosevelt (with Ambassador Grew's full concurrence) stopped exports to Japan of scrap iron and steel; and from that time on, the Roosevelt administration made only a limited effort to drive wedges between Japan and Germany by reaching some sort of understanding with the former. Politically, it was easier to be tough with Japan than accommodating. Roosevelt and his top advisers were always aware that the latter course could damage the morale of China, Holland, and Britain and perhaps lead to divisive partisan debate in America.

Moreover, American officials were privy to some of Tokyo's most secret messages (because Japan's codes had been broken), and they saw few signs that Japanese leaders were prepared to accept basic U.S. conditions for stability and peace in the Pacific. These conditions were set out repeatedly by Secretary Hull in a series of meetings with Ambassador Nomura, which

[6] The United States provided $50 billion in lend-lease aid to the Allies during World War II and received $10 billion worth of return aid. Settlement agreements covering items not consumed during the war were promptly negotiated with most countries after the war, under terms that were supposed (under the Lend-Lease Act) to be mutually advantageous and for the "betterment of worldwide economic relations." More than twenty-five years elapsed, however, before such an agreement was finally reached with the U.S.S.R.

lasted from April to December 1941. Hull's main requirements were that Japan indicate respect for the principles underlying the treaties signed in Washington in 1922, withdraw its
forces from China and Indochina, accept Chiang Kai-shek's
regime as the sole legitimate government in China (hence disown
the various puppet regimes created by Japan), and disavow the
Tripartite Pact, insofar as it was aimed at the United States.

In response, the Japanese insisted that the United States must
persuade Chiang Kai-shek to accept Japan's terms for ending
the "China incident" (as the war was officially called in Japan).
The United States must cease supporting Chiang if he refused
Japan's terms. Once political issues had been settled, Japan
would withdraw its forces from all but certain parts of North
China and Inner Mongolia. Meanwhile, if the United States
assisted Japan in obtaining the raw materials it needed from
Southeast Asia, Japan would promise not to use force for this
purpose. The United States would also have to restore normal
trade with Japan. As regards the Tripartite Pact, Japanese
leaders would only go so far as to say they would decide for
themselves whether they had to support Germany if the latter
went to war with the United States.

When Japan moved its forces into southern Indochina in
July 1941, Roosevelt responded by freezing Japanese assets
in the United States. Britain and the Netherlands quickly
followed suit. Japan was thereby cut off from vital sources
of raw materials in the United States, the Dutch East Indies,
Malaya, Singapore, and Burma. Its navy would probably have
inadequate supplies of oil to complete the conquest of the
"Greater East Asian Co-Prosperity Sphere" [7] unless that huge
task were begun before the winter monsoon season. This was
one of the main reasons the Japanese government decided, in
early September, to launch a full-scale invasion of Southeast
Asia in spite of the risk of war with Britain and America.

Japanese leaders decided to make one final effort to negotiate

[7] This area was usually described by Japanese radical expansionists such
as Foreign Minister Matsuoka as including China, Manchuria, Korea,
Taiwan, and all of Southeast Asia to the Indian border (possibly but not
necessarily excluding the Philippines, if the United States would comply
with the rest of the program).

an agreement with the United States that would leave Japan free to conquer East Asia. If this could not be achieved by early October, war must follow. The deadline was later extended a few weeks because the Imperial Court, the navy, and substantial elements of the army were reluctant to invite war with the United States, realizing this was an almost suicidal course. However, no one who opposed the war decision was willing to take the initiative to try to reverse it.

From Argentia to Pearl Harbor

Roosevelt and Churchill were unaware when they met at Argentia, Newfoundland, in August 1941, that the overt attack needed to bring the United States into the war was being prepared in Tokyo. Churchill had sought this first summit meeting of the war to "proclaim the ever closer association of Britain and the United States, . . . cause our enemies concern, make Japan ponder, and cheer our friends." The "enemies" in question were, of course, Hitler and Mussolini. In the Atlantic Charter, adopted at Argentia, Roosevelt and Churchill declared to the world that they hoped, "after the final destruction of Nazi tyranny, . . . to see established a peace which will afford to all nations the means of dwelling in safety within their own boundaries . . . in freedom from fear and want." [8]

Roosevelt and Churchill thus met and proclaimed their common purpose; the two countries were allied in war against Germany in fact, if not yet in name. Since Hitler's attack on the Soviet Union in June (which relieved the immediate pressure on Britain), American statesmen had been busy arranging with Stalin for the extension of lend-lease aid to Russia. This meant convoying merchant ships all the way to Murmansk. To permit the British Royal Navy to assume this added burden, the U.S. Navy began escorting British merchant ships from the United States to Iceland in July.

Roosevelt had already, several months earlier, assigned the American Navy to submarine patrol duty in the North Atlantic

---

[8] Churchill sought to avoid sweeping, Wilsonian commitments in the area of decolonization.

from the U.S. coast out to 26° west longitude. Until September 1941, U.S. vessels patrolling this vast area only signaled the position of German submarines to the Royal Navy. However, when a German U-boat fired its torpedoes at an American destroyer on September 4 (missing its target), Roosevelt took the opportunity to order U.S. ships to "shoot on sight" whenever they found a German submarine. Hitler, who was obviously trying to avoid war with the United States at this time, responded by stating simply that German submarines would defend themselves. Two American destroyers were sunk by torpedoes during October, the *Kearny* and the *Reuben James*, with 107 crew members killed.

While these grim events were taking place, Congress debated Roosevelt's October 9 request for an amendment to the 1939 neutrality law to allow arming of merchant ships. Congress went even farther, in spite of strong resistance by the isolationists, and gave the president a bill on November 17 that eliminated virtually all remaining restrictions.

The vote in favor of arming U.S. merchant ships was 50 to 37 in the Senate, 212 to 194 in the House. Many Congressmen (on both sides of the issue) believed that voting for this bill was tantamount to voting for war. Since an actual declaration of war required a majority vote of both houses of Congress, one could add the ayes and nays on the merchant ship bill and estimate that there were 262 votes for and 231 against war with Germany.

However, a poll conducted on November 5, 1941 [9] showed the American people strongly opposed (63 to 26 percent) to a declaration by Congress that a state of war existed between the United States and Germany. Knowing this, a good many Congressmen who voted to arm merchant ships might have thought twice about voting for an actual declaration of war. This is probably why Roosevelt held back from asking Congress to take the final step, although he almost certainly believed by this time that entry into the war was essential to U.S. security. This would also explain why he tried so hard to provoke Hitler

[9] By the American Institute of Public Opinion.

into striking the necessary first blow. And finally, this is one of the reasons why some historians have argued that Roosevelt deliberately invited Japan's attack on Pearl Harbor.

Roosevelt and his top advisers knew in early December that Japanese naval squadrons were poised to attack the Philippines, Malaya, and the Dutch East Indies. Their attention was on these danger points in the Pacific. They were pondering such questions as whether an attack on Singapore would cause Congress to declare war on Japan. They had no way of knowing how Hitler would respond to such a situation. (Nor, in fact, did the Japanese, given Hitler's record of duplicity.) They had not spotted Admiral Nagumo's task force heading for Hawaii. Earlier intelligence reports had told them of Japanese interest in U.S. air and naval bases there, but they failed to take these reports as seriously as they should have. And they failed to give U.S. commanders in Hawaii adequate warning and instructions to defend their bases against possible air attack. These failures add up to a picture of gross negligence.

However, there is no evidence that the Roosevelt administration invited or provoked a Japanese attack on Pearl Harbor. Roosevelt's stated aim in keeping the fleet at Hawaii was to discourage Japanese aggression in the western Pacific. This was altogether in keeping with his character—including a very Rooseveltian faith in seapower as an instrument of American policy. It is virtually impossible to believe he would have sacrificed such badly needed ships and men to gain a declaration of war against Japan. To believe he could, one must ignore not only the historic context of the Pearl Harbor attack (which could have embroiled the United States in a war with the wrong enemy) but also Roosevelt's extraordinary record of service to the United States before and after December 7, 1941.

Suggested Reading

BORG, DOROTHY. *The United States and the Far Eastern Crisis of 1933–1938.* Cambridge, Mass.: Harvard University Press, 1964.

BORG, DOROTHY, and SHUMPEI OKAMOTO (eds.). *Pearl Harbor as History: Japanese-American Relations, 1931–1941.* New York: Columbia University Press, 1973.

COLE, W. S. *America First: The Battle Against Intervention.* Madison: University of Wisconsin Press, 1953.

CRAIG, GORDON A., and FELIX GILBERT (eds.). *The Diplomats, 1919–1939.* Princeton, N.J.: Princeton University Press, 1953.

DIVINE, R. A. *The Illusion of Neutrality.* Chicago: University of Chicago Press, 1962.

FEIS, HERBERT. *The Road to Pearl Harbor: The Coming of War Between the United States and Japan.* Princeton, N.J.: Princeton University Press, 1950.

GARDNER, LLOYD C. *Economic Aspects of New Deal Diplomacy.* Madison: University of Wisconsin Press, 1964.

GREW, JOSEPH C. *Ten Years in Japan.* New York: Simon & Schuster, 1944.

HOOKER, NANCY H. (ed.). *The Moffat Papers: Selections from the Diplomatic Journals of Jay Pierrepont Moffat.* Cambridge, Mass.: Harvard University Press, 1956.

HULL, CORDELL. *The Memoirs of Cordell Hull.* 2 vols. New York: Macmillan, 1948.

IKE, NOBUTAKE. *Japan's Decision for War: Records of the 1941 Policy Conferences.* Stanford, Calif.: Stanford University Press, 1967.

JOHNSON, WALTER. *The Battle Against Isolation.* Chicago: University of Chicago Press, 1944.

LANGER, WILLIAM L., and S. E. GLEASON. *The Challenge of Isolation, 1937–1940.* New York: Harper & Row, 1952.

———. *The Undeclared War, 1940–1941.* New York: Harper & Row, 1953.

PRATT, JULIUS W. *Cordell Hull.* 2 vols. New York: Cooper Square, 1964.

WOHLSTETTER, ROBERTA. *Pearl Harbor: Warning and Decision.* Stanford, Calif.: Stanford University Press, 1962.

7

World War II:
Summitry and Strategy

Relations between Allied governments during the crowded years from Pearl Harbor to Hiroshima can be divided into two main periods: The first was a time of organizing victory, while Allied forces were still on the defensive; the second was a period of consolidating victory, in which Allied leaders tried to shape the postwar world.[1]

As described in the previous chapter, President Roosevelt had worked hard to place the United States on a wartime footing before any declaration of war was made. To nations still resisting Axis aggression he publicly promised "all aid short of war." Americans were conscripted; American industry was converted to war production; lend-lease began to supply the vast needs of embattled Britain and Russia. A declaration of war aims was issued in the form of the Atlantic Charter, and U.S. Navy ships were ordered to "shoot on sight" German submarines in the North Atlantic.

In the winter of 1941–42, with war formally declared, the tempo of these activities quickened; targets were raised with only one end in view—military victory over Germany first and then Japan. Only days after the Pearl Harbor attack, Churchill arrived at the White House with a large staff to meet with Roosevelt and his aides. This conference, code-named "Arcadia,"

[1] Chapter 8, "Origins of the Cold War," is concerned with the second period and events just after the war.

saw the establishment in Washington of the Combined Chiefs of Staff—American service chiefs and representatives of their British counterparts. Anglo-American strategy and operations were coordinated by this body throughout the war. General George C. Marshall, Chief of Staff of the U.S. Army, was the towering figure of the Combined Chiefs, the "architect of victory" in theaters where U.S. forces played the major role.

Arcadia also produced a "Declaration by United Nations," which amounted to an alliance, binding signatory nations to use their full resources to prosecute the war and not to make a separate peace with the enemy. Essentially an American-inspired document, the Declaration was also signed by representatives of the United Kingdom, the Soviet Union, China, the British Dominions, eight European governments in exile (whose countries had been overrun by Hitler), and nine Latin American nations. Eventually, forty-six nations signed. Roosevelt never bothered to submit this Declaration to the Senate for ratification; little criticism was voiced about this procedure.

Roosevelt, Churchill, and Stalin

The leaders of the "Big Three" powers, Churchill, Roosevelt, and Stalin, met twice: at Teheran (November–December 1943), when the tide of battle had unmistakably shifted in the Allies' favor; and at Yalta (February 1945), when victory in Europe was in sight. In addition, Roosevelt and Churchill met at roughly six-month intervals from Argentia (August 1941) to Yalta.[2]

Churchill and Roosevelt relied on one another more completely than any other two British and American leaders in history. Their relationship of profound friendship, trust, and respect was the cornerstone of the Anglo-American alliance, enabling their top military and civilian advisers to disagree frankly and eventually resolve the hundreds of issues, great and small, that arose in this unique combination of the world's greatest powers.

Temperamentally, the two leaders had much in common. Both were aristocrats who believed deeply in the values of liberal

[2] Roosevelt died on April 12, 1945, one month before Germany surrendered.

Anglo-Saxon democracy and were master practitioners of its politics. Each inspired almost as much affection and support among the other's people as from his own. Intellectually, and in terms of resources at their command, they complemented each other brilliantly. Churchill had the keener intelligence of the two, and a much broader sense of history and world affairs. Roosevelt was intuitive, bold, "foxy," a poor administrator but a born leader; he presided over the intersection of U.S. domestic and foreign policy, keeping both in a state of active ferment and somehow making events in one sphere reinforce progress in the other.

Churchill and Roosevelt communicated almost constantly throughout the war, by letter, cable, phone, and private emissary as well as in their face-to-face meetings. The prime minister tended to take the initiative, the president generally responded. A steady barrage of ideas, on everything from grand strategy to the politics of remote countries, was fired westward across the Atlantic, together with requests for joint action and logistic support. Amendments, decisions, warm notes of encouragement, and spontaneous offers of aid formed the bulk of FDR's responses.

Each was on familiar terms with the other's official family. Secretary Stimson, for example, was by no means always in accord with Churchill—particularly on the great issue of when and where to invade Europe—yet he could write that

. . . Roosevelt and . . . Churchill established and sustained a wartime collaboration which grew ever stronger in the settlement of successive differences. When all the arguments have been forgotten, this central fact will remain. The two nations fought a single war, and their quarrels were the quarrels of brothers.[3]

The Anglo-Saxon leaders did not always face Stalin in full harmony, though they trusted each other far more deeply than either trusted "Uncle Joe" (as they called him in private). Churchill, the realist, never lost sight of the fact that a strong Communist Russia was almost as great a threat to British interests

[3] Henry L. Stimson and McGeorge Bundy, *On Active Service in Peace and War* (New York: Harper and Brothers, 1947), p. 448.

as Nazi Germany. Roosevelt, who believed that Soviet collaboration would be essential after the war, never quite lost his naïve
hope that Stalin would respond to charm, generosity, and expressions of good will. Churchill felt no pangs of guilt for having
urged Allied intervention in Russia in 1918. Roosevelt, who had
reversed Wilson's policy of not recognizing the U.S.S.R., still
felt the need to atone for past wrongs to Russia.

As for Stalin, he had disowned much of the ideological fervor
with which his former rival, Trotsky, conducted foreign affairs.
Stalin's 1939 pact with Hitler was the ultimate expression of
conventionally cynical, power-oriented diplomacy. Churchill in
the past had made no great secret of his wish to see Hitler's
and Stalin's forces destroy each other; yet he developed a fairly
close and frank relationship with the Soviet dictator. This was
epitomized by Churchill's October 1944 visit to Moscow, in
which he and Stalin quickly divided up the Balkans into British
and Russian spheres of influence.

At their first meeting, in Teheran, Roosevelt rashly tried to
win Stalin's friendship by siding with him against Churchill on
such issues as the future of France. Churchill, who knew Roosevelt well by this time, seems to have realized that little of
substance would be decided on this occasion. Although Stalin
seemed responsive to FDR's gambit, he was probably more at
ease with Roosevelt when they spoke the common language of
political pragmatism.

Cross-Channel Invasion Versus "Periphery-Pecking"

The different historical experiences of the British and American peoples contributed to their leaders' sharp disagreement
over the correct strategy for defeating Hitler. For Americans,
whose army had seen less than a year of combat in World War I,
the obvious strategy was to send another large expeditionary
force to France as soon as possible and push the Germans
back toward their border. Whatever would bring a decisive
victory in the shortest possible time seemed obviously the best
strategy to pursue.

The British had lost a whole generation of young men in the

endless, agonizing trench warfare of 1914–18, and they barely evacuated their expeditionary force from Dunkirk in 1940. They were understandably loath to invade the Continent again without overwhelming odds in their favor. If the war could be won by letting Hitler overextend himself (especially in the east against Russia) and by chopping away steadily at his southern perimeter, victory might take longer but the cost in British and American lives might also be far less. In addition, Britain had a much greater economic and political stake in the Mediterranean basin than the United States had. And finally, Churchill believed that an attack through Europe's "soft underbelly" would enable the Allies to pre-empt the heart of the Continent from Soviet occupation.

The two strategies—a cross-channel invasion and what General Marshall labeled "periphery-pecking"—tended to be mutually exclusive. There were enough men and material to carry out one strategy but not both. Mediterranean operations might be described as preliminary to a cross-channel push, but they tended to prevent or delay the necessary concentration of forces for a full-scale attack. Thus, throughout all of 1942 and much of 1943, the question of basic strategy remained in a fluid state.

Roosevelt irritated subordinates like Stimson by seeming to waver between the two basic concepts. On several occasions, Churchill agreed in principle to the cross-channel attack, then later reopened the issue by urging peripheral campaigns in the Balkans and southern France. When Molotov visited Washington in May and June of 1942, he was assured that a second front would be opened within the year. When this proved impossible, Churchill assumed responsibility for explaining to Stalin that a North African invasion was all the Western powers could do in 1942 to take the pressure off the eastern front.

The North African campaign was carried out successfully between November 1942 and May 1943. It was followed by an invasion of Italy, leading to Mussolini's fall and that country's surrender in September 1943. While these efforts probably delayed the cross-channel invasion, they served an important political function in rallying the support of the American people behind the more basic concept of giving priority to the war in

Europe. Due to the attack on Pearl Harbor, it was natural for Americans to regard Japan as the major enemy. Besides, the island-hopping strategy of the United States in the Pacific could be pursued without such lengthy preparations as were required to invade Europe. Thus, there was public pressure, as well as private lobbying by U.S. commanders in the Far East, to give Japan's defeat greater priority.

Roosevelt steadfastly resisted these pressures, but it was not until late in the summer of 1943 that he made a firm choice between the two main alternative strategies for defeating Hitler. At Teheran (November 1943), it was decided that the Normandy landing would take place the following May or June. To help compensate for the long delay, Roosevelt made every effort to be forthcoming in providing lend-lease aid to the Soviet Union, ignoring the Russians' stubborn pettiness in negotiations. However, Roosevelt was naïve to believe that this form of generosity would soften the blow of postponing the cross-channel invasion. To a man of Stalin's mentality, such tactics probably seemed to confirm that the Western powers were at fault.

One of the great ironies of the whole subject of the cross-channel invasion is that Soviet-American relations began to deteriorate sharply as soon as large numbers of U.S. forces were on the Continent and moving eastward—in competition, whether they realized it or not, with the Red Army to occupy the heart of Europe.

Unconditional Surrender

One of Roosevelt's most fateful acts as president was designed to prove to Stalin the sincerity of the Western powers' intentions. On January 26, 1943, at the end of the Casablanca conference, he announced that "The democracies' war plans were to compel the 'unconditional surrender' of the Axis." He later indicated that the statement was impromptu and had not been cleared in advance with Churchill. However, the prime minister immediately supported its use; the fact that victory was still a long way off seemed to Churchill to justify a tone of defiance toward the Axis.[4] Both Roosevelt and Churchill wished to avoid having to haggle with the Germans over peace terms; they believed that unconditional surrender would eliminate this problem by depriving Germany of any claim to treatment in accordance with the Atlantic Charter.[5]

However, the unconditional surrender doctrine played into the hands of Nazi propagandists by reviving the German people's bitter memories of being saddled with moral and financial responsibility for World War I—after Wilson promised them "peace without victory" and negotiated a pre-armistice agreement on the basis of his Fourteen Points. There is little room for doubt that the unconditional surrender doctrine stiffened the resistance of the German people.

To the Japanese, the term "unconditional surrender" sounded very much as if America planned to destroy the institution of the emperor and the entire Japanese sociopolitical system over which he presided. Unquestionably, this perception of Allied aims tightened the already close bonds between the Japanese people and their leaders. Only in the case of Italy, where individual and group commitments to the Axis cause were weaker and more opportunistic, could it be argued that the unconditional surrender doctrine may have helped produce division and defections from Mussolini's Fascist order.

An important reason for announcing the unconditional surrender doctrine was to demonstrate to Stalin that the Western powers were unshakably committed to the war against Hitler, in spite of delays in launching the invasion of Europe. Did it achieve this purpose? The brief answer seems to be no; Stalin

[4] Robert E. Sherwood quotes both Churchill and Roosevelt on this episode in *Roosevelt and Hopkins: An Intimate History* (New York: Harper and Brothers, 1948), pp. 695–96. Roosevelt said, "We had so much trouble getting those two French generals [de Gaulle and Giraud] together that I thought to myself that this was as difficult as arranging the meeting of Grant and Lee—and then suddenly the press conference was on, and Winston and I had no time to prepare for it, and the thought popped into my mind that they had called Grant 'Old Unconditional Surrender' and the next thing I knew, I had said it."

[5] See the volume of Churchill's history of World War II entitled *The Hinges of Fate* (Boston: Houghton, Mifflin, 1950), p. 689.

emphasized in frequent messages to Roosevelt and Churchill that mere words could not possibly make up for the lack of a second front. However, Stalin did welcome the Western powers' commitment to the total defeat of Germany. He could not fail to recognize that this would open immense opportunities for the Soviet Union.

Wartime Relations with China

An added aim of the unconditional surrender doctrine was to raise the morale of Chiang Kai-shek's regime, which may have been weighing the merits of a separate peace with Japan. However, Roosevelt's announcement had no discernable effect on Chinese morale, unless measured by increasingly vigorous complaints about the quantity of aid received from the United States.

In the months immediately following Pearl Harbor, when Allied forces were unable to make a firm stand anywhere in Asia, Chiang's large army was a potentially vital factor, in spite of its poor performance against the Japanese. But the battle of Midway marked the turning point in the Pacific naval war, and it became increasingly evident that the American island-hopping campaign would be the decisive factor in defeating Japan.

Moreover, from early 1942 to late 1944, Japanese troops occupied the only possible land route across northern Burma by which lend-lease supplies could be trucked to Chiang's forces. This meant that every ton of supplies that reached the Chinese had to be flown across the Himalayas from India at a cost that was incomparably greater than shipping it to Britain to support the build-up for Normandy. Finally, Chiang himself knew, after Pearl Harbor, that he could count on Japan's eventual defeat by vastly superior U.S. forces; he therefore began to worry more about the Chinese Communists. Although they were nominally his allies against Japan, they were really his main long-term obstacle in reunifying China.

Nevertheless, American aid to Chiang's regime was far from negligible. It amounted to some $120 million between 1937 and 1941, when China became eligible for lend-lease; from Pearl

Harbor to V-J Day, the United States provided large quantities of lend-lease aid and a $500 million economic stabilization loan; and another $2 billion was sent during the first four postwar years.[6] In addition, U.S. military aid included the "Flying Tigers," the American-staffed air arm of Chiang Kai-shek's forces, which was led by General Clair Chennault.

General Joseph Stilwell commanded U.S. ground support forces in China, and served as Chiang Kai-shek's chief of staff. He greatly increased the fighting potential of the Chinese Nationalist army and reopened a supply route through the mountains of northern Burma. Although passionately devoted to the cause of China's victory, Stilwell took issue with Chiang's decision to reserve his best units to block or fight the Chinese Communists. His unwanted political advice made him *persona non grata* in Chungking, and he was recalled in the fall of 1944.

Until V-J Day, the United States sought to keep China (meaning Chiang Kai-shek's regime in the southwest and the Chinese Communists in northern Hunan province) engaged against Japan. Even if these forces were not destined to play the decisive role in Japan's defeat, they could tie down Japanese divisions that might otherwise be used against India or Russia or to defend the home islands. U.S. planners also believed that air bases might be needed on the China mainland to attack Japan, and these would have to be defended by Chinese ground troops.

America's second major aim in regard to China looked beyond such tactical considerations to the strategic balance of power in postwar Asia. With Japan's defeat, U.S. leaders expected China to assume the role of a major world power and the main stabilizing force in East Asia. This explains why American officials (including Stilwell's military mission and the U.S. embassy in Chungking) tried time and again to persuade the Chinese Nationalists and Communists to bury their differences and cooperate on both the political and military levels. Without internal unity and political stability, China would obviously be unable to serve as a stabilizing force in East Asia.

Churchill and Stalin both regarded the American aim of

[6] Postwar U.S. aid to China and its objectives are discussed in Chapter 10.

making China a great power and one of the world's "four policemen" as totally unrealistic.[7] However, for reasons of their own, they cooperate with Roosevelt on this matter up to a point. In a treaty made with Chiang Kai-shek in January 1943 (just before Roosevelt and Churchill were due to meet at Casablanca), the United States surrendered all the special rights of extraterritoriality it had enjoyed for a century at Peking and at coastal cities such as Amoy, Tientsin, and Shanghai. The British followed suit the same day, undoubtedly believing that any gain in U.S. good will more than offset the loss of purely hypothetical privileges in areas of China still occupied by Japan. Later in 1943, Congress passed a law permitting Chinese to immigrate to the United States on the same basis as Europeans (but with an annual quota fixed at only 104). Thus, Sino-American relations were finally placed on a basis of full legal equality.[8]

The next step in U.S. efforts to elevate China to the status of a major power came in the series of Allied conferences at Moscow, Cairo, and Teheran in late 1943. At the meeting of foreign ministers in Moscow, Secretary Hull managed to associate the Republic of China with some of the basic decisions of the "Big Three" regarding the formation of the United Nations organization. Next, Roosevelt persuaded Churchill to allow Chiang Kai-shek to join their meeting at Cairo, where they issued a declaration containing an important section on Asia:

[7] Churchill expressed himself on the matter in an August 23, 1944, message to Foreign Secretary Eden:

That China is one of the world's four Great Powers is an absolute farce. I have told the President I would be reasonably polite about this American obsession, but I cannot agree that we should take a positive attitude on the matter. The latest information from inside China points to the rise already of a rival Government to supplant Chiang Kai-shek, and now there is always a Communist civil war impending there. While not opposing the President's wish, I should object very much if we adopted other than a perfectly negative line, leaving him to do the needful with the Russians. From *Triumph and Tragedy*, p. 701.

[8] To compare the evolution of U.S.-Japanese relations in the twentieth century, see Chapters 2 and 5.

Japan shall be stripped of all the islands in the Pacific which she has seized or occupied since the beginning of the first World War in 1914, and . . . all the territory Japan has stolen from the Chinese, such as Manchuria, Formosa and the Pescadores, shall be restored to the Republic of China. Japan will also be expelled from all other territories which she has taken by violence and greed. The aforesaid three great powers, mindful of the enslavement of the people of Korea, are determined that in due course Korea shall become free and independent.

At the Churchill-Roosevelt-Stalin meeting in Teheran, which followed the Cairo conference, Stalin repeated his earlier promise that Russia would enter the war against Japan once Germany was defeated. Churchill suggested that Russia might gain an ice-free port by this action, and Roosevelt suggested obtaining access for Russia to Dairen in southern Manchuria. It was finally agreed at the Yalta meeting of February 1945 that Russia's price for entering the Pacific war would be all the territorial rights and privileges lost to Japan in 1905. However, Chinese officials were not consulted before President Roosevelt struck his bargain with Stalin at Teheran and Yalta. When they learned of this deal, Chinese officials complained that it made a mockery of their country's supposedly enhanced status.

Wartime Relations with France

When discussion turned to the place that France should occupy in the postwar world, Churchill and Roosevelt exchanged positions. The prime minister vigorously defended his view that France should be allowed to regain a place among the great powers after victory was won. Roosevelt was deeply skeptical of France's ability to make any major contribution until ruled by a generation that had played no part in the ignominious surrender of 1940.

Both Churchill and Roosevelt believed France would be unable to play a major power role unless it regained its former empire. Churchill, a staunch imperialist, argued that peace and stability would not exist in Europe without a strong France; hence France must be allowed and even assisted to regain its colonies. Roosevelt, on the other hand, believed that France had exploited and misgoverned its former colonies (particularly Indochina) to a shocking degree. He lost no chance to propose that Indochina be placed under an international trusteeship after the war. The idea was defeated when the task of liberating Southeast Asia was assigned to Britain at Yalta and the assignment confirmed (after Roosevelt's death) at Potsdam.

These differing viewpoints were reflected in the relations of Britain and the United States with the two governments that claimed to speak for France after the German defeat in June 1940. Washington maintained diplomatic relations with the pro-Axis regime of Marshal Pétain at Vichy, France, until the North African invasion of November 1942, when Pétain broke relations. Britain attacked the French fleet off Algeria to prevent it from falling into Axis hands, which caused Pétain to break relations with England as early as July 1940.

Churchill let General Charles de Gaulle establish his Free French National Committee in London before the liberation of Algeria (when he was able to move to that French colony). Although Washington provided lend-lease aid to the Free French, it refused to grant de Gaulle diplomatic recognition until after the liberation of France in 1944. (The general had antagonized Hull by seizing the islands of St. Pierre and Miquelon in 1941.) Roosevelt's antipathy for de Gaulle was part of his general phobia for the French; he may also have been influenced by Admiral Leahy, the first U.S. ambassador to Vichy, who became his chief of staff in May 1942.

De Gaulle managed to reassert control over many former French colonies. In the summer of 1944 he paid a successful visit to Roosevelt in Washington, which improved the climate of Franco-American relations. Free French forces under General Le Clerc carried out the liberation of Paris, and de Gaulle himself received a tremendous welcome when he entered the city on August 25, 1944. Soon after, Roosevelt provisionally recognized de Gaulle's government.

Plans for the Postwar World

Almost a year before the United States entered the war, Secretary Hull (who was often bypassed by Roosevelt in the making of current foreign policy) began to think about postwar interests. He assigned interdepartmental committees within the U.S. government the task of developing plans for the treatment of areas that might be liberated and occupied by U.S. and Allied forces. For the most part, these committees worked in a political vacuum, isolated from the big three leaders' crucial policy discussions. As might be expected, the plans for postwar Europe which were developed in this manner often failed to take into account such basic realities as the growing conflict of aims between Russia and the West.

By the fall of 1943, Italy had been defeated and Germany and Japan were being forced onto the defensive. The Allied foreign ministers (meeting before the Teheran conference) grappled with the pressing problem of who would govern the liberated areas. Their failure to agree on many urgent matters was hidden by the time-honored device of creating a committee, the European Advisory Commission, to study both current and future problems. The foreign ministers also issued a number of declarations, setting forth general principles on Italy, Austria, and the broad subjects of postwar Allied cooperation. Secretary Hull, confusing pious words with accomplishments, told Congress that, once these principles had been carried into effect,

. . . there will no longer be need for spheres of influence, for alliances, for balance of power, or any other of the special arrangements through which, in the unhappy past, the nations strove to safeguard their security or to promote their interests.

One of the strangest misadventures in Allied planning for postwar Europe was the Morgenthau Plan, a "programme for eliminating the war-making industries in the Ruhr and in the Saar" and converting Germany into a country "primarily agricultural and pastoral in its character." Roosevelt allowed

Henry Morgenthau, his friend and secretary of the treasury, to persuade Churchill to agree to this plan at their September 1944 meeting in Quebec, although Hull and Stimson were known to be against it.

Churchill later recorded the fact that he had been violently opposed to the idea of destroying Germany's industrial capacity, but he had agreed because he needed Morgenthau's support for continued financial aid to Britain. Churchill hoped that it would be possible to revise the plan for Germany at a later date; this indeed proved to be the case, when both he and Roosevelt realized the absurdity of destroying the main element of Europe's industrial prosperity.

While plans for postwar Europe involved the interests of Britain and Russia even more directly than those of the United States, Churchill and Stalin tended to defer to American planners as far as postwar Asia was concerned. The reasons for this are not hard to find. Stalin was fully occupied with the defeat of Germany and only afterward declared war on Japan. Having set a very high price on this action, he seemed willing for the moment to let the rest of Asia find its own level. He apparently did not expect the Chinese Communists to be able to seize control of China for many years.

Britain's prime interest east of Suez was of course India, though major responsibilities in Southeast Asia grew out of Britain's position on the subcontinent. As the main contributor to Japan's defeat, the United States sought and gained a virtually free hand in deciding that nation's future. Churchill was willing to let the United States try to influence China's destiny as well, the more so if Britain were given a free hand in Southeast Asia.

Political guidelines for East Asia produced by State Department planners (in conjunction with other departments) were generally more realistic than American policy papers on postwar Europe. For example, the State Department planners foresaw the need to rebuild Japan's industrial base and allow the country access to world trade in order to become economically self-sufficient. Efforts by Secretary Morgenthau to impose a harsh, vindictive peace settlement on Japan were therefore firmly resisted by the State Department. As signs of Soviet-American competition began to appear in the latter part of the war, the State Department began thinking of the need to deny Russia control of Japan's vast industrial potential.

Suggested Reading

BALDWIN, HANSON W. *Great Mistakes of the War*. New York: Harper & Row, 1950.

CHURCHILL, WINSTON S. *The Second World War*. 6 vols. Boston: Houghton, Mifflin, 1948–53.

DE GAULLE, CHARLES *The War Memoirs of Charles de Gaulle*. 2 vols. Vol. 1, New York: Viking, 1955; Vol. 2, New York: Simon & Schuster, 1959.

DEANE, J. R. *The Strange Alliance*. New York: Viking, 1947.

FEIS, HERBERT. *The China Tangle: The American Effort in China from Pearl Harbor to the Marshall Mission*. Princeton, N.J.: Princeton University Press, 1953.

———. *Churchill-Roosevelt-Stalin: The War They Waged and the Peace They Sought*. Princton, N.J.: Princeton University Press, 1957.

HAYES, CARLTON J. H. *Wartime Mission in Spain, 1942–1945*. New York: Macmillan, 1945.

HIGGINS, TRUMBULL. *Winston Churchill and the Second Front, 1940–1943*. New York: Oxford University Press, 1957.

LEAHY, WILLIAM D. *I Was There*. New York: McGraw-Hill, 1950.

McNEILL, WILLIAM H. *America, Britain and Russia: Their Cooperation and Conflict, 1941–1946*. London: Oxford University Press, 1953.

SMITH, GADDIS. *American Diplomacy During the Second World War, 1941–1945*. New York: John Wiley & Sons, 1965.

STILWELL, J. W. *The Stilwell Papers*, arranged and edited by T. H. WHITE. New York: Sloane, 1948.

STIMSON, HENRY L., and McGEORGE BUNDY. *On Active Service in Peace and War*. New York: Harper & Row, 1948.

8

Origins of the Cold War

During the summer of 1943, relations between Russia and the Western Allies grew strained and contentious, mainly over Soviet policy toward its East European neighbors. Russian leaders ceased to recognize the Polish exile government in London and began assembling a more compatible group of Poles in Moscow. The Soviets also pressed for closer bilateral ties with the Czech government in exile, apparently in part to isolate the London Poles. Finally, Moscow Radio began broadcasting a propaganda line to the German people and army which seemed to imply that terms less stringent than unconditional surrender might be had if they overthrew Hitler.

Roosevelt and Churchill had proposed a Big Three summit meeting, but Stalin was unresponsive, claiming that he was needed personally to supervise the Soviet summer offensive. For weeks, while he was at the eastern front, he left messages from Roosevelt and Churchill unanswered and even omitted the customary congratulations after their successful Sicilian campaign. When he deigned to communicate with his Western colleagues, it was usually to chide them for delays in launching the cross-channel invasion.

Churchill was often irritated by Stalin's attitude during this period, but Roosevelt tried to play a moderating role. He would have found it easier to let the British and Russians deal with Eastern Europe alone, not least because he believed the American people would insist on bringing all U.S. troops home soon after the war. But he was also convinced that no

U.S. administration could survive unless it did everything short of war to support self-determination for the peoples of Eastern Europe.

September 1943 marked the start of a new phase in the war. Anglo-American forces finally began to see action against German divisions on the continent of Europe. This produced the period of greatest cordiality in Big Three relations, although it forced the leaders to begin grappling with the question of who would govern the territory that fell under their control.

The Italian Precedent

On the night of September 8, 1943, British and American forces crossed the sea from Sicily (where their recent victory had caused the fall of Mussolini) to Salerno in southern Italy. A few days earlier, Roosevelt and Churchill had informed Stalin of their firm decision to launch the Normandy invasion within eight or nine months. This news had greatly pleased Stalin; he had even agreed to go as far as Teheran to meet the other two leaders. Arrangements were thus under way for the first Big Three summit.

As the Anglo-American forces approached the beaches of Salerno, the news of a military armistice was broadcast by the Badoglio government to the Italian people.[1] The armistice had been signed five days earlier in secret to avoid Nazi retaliation against the Italian people and their leaders. General Eisenhower's chief of staff signed for the Allies, including Stalin, who had given his advance approval. Eisenhower's position was described in the surrender document as "Commander-in-Chief of the Allied Forces, acting by authority of the Governments of the United States and Great Britain and in the interest of the United Nations."

The agreement gave the Allied commander full authority to enforce its terms, without stating which members of the United Nations should take part in supervising Italian affairs. The U.S. government was inclined to give its military com-

[1] General Pietro Badoglio had replaced Mussolini and had tried, unsuccessfully, to link Italy with the Allied cause.

mander broad political and administrative latitude to allow him to accomplish his mission as efficiently as possible. The British would have preferred to have on-the-spot political decisions made by trained diplomats. But neither Western power wanted the Soviets involved in deciding Italy's future, because the large and active Italian Communist Party offered them too great a potential lever. The fact that German forces in Italy stubbornly resisted the Allied invasion made it easier for the Western leaders to rationalize keeping political and administrative power in the hands of the military commander.

Stalin strongly urged the Western powers to agree to a tripartite military-political commission for Italy and announced his intention of naming Andrei Vishinsky as the Russian member.[2] He complained that the Western Allies "made agreements but the Soviet Union received information about the results . . . just as a passive third observer." Roosevelt replied soothingly, inviting Stalin to send an officer "to General Eisenhower's headquarters in connection with the commission." Stalin was not fooled by this response and continued to press his claim, but the Western powers held firm. Eventually, the Soviets accepted membership in a powerless Adivsory Council. But they plainly intended to turn this setback to good account by making it a precedent for denying the Western powers a voice in the control of East European countries liberated by the Red Army.

From Teheran to Yalta

The first summit conference of the Big Three at Teheran (December 1943) took place in an atmosphere of warm camaraderie and collaboration, as had the preparatory meeting of foreign ministers in Moscow. The Allies had turned the corner militarily, but they knew they still had many months of hard fighting ahead and much to ask of each other before victory

---

[2] Vishinsky was assistant foreign minister in charge of U.S. and British affairs. His nomination underscored the importance Stalin attached to asserting political control over the military—both as a general rule of Soviet administration and particularly in the control of liberated areas where Soviet interests were involved.

would be won. Brave beginnings were made on a wide range of difficult political issues at Teheran including Italy, Austria, Germany, Eastern Europe, Soviet entry into the war against Japan, and postwar cooperation by the Big Three. Roosevelt reported afterward to Congress and the American people that he "got along fine with Marshal Stalin," and he predicted that "we are going to get along well with him and the Russian people—very well indeed."

As noted in the previous chapter, Secretary Hull was pleased that the Moscow meeting yielded several high-sounding declarations of principle. Other delegates may have been more concerned about the lack of agreement on specifics. (Stalin once told Foreign Minister Eden that he regarded a declaration as algebra while an agreement was practical arithmetic. "I do not wish to decry algebra," he added, "but I prefer practical arithmetic.") Molotov announced blandly at the Moscow conference that Russia had no interest in dividing Europe into spheres of influence. However, when Churchill raised the question of Soviet territorial aims, Stalin replied, "There is no need to speak at the present time about any Soviet desires, but when the time comes we will speak."

The time came soon after the Normandy landings (which Stalin assisted by mounting a large offensive that tied down scores of German divisions on the easten front). For more than a year prior to Normandy, there had been signs that Russia planned to settle the future of Eastern Europe unilaterally. Now, with Western ground forces fully committed to Hitler's destruction, he proceeded to act more boldly. He could not be sure how soon the Anglo-American forces would reach Central Europe.

In August 1944, Moscow Radio incited the mainly anti-Soviet Polish underground to rise up against the Nazis in Warsaw. For two months, the Poles fought heroically against the well-armed German garrison, while Red Army tank units waited nearby on the banks of the Vistula, and Stalin refused to help the Western Allies resupply the Poles from the air. In the West, this was seen as a cold-blooded maneuver to destroy the main opponents of a Soviet-dominated Poland. However, in Stalin's eyes it was a legitimate move to prevent Poland from falling into anti-

Soviet hands—justifiable because Poland had served as a corridor for so many invasions of Russia.

In September 1944, Ambassador Averell Harriman reported from Moscow that Soviet officials who opposed cooperation with the United States seemed to be winning out over those who favored good relations and "the policy appears to be crystallizing to force us and the British to accept all Soviet policies backed by strength and the prestige of the Red Army."

Nevertheless, Prime Minister Churchill visited Moscow in October and struck his celebrated deal with Stalin over spheres of influence in the Balkans. For the remainder of the war period, Russia would have 90 percent predominance in Rumania, and 80 percent in Bulgaria and Hungary; Britain would have 90 percent predominance in Greece. In Yugoslavia, the two powers would have equal influence.[3] The agreement was tested before the end of 1944, when Churchill found it necessary to send British Army units to Greece to quell an uprising by Communist-dominated guerrillas. Although this action was widely condemned in Britain and America (and the U.S. government formally dissociated itself from the move), no criticism appeared in the controlled Soviet press. Churchill felt that Stalin had lived up to his word in this instance.

Yalta: European Questions

At the Yalta summit conference in February 1945, the Big Three leaders discussed the questions of Poland, Germany, Russia's entry into the Pacific war, and the United Nations. Of these four topics, the first had the greatest significance in the development of the Cold War, because the growing dispute convinced many key Western diplomats and political leaders in early 1945 that Stalin's aims were ruthlessly expansionist and his promises could not be believed.

Two years after breaking relations with the Polish exile gov-

---

[3] The previous June, Churchill and Stalin had recognized each other's primary influence in Greece and Rumania respectively. This deal had been for a three-month trial period only. It was approved by Roosevelt when Hull was away from Washington for a few days, thus illustrating the fact that Roosevelt was sometimes open to spheres of influence deals, even though he was basically a Wilsonian.

ernment in London, with Red Army units moving rapidly through Poland, Stalin apparently saw no need to yield anything to his Western colleagues on the Polish question. Churchill reminded Stalin that Britain had entered the war because of Poland; hence that country's fate was a question of honor to Britain. Stalin answered, "It is not only a question of honor for Russia, but one of life and death."

The two main issues were: Who would govern Poland? And what should Poland's borders be? On the first question, the Soviets sought to make the Polish Provisional Government (which they had created as an instrument of Soviet influence) the nucleus of the government that would preside over liberated Poland. Roosevelt and Churchill fought hard for a completely new Polish government, in which the Communists who comprised the Provisional Government would be only one of several elements. In spite of long and arduous negotiation at Yalta, Stalin held all the cards. The best the Western Allies could obtain was a Soviet pledge that the Provisional Government would be expanded to include other democratic elements and that free elections would be held as soon as possible.

On the subject of Poland's borders, a verbal formula was devised that made the eastern border conform fairly closely to the Curzon line drawn at the Versailles peace conference in 1919 and left it to the Polish Provisional Government—in other words, to Stalin—to decided how much German and Czech territory should be absorbed on the north and west. This opened the way to a Soviet-dominated "large Poland," extending into western Europe, which the Soviets regarded as an essential part of their defense system. The Western Allies feared that it might have offensive implications as well, and they were disturbed by the fact that it meant vast hardship and lasting bitterness for millions of Germans who would be forced to move off the lands gained by Poland.

The Big Three leaders and their staff members devoted a lesser amount of time at Yalta to reviewing the current situation in Italy, Greece, and Yugoslavia and discussing certain demands raised by the Western Allies about Rumania, Bulgaria, and Hungary. Stalin reaffirmed his October spheres of influence agreement with Churchill (giving Britain 90 percent control in Greece and 50 percent in Yugoslavia). The main discussions about Italy at Yalta took place between British and American representatives, with the former eager and the latter reluctant to grant the Italians the status of cooperating allies.

The Soviets continued to stress the Italian precedent whenever the Western Allies sought a more substantive role or greater freedom of action for their representatives on Control Commissions in East European states. For example, in the case of Hungary the Western powers were ready to concede that the Soviet chairman of the Control Commission would have the final say as long as the fighting continued. But they wanted the Western members to be told of policy directives before they went into effect—to give them time to register a protest if they disagreed. Molotov first parried this request by claiming that the Soviet representative in Italy had not been consulted for over a year, but he eventually gave in to this particular Western demand.

On the subject of Germany, which was destined to become the most sensitive zone of East-West contact in the Cold War, the Big Three leaders achieved some useful results at Yalta. They quickly agreed on an instrument of unconditional surrender, by which the Nazi regime and German military forces would be dismantled and the German people forced to submit to Allied control.

It was further decided that the Allied occupation would combine the two principles of tripartite rule and spheres of influence. American, British, and Soviet commanders would exercise supreme authority in their respective zones, but they would also sit together on a Control Council which would be responsible for matters concerning Germany as a whole. The decisions of this body would have to be unanimous and, in case of deadlock, responsibility would revert to the individual zone commanders.

After some initial opposition from Stalin, the Big Three leaders invited General de Gaulle to accept an occupation zone for France carved from those assigned to the United States and

Britain. France was also given a seat on the Control Council.

The district of Greater Berlin, which was divided into four separate Allied sectors, was located deep inside the Soviet zone. Therefore, the American, British, and French commanders needed access across the Soviet zone of Germany to Berlin in order to administer their sectors of the city. American and British staff officers reached agreement on this matter at Yalta, but their Soviet colleague hung back.[4]

The Big Three leaders could agree only to keep their options open on the complex issues of reparations and the dismemberment of Germany. Churchill was not opposed to reparations or dismemberment in principle, but he believed it a great mistake to try to decide such far-reaching matters before the Allies had some experience with actual postwar conditions in Europe. Churchill was now fully alive to the dangers of a drastic approach such as the Morgenthau plan (discussed in the previous chapter). He and Eden pointed out that if Germany were stripped of all industry, it might have to depend on British and American charity merely to survive. In effect, the Western Allies would also be paying Germany's reparations bill.

Stalin made an impassioned speech which left no doubt of his determination to exact large-scale reparations from Germany, both to prevent its revival as a military threat and to help in Russia's reconstruction. He said he expected to receive about $10 billion worth of reparations, but he wanted it in kind, not in money. He demanded large transfers of heavy machinery as well as the products of German industries that were left in place. Moreover, he demanded two or three million German people to work as slave laborers on reconstruction tasks in the Soviet Union over a period of ten years. He said that these workers would be selected first from the lesser German war

---

[4] Soviet restrictions on access routes to Berlin were a major source of East-West friction throughout the Cold War period, because Berlin remained under joint Allied occupation long after the Western powers' occupation zones became the Federal Republic of Germany and the Soviet zone became the German Democratic Republic. Not until 1972 was an agreement reached by the Soviet, British, and American governments that spelled out the Western powers' right of access to Berlin.

criminals, then from the ranks of active Nazis, and lastly from the unemployed.[5]

Roosevelt supported the idea of reparations in principle, but he was concerned about the pitfalls described by Churchill. For the United States, he claimed only German assets located in America and possibly some German raw materials. Beyond that, Roosevelt seemed to want to give Stalin as much support as possible (to maximize the chances of Soviet cooperation in the occupation of Germany), but he tried to defer definite decisions to a future date. He agreed with Stalin and Churchill that a Reparations Commission should be established in Moscow, and he agreed with Stalin that the commission should take the Soviet figure of $20 billion (half reserved for the U.S.S.R.) "as a basis for discussion." This agreement was announced publicly after Yalta, along with the British position that no reparations figure should be mentioned pending consideration of the question by the Reparations Commission.

On the question of dismembering Germany, Stalin was for making detailed plans at once. Churchill argued that it would be a grave mistake to dispose of the fate of 80 million people in eighty minutes. Roosevelt's failing health prevented him from giving sustained thought to this as well as other difficult questions. However, his somewhat rambling remarks about dismembering Germany indicated that he, like Churchill, thought it best to wait and see how the situation developed rather than try to impose a solution beforehand. The three leaders decided to reserve the right to dismember Germany in the surrender instrument, so there would be no question of the legality of such a move if they chose to proceed at a later date.

It is impossible to know to what degree Churchill's views at Yalta were influenced by balance-of-power considerations. Stalin plainly suspected that he wanted to keep a strong German state intact to restrain or coerce the Soviet Union. At one point in their discussions, he told Churchill sarcastically that if he didn't

---

[5] Stalin's plan to exact reparations in the form of slave labor was not announced publicly, but it was carried out. The Western powers seem to have acquiesced in this monstrous program because they had no means of preventing it.

think Russia should get any reparations, it would be better to say so openly. However, Churchill said that he favored "large reparations" for Russia. To Eden, Churchill explained why he preferred to move a step at a time: "It is a mistake to try to write on little bits of paper what the vast emotions of an outraged and quivering world will be either immediately after the struggle is over or when the inevitable cold fit follows the hot." Churchill was not yet prepared to announce the start of the Cold War between Russia and the West, but he had lived long enough to know that one could not rule out such a development.

Yalta: Asian Questions

When the Big Three turned their attention to Asia, they promptly began writing on little bits of paper. They produced a secret agreement in which Russia was promised large territorial rewards from the crumbling Japanese Empire in return for attacking Japan three months after Germany's defeat.

Roosevelt has since been much criticized for this agreement. He is said to have paid with Chinese coin for the unnecessary and dangerous presence of Soviet armies in China, without consulting or even informing Chiang Kai-shek. Thus, the Soviets and their Asian Communist allies are said to have been given a tremendous advantage in their struggle to dominate Asia. Roosevelt's milder critics say he acted from ignorance; his most bitter foes claim he worked with masterful precision. Perhaps no other agreement made at Yalta did more to poison the atmosphere in which U.S. foreign policy was debated in the early postwar years.

Roosevelt acted at Yalta on the basis of military advice that Russian entry into the Pacific war would be of great value in reducing American casualties. In spite of U.S. control of the air and sea around Japan and the expected availability of small atomic bombs, the Joint Chiefs of Staff were still basing their estimates on the cautious assumption that Japan would not surrender unless U.S. forces invaded and seized the home islands. Although the Joint Chiefs and Roosevelt hoped this would not be necessary, they considered it prudent to plan on this basis and to assume that V-J Day might come as much as eighteen months after the defeat of Hitler.

East Asia had not figured prominently in the discussions at Teheran. At Cairo, Roosevelt, Churchill, and Chiang Kai-shek had declared that Japan would be deprived of its overseas empire, and that China would regain Manchuria, Formosa, and the Pescadores. But what was to be done with the rest of Japan's holdings on the Asian mainland and in the Pacific? Morever, what could be done about Sino-Soviet feuding along their lengthy border? And what kinds of diplomatic pressures might help snuff out the nascent civil war between Chinese Nationalists and Communists? These conflicts augured poorly for the U.S. policy of making China the great stabilizing force of postwar Asia.

The steady progress being made toward Japan's defeat might well have caused Roosevelt to sound out Stalin's Asian ambitions, if Stalin himself had not taken the initiative. In the last three months of 1944, he had spelled out his territorial demands in return for entering the Pacific war. These would restore the position held by the Russian Empire before losing the Russo-Japanese War; the terms included a lease on Dairen and Port Arthur, a lease on the Manchurian railways, transfer to Soviet ownership of the southern half of Sakhalin Island and the Kurile Islands, and recognition of Soviet hegemony in Outer Mongolia. Ambassador Harriman, to whom Stalin presented these terms, had raised a number of questions, but the subject had been left for decision at Yalta.

Roosevelt, in face-to-face bargaining with Stalin, agreed to everything the latter demanded, with two minor exceptions: Dairen was to become an internationalized port instead of a leased port (but with due regard for the "pre-eminent interests of the Soviet Union"). The Manchurian railways were to be under a joint Sino-Soviet company instead of a leasing arrangement. Again, "pre-eminent" Soviet interests would be protected (the agreement did not say how). Finally, the Big Three leaders stated that Russia's claims should be "unquestionably satisfied after Japan's defeat," meaning that China's concurrence was not necessary. However, Roosevelt agreed to approach Chiang

Kai-shek and seek his approval for the terms, and Stalin indicated his willingness to enter into a treaty of friendship and alliance with the Chinese Nationalist government to aid it in "liberating China from the Japanese yoke." [6]

The United Nations

The broad outlines of the United Nations Organization had already been drawn at the Dumbarton Oaks conference.[7] Members of the American delegation at Yalta attached greater importance than their Soviet or British colleagues to launching the proposed world organization. This was because most senior American officials at this time, including President Roosevelt himself, were at heart believers in the Wilsonian ideals that had led to the formation of the League of Nations. Most of them believed, rightly or wrongly, that America's failure to join the League had helped to bring about World War II.

The Roosevelt administration was anxious not to repeat the political errors which had led Congress to reject the League in 1920. Due care would be taken to involve the Senate in creating the United Nations. To take advantage of wartime bipartisanship, it was deemed necessary to organize the United Nations before the end of the war. Churchill and Stalin agreed to hold the organizing meeting in San Francisco on April 25, 1945.

Some American officials were more committed than others to the view that the United Nations would play a central and vital role in postwar international relations. The more seasoned American diplomats tended to agree with their British colleagues

[6] Churchill signed the agreement on Russian entry into the Pacific war, although he and Eden took very little part in the negotiations. Churchill recorded in his history of the war that he considered it an "American affair. . . . To us the problem was remote and secondary." He may have felt that supporting the U.S. position in Northeast Asia was a fair exchange for being given the initiative in Southeast Asia.

[7] Dumbarton Oaks is a Washington estate; representatives of the Big Three powers met there in August and September 1944 to begin drafting the U.N. Charter. Because of the U.S. desire to include China as a permanent member of the U.N. Security Council, American, British, and Chinese representatives met September 29 to October 7. The U.S.S.R. excused itself from this meeting on the grounds that it was still neutral in the Pacific war.

that the United Nations could do little harm (except perhaps by raising unjustified expectations), and that it might do considerable good by providing a forum in which to air disputes. But, as Churchill noted, he "did not believe that the world organization would eliminate disputes between powers and that would remain the function of diplomacy."

The three main U.N. questions decided at Yalta were: (1) voting procedures in the Security Council, (2) countries to be invited to join, and (3) principles governing trusteeships. Concerning voting procedures, the United States proposed that parties to a dispute (including the major powers) should abstain from voting while the Council was trying to bring about a voluntary, peaceful setlement by advice, conciliation, or adjudication.

Stalin at first objected to this idea, but he gave in during the Yalta conference. He then promptly made a request of the Western Allies—that two or three of the constituent Soviet republics of the Soviet Union be invited to join as regular voting members of the United Nations, in effect giving Russia extra votes. Churchill and Roosevelt agreed. The president then realized that he might have created an obstacle to Senate approval of the U.N. Charter. So he obtained agreement from Churchill and Stalin to seek extra votes in the United Nations for the United States, if this proved politically necessary.

The U.S. government proposed a system of U.N. trusteeships to replace the old League mandates over territories not yet ready for self-government. This triggered a tirade by Churchill against any and all efforts to break up the British Empire. After some debate, it was agreed that the trusteeship system would apply only to (1) former League mandates, (2) territories detached from the Axis powers, and (3) territories that were voluntarily placed under U.N. supervision.

From Collaboration to Conflict

In the weeks following Yalta, Europe's spring thaw came more quickly than the Allies expected; as soon as muddy roads and fields had dried, Allied tanks began to advance rapidly on both the eastern and western fronts. American and British bombers destroyed what remained of the German transportation system, and scores of Nazi divisions were trapped before they could regroup in new defensive positions.

This long-awaited triumph of Allied arms provided an ironic backdrop to the steadily increasing bitterness of East-West relations that followed Yalta. Each side believed the other had reneged on important aspects of the Polish agreement, which each chose to regard as the acid test of continued Allied unity. As a result, by the time of Roosevelt's death on April 12, the Western Allies were losing hope of Soviet cooperation in the United Nations and in the administration of conquered Germany.

In the Declaration on Liberated Europe issued at Yalta and in subsequent statements, Roosevelt and Churchill tried to put their agreement with Stalin in the best possible light. However, the Yalta agreement left Poland largely at Stalin's mercy. In jailing known anti-Communists, in barring any independent Poles of stature from entering the Warsaw government, and in handing over large chunks of German territory to Poland's puppet regime Stalin may or may not have technically violated the ambiguous Yalta agreement. But he made his Western colleagues highly vulnerable to attack in their own democratic political systems, because they had based their policies on tripartite cooperation. The crowning blow was the mutual aid treaty between Moscow and the Warsaw government, published a week after Roosevelt's death.

Stalin's police-state methods in Poland were all the more abhorrent to the West in contrast to his handling of relations with Finland and Czechoslovakia (two countries only somewhat less vital to Soviet security interests than Poland).[8] More than likely, the hardening of Stalin's policy on the Polish question was linked to his reaction to the news Roosevelt sent him in March about the efforts of German generals in Italy to arrange

---

[8] In each of these countries, the Soviets abstained from direct efforts to prevent non-Communist regimes from coming to power. While both governments found it expedient to adopt pro-Soviet foreign policies, they were left relatively free to run their own internal affairs in the initial postwar years.

to surrender their forces. Stalin reached the entirely fanciful conclusion that he had been betrayed by a deal between his Western Allies and Germany, which would allow Hitler to transfer his armies from the western to the eastern front. Although Stalin's messages openly accused Roosevelt of treachery, the president preserved a moderate and reasonable tone in response.

Thus, the pattern of mutual suspicion known as the cold war, which dominated U.S.-Soviet relations until the early 1970s, was established before the defeat of Nazi Germany. Which side began the cold war and why? Was it inevitable, or could it have been avoided? And how was it finally ended (if indeed it has been)? These questions are still the subject of intensive debate among historians, and each student of the postwar period must reach his own conclusions. The following thoughts will serve as an introduction to the analysis presented in the remaining chapters of this book.

Who Began the Cold War?

Was the cold war started by the United States, when it violated the "Italian precedent" by seeking undue influence in Poland and Eastern Europe? Did the United States decide to drop atomic bombs on Japan mainly to intimidate Stalin? Were the politics of the Truman and Eisenhower administrations mainly designed to create a universal "open door" for U.S. trade? The analysis begun in Chapter 8 and continued in Chapter 9 answers these questions with a qualified no. The publicly declared U.S. aim of increasing its political influence in Eastern Europe was obviously unrealistic and mainly for domestic consumption. As we have seen, Stalin learned at Yalta that Roosevelt and Churchill were by no means set on denying him the essence of power in Poland or the rest of Eastern Europe—provided he allowed these countries a very modest degree of internal political autonomy.

Stalin's heavy-handed methods in Eastern Europe *might* have provoked the United States to seek some kind of military showdown—either by taking the lead in dividing the world into hostile armed camps or even by trying to force a reduction of

Moscow's sphere of influence. But in spite of possessing an atomic monopoly and (in the initial postwar months at least) strong conventional forces, President Truman and his top advisers did not seek to intimidate Russia. Instead, they pursued the ever-dwindling prospects of collaboration during their entire first two years in office. When they finally adopted the policy of containment and rebuilding Western Europe, they did so with the express hope that this would eventually lead to collaboration between the Eastern and Western blocs.

Does it follow that Stalin deserves the main onus for starting the cold war? As head of a totalitarian police state, he was presumably not subject to domestic political pressures of the kind that caused Roosevelt to make a show of standing up for the rights of the Polish people. Yet in his headlong rush to establish full political control over areas liberated by the Red Army, he provoked a predictable Western response which, while it could not be regarded as threatening, would almost certainly have been even milder had Stalin used the same restraint he showed in dealing with Czechoslovakia and Finland.

Morever, Stalin proved to be unstable and paranoid to a dangerous degree in his reaction to the Western Allies' negotiations with German generals for surrender in Italy. Yet if the Soviet leader made things difficult for his Western Allies, Roosevelt too must have seemed highly erratic to Stalin and Molotov. One moment he would ply them with war booty and aid; the next moment he would be making unreasonable demands regarding Poland; and then he would talk as if he believed the world could be jointly run by the major powers. Thus, both sides had a part in establishing the pattern of mutual misunderstanding and hostility that soon became the dominant fact of U.S.-Soviet relations.

Was this pattern inevitable or could wiser statesmen on both sides have prevented it? In retrospect, Soviet leaders of the 1940s often seem to have been more realistic (as well as more stubborn and selfish) than their American counterparts. They saw that the postwar interests of the two superpowers would rarely coincide, and they were the first to realize that acknowledging each other's spheres of influences might be the only basis for coexistence.

Eventually, American leaders also adopted the spheres of interest approach, resulting in the Truman administration's policy of containment and the rebuilding of Western Europe (discussed in Chapter 9). The U.S. government believed during this period (1947–48) that bold efforts to revive Western Europe combined with firm but patient resistance to Soviet expansion would lead eventually to reduced hostility. It even looked forward to eventual collaboration between the two blocs. However, Stalin's initial response to the U.S. containment policy was to tighten controls over his European satellites and start a war of nerves with the West by such means as the Berlin blockade.

It is not unlikely that some reduction of East-West tensions might have come about as the growing political and economic strength of the two blocs made their leaders more self-confident in dealing with each other. It would not have been hard to develop joint cultural, scientific, and economic programs to explore the principle of collaboration. However, just when the ending of the Berlin blockade gave grounds for cautious optimism that an "era of negotiation" might be at hand, the victory of Mao Tse-tung's forces in China changed everything.

Stalin evidently felt compelled to give top priority to incorporating the People's Republic of China into his Soviet-led bloc; this meant, among other things, not being outdone by Mao in the militancy of his anti-Western propaganda. In the United States, the "loss" of China by the Democratic administration became an emotion-charged political issue (discussed in Chapter 10). Truman and Secretary of State Acheson increasingly lost control of the containment policy to right-wing extremists whose main aim was to discredit the party in power. Reluctantly at first, but with growing conviction after the Soviet-inspired invasion of South Korea, the Truman administration evolved the "China containment" policy. China's subsequent entry into the Korean war brought on one of the most dangerous crises of the cold war period.

In Chapters 11 and 12, it is argued that for the next twenty years after Truman, no U.S. administration chose to base its Far Eastern policy on grounds more realistic than militant anti-

Communism. The Eisenhower, Kennedy, and Johnson administrations, I believe, all acted out of conviction rather than political expediency. The ultimate disaster to which this policy led was the ill-conceived effort to "pacify" Indochina (Chapter 13).

After tensions between Russia and China became acute in the late 1960s, these powers each sought to improve relations with the U.S. government. The Nixon administration (Chapter 14) proved to be receptive to such overtures, because for the first time in the postwar period, the White House was occupied by a president without any strong convictions in domestic or foreign affairs. The fact that Mr. Nixon had been a leading spokesman, during the late 1940s and the 1950s, for a policy of militant anti-Communism made his reversal of this policy in the early 1970s both dramatic and politically painless. Secretary of State Kissinger skillfully unraveled many of the tangled issues that had grown up around conflicts that, since the cold war, had come to threaten world stability. But his task was made more difficult by the steady erosion of the administration's political base due to unscrupulous conduct that was condemned by broad segments of the American public.

As discussed in Chapter 15, a major test of the policy of normalizing relations with the Soviet Union and China would be the ability of President Nixon's successors to (1) sustain the positive aspects of such a policy while repairing the damage done to relations with the West European Allies and Japan and (2) develop widespread support in the United States for a realistic and moderately active foreign policy without resorting to the creation of some new and artificial external threat to replace Communism.

Suggested Reading

ACHESON, DEAN. *Present at the Creation: My Years at the State Department.* New York: Norton, 1969.

ALPEROVITZ, GAR. *Cold War Essays.* Garden City, N.Y.: Anchor Books, 1970.

BUTOW, R. J. C. *Japan's Decision to Surrender.* Stanford, Calif.: Stanford University Press, 1954.

BYRNES, JAMES F. *Speaking Frankly*. New York: Harper & Row, 1947.

FEIS, HERBERT. *The Atomic Bomb and the End of World War II*. Princeton, N.J.: Princeton University Press, 1966.

———. *From Trust to Terror: The Onset of the Cold War, 1945–1950*. New York: Norton, 1970.

GADDIS, JOHN LEWIS. *The United States and the Origins of the Cold War, 1941–1947*. New York: Columbia University Press, 1972.

GREW, JOSEPH C. *Turbulent Era: A Diplomatic Record of Forty Years, 1904–1945*. Boston: Houghton, Mifflin, 1952.

HARRIMAN, W. AVERELL. *America and Russia in a Changing World*. Garden City, N.Y.: Doubleday, 1971.

HARRIMAN, W. AVERELL, with ELIE ABEL. *Ambassador Extraordinaire* (tentative title). New York: Random House, 1975.

KENNAN, GEORGE F. *Memoirs:* Vol. 1, *1925–1950*. Vol. 2, *1950–1963*. Boston: Atlantic Monthly Press, 1967, 1972.

KHRUSHCHEV, NIKITA S. (alleged author). *Khrushchev Remembers*. With introduction, commentary, and notes by EDWARD CRANKSHAW. Translated and edited by STROBE TALBOTT. Boston: Little, Brown, 1970 (supplement issued by same editor and publisher in 1974).

KOLKO, GABRIEL. *The Politics of War: The World and the United States Foreign Policy, 1943–1945*. New York: Random, 1969.

LIPPMANN, WALTER. *The Cold War*. New York: Harper & Row, 1947.

SNELL, JOHN L. (ed.). *The Meaning of Yalta*. Baton Rouge: Louisiana State University Press, 1956.

TRUMAN, HARRY S. *Memoirs*. 2 vols. Garden City, N.Y.: Doubleday, 1955, 1956.

WILLIAMS, WILLIAM A. *The Tragedy of American Diplomacy*. New York: Dell, 1962.

9

Containment and Reconstruction

During the final year of the war, American diplomats serving in Moscow had grown increasingly concerned about the way Roosevelt and some of his top advisers dealt with Soviet leaders. They tended to yield on secondary matters whenever the Russians produced a display of bad temper or rudeness —hoping this would earn them Soviet gratitude and cooperation on primary issues, such as postwar cooperation in Germany and the United Nations.

Ambassador Harriman and his deputy, George Kennan, and General John Deane (chief of the U.S. military mission) all believed that President Roosevelt was right in wanting to maintain the three-power coalition after the war. They believed that East-West cooperation was both desirable and attainable, although they knew from experience the difficulty of working with the Russians.

These diplomats felt, however, that Washington officials tended to overrate the importance of Soviet cooperation to the achievement of America's postwar aims. The United States would emerge from the war incomparably stronger than Russia, both militarily and economically. Its sociopolitical system based on individual freedom had survived for over a hundred and fifty years, while the Soviet police state was relatively new and untried.[1]

To attain maximum cooperation with Russia, U.S. officials in Moscow favored the exact reverse of the tactics Roosevelt had been using. American negotiators should avoid placing themselves in the position of supplicants by constantly stressing America's dependence on Soviet cooperation to achieve its postwar objectives. Americans should refuse to let themselves be browbeaten into yielding on secondary matters by calculated Russian displays of anger and rudeness. They must avoid loose, platitudinous agreements and get down to specifics. They must match their Soviet counterparts in stubborn patience, making certain that each aspect of any agreement was clearly understood, and based on mutual advantage. Then, but only then, according to the most experienced American diplomats, would Soviet leaders abide by their agreements.

The Transition to Truman

In the last weeks of Roosevelt's life and the first weeks of Harry Truman's administration, Americans in Moscow began to fear that Washington officials might suddenly swing to the other extreme in their dealings with the Soviet Union. Having tried to charm the Russians into cooperating with America's plans for the postwar world—and having gained little in return except abuse—some U.S. officials were beginning to look upon Russia as a virtual enemy and a serious threat to American security interests.

Stalin was obviously shaken by Roosevelt's death on April 12; he expressed his concern to Ambassador Harriman about the continuity of American policy. Harriman assured him that U.S. policy remained the same and used the occasion to ask Stalin to reverse an earlier decision and send Foreign Minister Molotov to San Francisco to take part in the founding of the United Nations. Stalin agreed, and Molotov stopped off in Washington

[1] See George F. Kennan, *Memoirs, 1925–1950* (Boston: Little, Brown, 1967), pp. 213–264. Secretary of War Stimson's views on Russia were very similar to those of Harriman and Kennan in Moscow. See Stimson and Bundy, *On Active Service in Peace and War*, pp. 605–611.

on the same day that Moscow published its mutual aid treaty with Warsaw. This treaty caused a furor in Washington and resulted in a tense meeting between Molotov and President Truman.

Molotov stated that the only obstacle to a smooth settlement in Poland was Western opposition to the Soviet formula of twenty-one Communists and six non-Communists in the Warsaw government. Truman told the foreign minister bluntly that the Soviet Union had made an agreement on Poland and all that was needed was for that government to keep its word. He said he wanted friendship with Russia but this could not be a "one-way street." Molotov said he had never been spoken to that way in his life. The president advised him to keep his agreements and he would not be spoken to that way.

Some historians have argued that this incident reveals a sudden hardening of U.S. policy after Roosevelt's death. However, although President Truman adopted a somewhat firmer tone than Roosevelt in his dealings with the Soviets, he did his best to salvage FDR's policy of collaboration.

Truman had little background in foreign affairs before Roosevelt's sudden death brought him to the White House. However, this allowed him to look at the Yalta agreements with a more critical eye than some people who took part in their negotiation. He proved to be a voracious reader of briefing papers, cables, and memoranda and a far more orderly administrator than Roosevelt. One of his outstanding characteristics as president was his ability to make difficult decisions and stick to them, whether or not they attracted political fire.[2]

Truman and the man he chose to be his first secretary of state, James Byrnes, shared the country's buoyant optimism in the summer of 1945. Neither the American people nor their new leaders were prepared to launch a new struggle against an ally they had worked so hard to sustain. The problems of peace

[2] During his first week in office, Truman surprised Ambassador Harriman and other subordinates by the speed with which he grasped the complexities of Soviet-American relations. See W. Averell Harriman, *U.S.-Soviet Relations and the Beginning of the Cold War: A Half-Century of Personal Observation* (New York: Doubleday, 1970), pp. 31–44.

were already beginning to crowd in on the new administration, and the first rumblings of partisan attack on its foreign policy could be heard, but Truman and Byrnes believed in the strength of the American system and in the tripartite coalition which had produced so great a victory. They regarded the new United Nations as a major asset to the U.S. policy of world peace and stability. They had faith in their own abilties as negotiators, and they believed it their duty to do all in their power to make the promise of lasting peace a reality.

One of the reasons for the steadiness of U.S. policy during these transitional months—from war to peace and from Roosevelt's leadership to Truman's—was the continuity provided by men of long experience like Henry Stimson. As he recorded in his diary on April 3, 1945:

> It seems to me that it is a time . . . to use all the restraint I can on these other people who have been apparently getting a little more irritated. I have myself been in the various crises enough to feel the importance of firm dealing with the Russians but . . . what we want is to state our facts with perfectly cold-blooded firmness and not show any temper.

Stimson was by no means the only moderating influence in Washington during the final months of war. Joseph Grew, acting secretary of state during most of this period, held much the same views, as did General George Marshall, chief of staff of the Army.[3] Averell Harriman was soon called back from Moscow to the center of policy-making in Washington. But Stimson, with the weight of forty years of distinguished service in public life, was Washington's elder statesman at this time. He took the position that the U.S. government should continue to regard the Balkan states as "beyond the sphere of proper United States action" (although he later reversed this position and supported

[3] Marshall became an almost indispensable figure in the Truman administration, serving as special mediator in China during 1946, then as secretary of state during 1947 and 1948, and finally as secretary of defense. Grew, whose role as ambassador to Japan is traced in Chapters 5 and 6, retired as undersecretary when the war ended; he was succeeded by Dean Acheson, who became secretary of state in 1949.

aid to Greece and Turkey). In Eastern Europe generally, he believed that it was a mistake for the United States to press for more political influence; he pointed out that the Russians "perhaps were being more realistic than we in regard to their own security."

Japan's Surrender and the Atomic Bomb

Stimson and Grew both saw the importance of letting Japan know that "unconditional surrender" would not entail abolishing the institution of the emperor, for whom many Japanese were prepared to fight to the death. Their idea met stiff opposition from Byrnes and others, who feared that such a move would be regarded by the American people as shameful "bargaining" with the Japanese militarists. Grew and Stimson prepared a declaration for issuance by the Big Three at Potsdam (July 1945); it called on Japan to surrender and contained a straightforward statement that the institution of the emperor would be preserved.

Although this direct language was eliminated, the Potsdam declaration contained some assurances of the Allies' intentions regarding Japan. Nevertheless, the Japanese government delayed its response, hoping to gain time to arrange Russian mediation. Press reports distorted this decision into an announcement that Japan would "ignore" the Potsdam declaration—an unintended gesture of defiance which may have contributed to the Truman administration's decision to drop atomic bombs on Hiroshima and Nagasaki on August 6 and 9.[4]

At the time, American officials could only guess at the strength of Japanese leaders' determination to continue the war. Stimson and Grew proved correct in believing that it was essential to provide positive assurances that the emperor would be preserved. But Truman, Stimson, and other leading officials have stated

[4] The Soviet Union entered the war on August 8, swiftly occupying large areas of Manchuria and Korea. On August 10 at Japan's request, Secretary Byrnes provided somewhat stronger assurances than those contained in the Potsdam declaration that the emperor's position would not be compromised. The emperor himself then cast the deciding vote for surrender.

that they believed at the time it would also be necessary to use atomic bombs to convince the Japanese that further resistance was futile.

Was this the *main* reason the atomic bombs were used? Some historians have argued that forestalling Russia's entry into the war and demonstrating the terrible power of atomic weapons to Stalin was a more likely motive for dropping the bombs. These historians point out that Japan had not definitively rejected the Potsdam declaration; thus, the decision to drop the bombs seems to have been made with undue haste. Moreover, Stimson's memoirs show that he had been growing more distrustful of the Russians; he was also beginning to doubt that their help was essential to defeat Japan, now that atomic bombs were available.

However, Truman states in his memoirs that his main consideration in ordering the use of the bomb was to defeat Japan as quickly as possible with the fewest American casualties. The president's military advisers still believed that Russia's entry into the war *and* the use of atomic bombs were desirable from this standpoint. Although many people would question the soundness of this advice, especially with the advantage of hindsight, the crucial point is that it probably seemed valid to President Truman at the time. Thus, it appears unlikely that the main reason for the president's decision to bomb Hiroshima and Nagasaki was to impress Stalin or to preclude Soviet entry into the Pacific war, although some idea of achieving one or both of these aims may have been in the minds of President Truman and his advisers.

The U.S. government sought, during the remainder of 1945 and 1946, to take the lead in placing all dangerous forms of atomic energy under international control. A plan was devised by a committee, on which Undersecretary of State Dean Acheson and David E. Lilienthal played the leading roles.[5] Under this

---

[5] Lilienthal was Chairman of the Tennessee Valley Authority. The members of the committee were: Vannevar Bush, president of the Carnegie Institution; James B. Conant, president of Harvard; General Leslie Groves, commandant of the Manhattan Project that built the first atomic bombs; and John J. McCloy, former assistant secretary of war. The panel of consultants included J. Robert Oppenheimer, former director of the Los Alamos Atomic Laboratory.

plan, all nations would be invited to sign a treaty in which they would relinquish to an international Atomic Energy Authority the right to make atomic bombs or the materials for them. The committee believed that the only practicable safeguard in case of violations would be public warnings by the Atomic Energy Authority that violations were taking place. This would allow the various governments of the world to take whatever action they could to protect their people.

When Bernard Baruch, the financier, was appointed U.S. representative to the U.N. Atomic Energy Commission, he revised the Acheson-Lilienthal plan in two important respects. First, any country that engaged in illegal production of atomic weapons would receive prompt and severe punishment; second, the major powers would not have any right to veto such punishment. Although it was not Baruch's (or Truman's) intention, these amendments probably destroyed whatever small chance then existed that the U.S.S.R. would agree to international control of atomic energy. Most other U.N. members accepted the U.S. proposal. Moscow escaped a propaganda defeat by proposing the immediate destruction of all atomic weapons; this was not acceptable to Congress or the Truman administration.

1946: The Year of Disillusion

International control of atomic energy was by no means the only issue on which U.S. leaders, who had hoped for collaboration with Russia, experienced frustrations during 1946. Secretary of State Byrnes was abroad a good part of the year attending meetings of the Big Four foreign ministers; these long weeks of negotiation finally produced peace treaties for the former Axis satellites: Bulgaria, Finland, Hungary, Italy, and Rumania. Except for the treaty with Italy, these merely confirmed the terms Russia had dictated to its smaller neighbors in wartime armistice agreements. George Kennan described Byrnes's negotiating technique at a December 1945 foreign ministers' meeting in Moscow:

> He plays his negotiations by ear, going into them with no clear or fixed plan, with no definite set objectives or limitations. He relies

entirely on his own agility and presence of mind and hopes to take advantage of tactical openings. In the present conference his weakness in dealing with the Russians is that his main purpose is to achieve some sort of an agreement, he doesn't much care what. The realities behind this agreement, since they concern only such people as Koreans, Rumanians, and Iranians, about whom he knows nothing, do not concern him. He wants an agreement for its political effect at home. The Russians know this. They will see that for this superficial success he pays a heavy price in the things that are real.[6]

At each succeeding conference, prominent Republicans in the U.S. delegation (who were more aware than Byrnes of the American public's growing irritation with Russia) became increasingly critical of the secretary of state. In Washington, President Truman and Undersecretary Acheson were annoyed by Byrnes's failure to keep them informed of what he was doing. Byrnes's British colleagues also criticized his reluctance to coordinate strategy on matters of mutual interest. By mid-1946, President Truman had decided that he would have to replace Byrnes with General Marshall. Few people were aware of the impending change; even fewer foresaw that the change of personalities would be accompanied by a change of policy toward Russia.

Meanwhile, General Marshall, weary and anxious for retirement, accepted the arduous task of trying to mediate the Chinese civil war. He spent 1946 in China, returning to the United States at the end of the year to take up his new duties as secretary of state. During his year in the Far East, he became thoroughly disillusioned with both the Chinese Nationalists and the Communists. In Marshall's view, there was little the United States could do, short of direct military intervention, to prevent victory by the more highly motivated Communists over Chiang Kai-shek's demoralized regime and army.

Marshall was firmly opposed to U.S. military intervention on the Asian mainland, and he knew that there was no political

[6] Kennan, *Memoirs: 1925–1950*, pp. 302–303.

support in the United States for such action.[7] Under these circumstances, it would have made sense for the United States to withdraw its support of Chiang Kai-shek's regime. However, the Truman administration chose to avoid a confrontation with Chiang's supporters in the U.S. Congress, because their votes were needed on other matters.

In Japan, General MacArthur and U.S. occupation forces faced the eerie silence of a nation that had almost reached a standstill. The winter of 1945–46 was unusually cold; millions of people were without adequate food or shelter. Many were still too numbed by defeat to search among the wreckage of their burned-out cities and frozen fields for the means of staying alive. As the occupation forces struggled to prevent mass starvation and epidemics, Soviet leaders angrily demanded a voice in occupation policy and the "right" to strip reparations from this ruined country. But the U.S. government saw no reason to yield on either point.

More complex problems confronted American officials in Germany, where the vital interests of many nations were involved. As in Japan, the occupying powers faced an enormous task in simply keeping the destitute and demoralized German people alive. The problem was aggravated by the fact that the Soviet Union, in redrawing the map of Poland, had forced 9 million Germans out of areas east of the Oder-Neisse line. These people, along with 2.5 million Germans expelled from Czechoslovakia and 0.5 million from Hungary, had to make a new life for themselves within Germany's reduced boundaries.

Instead of cooperating with international relief efforts, Soviet officials concentrated on extracting whatever they could in the way of reparations from their zone of Germany; they also refused to meet their commitments to send surplus food to the Western Allies' zones. The Four-Power Control Council, which could only operate on the basis of unanimity, was often deadlocked by Soviet dissent.

[7] U.S. ground forces were reduced from 3.5 million in May 1945 to four hundred thousand in March 1946. The Republicans gained control of Congress in the 1946 elections and promptly announced their aim of cutting the budget enough to reduce taxes by 20 percent.

To protest Soviet obstruction, the United States suspended shipments of reparations from its zone to Russia's in May 1946. A few months later, the United States and Britain joined their occupation zones in a single economic unit. Russia refused an invitation to link its zone to the two Western ones; France did the same to avoid offending the Russians and because its leaders feared a revival of German power.

By September 1946, events were clearly moving toward a formal division of Germany. Secretary Byrnes tried to reverse this trend (or prevent the ultimate blame from falling on the United States) by making a speech at Stuttgart in which he called for a unified federal German state. To relieve French and Soviet anxieties, he proposed that Germany remain disarmed under a long-term extension of the four-power military occupation. The Soviet Union rejected the entire concept.

The idea of a unified Germany was raised again in March 1947 by Byrnes's successor, General Marshall. The Soviets countered with two important conditions: (1) recognition of their earlier demand for the full $10 billion in reparations discussed at Yalta (which they had waived at Potsdam) and (2) a share in the control of the Ruhr industrial region. On both questions, the United States and Great Britain were firmly opposed. As regards the political organization of a reunited Germany, the Soviets wanted a highly centralized government. Believing that this might facilitate a Communist takeover of Germany, the Western powers insisted on a federal structure. The failure to find common ground on German reunification convinced Marshall and other American leaders that the division of Europe into two separate spheres was inescapable.

The Containment Policy

On February 22, 1946, George Kennan was in charge of the American embassy in Moscow. (He was also suffering, his *Memoirs* tell us, from a cold, fever, sinusitis, tooth trouble, and the aftereffects of a sulfa drug.) Among the papers brought to his sickroom that morning was a message from the U.S. Treasury Department asking why the Russians were unwilling to join the new World Bank and Monetary Fund. Kennan's scorn for this naïve query gave him strength to respond with an eight thousand word telegraphic essay, in which he described Soviet policy as expansionist and unable to conceive of permanent coexistence with the United States. Coping with this force, he said, "is undoubtedly [the] greatest task our diplomacy has ever faced."

Kennan did not offer a detailed plan in his "long telegram," as it came to be known. But he stated his belief that "the problem is within our power to solve," because the Soviet Union was "highly sensitive to [the] logic of force. . . . Thus, if the adversary has sufficient force and makes clear his readiness to use it, he rarely has to do so." Much would depend on the "cohesion, firmness, and vigor which [the] Western world can muster" and on "the health and vigor of our own society." [8] As conceived by Kennan, "containment" bore no resemblance to a policy of military encirclement of the Soviet Union.

Kennan's "long telegram" reached Washington just when top officials were in a mood to pay attention to it. Two weeks earlier, Stalin had delivered a speech restating the Marxist-Leninist dogma of "inevitable war" between Communism and capitalism; he proposed a series of Five-Year plans to prepare the Soviet Union for this struggle. Two weeks after Kennan's long telegram, Churchill delivered his "iron curtain" speech at Fulton, Missouri, calling for a "fraternal association of the English-speaking peoples" to defend the Western world.

Gradually, the Truman administration adopted (and then began to modify) Kennan's concept of "containing" the Soviet Union. The process by which this new foreign policy consensus evolved was extremely complex. As we have seen, Kennan and a few others with experience in Russia began advocating various features of the containment policy during the final year of the war. Their influence grew steadily in the early postwar years. During 1945 and 1946, political leaders of both major U.S.

[8] George Kennan, *Memoirs: 1925–1950*, pp. 583–598. Kennan was assigned to lecture at the new National War College in the fall of 1946. In 1947, he played an important role in developing the Marshall Plan. He later served as ambassador to Russia and to Yugoslavia.

parties began to be increasingly annoyed by Soviet tactics and disillusioned about the prospects for collaboration. At times, the Truman administration took the lead in trying to build public understanding and acceptance of this new doctrine. At other times, the administration seemed to respond to pressures from public groups and from key Republicans such as Senator Vandenberg and John Foster Dulles.

During 1945 and 1946, the Soviet Union helped to crystallize the U.S. government's containment policy by its pressures in Iran, Greece, and Turkey. In Iran, Soviet and British forces had each occupied portions of the country during the war to forestall growing German influence. After the British withdrew, the Soviets appeared to want to consolidate their influence in the country. However, faced with Anglo-American warnings, Soviet forces were pulled out in March 1946. In the case of Turkey, the Soviets steadily increased their demands for political and military rights which would have reduced the country to a Soviet protectorate. In August 1946, the United States responded by sending a naval task force into the eastern Mediterranean.

The internal political situation in Greece was typically chaotic. A British-backed conservative government lacked the means to begin rebuilding the war-shattered economy, and many of the people were reduced to a hand-to-mouth existence. Inflation, fed by the cost of maintaining a large army, sapped the government's popular support. The army's power was justified by alleged foreign backing of Greek Communists in the northern part of the kingdom.

Undersecretary Acheson and other U.S. officials spent considerable time and effort responding to these crises even before their government evolved a definite policy of containing Soviet ambitions in the eastern Mediterranean. In early 1946, emergency loans of $25 million each were extended to Greece and Turkey. U.S. ground and air forces in Trieste and northern Italy were reinforced during the midsummer crisis in which Tito's forces shot down two U.S. planes. Iran was given political advice and support in regaining control of its northern provinces. Warning notes were sent to the U.S.S.R. detailing as carefully as possible the consequences of continued Soviet agitation.

Each of these moves appeared to temporarily reduce the Soviet pressures, or at least redirected them to other areas. They neither led to war nor produced any permanent relaxation of tensions; Soviet advances always seemed to follow the course of least resistance. As Acheson later recalled, "The year 1946 was for the most part a year of learning that minds in the Kremlin worked very much as George F. Kennan had predicted they would."

The Truman Doctrine

At the end of January 1947, General Marshall was sworn in as secretary of state. His first major task was to prepare for the foreign ministers' meeting in Moscow in early March. He assigned broad responsibilities to Acheson, his deputy, who would take charge in his absence.

During February, the Greek situation deteriorated rapidly. State Department officials estimated that only a coalition government and substantial foreign aid could save the country from an early Communist takeover. On Friday, February 21, when General Marshall was out of town, the British embassy delivered copies of two very important messages to Acheson. One applied to Greece, the other to Turkey; Britain could no longer afford to carry the main burden of aiding either of these countries and would cease to do so in six weeks. The British government hoped that the United States could assume this responsibility. They estimated the initial foreign exchange needs of Greece at from $240 million to $280 million; smaller but still substantial sums, would be needed by Turkey, which had a stronger government.

Acheson knew that the United States was faced with an historic challenge. As he and a team of State Department officials worked through the weekend on staff papers to brief the secretary and president, he realized there could be only one decision. By the afternoon of Monday, February 24, General Marshall and President Truman shared his conviction that strengthening of Greece and Turkey was vital to U.S. security, and that the United States was the only country that could perform this task. However, funds and authority would have to be obtained from Congress. Since Marshall would leave for

Moscow in less than a week, he asked Acheson to continue to direct the preparation of administration policy.

On Wednesday, February 26, the leaders of Congress (which was controlled by the Republicans) met with Truman and Acheson in the president's office. Both parties had already expressed deep skepticism about the wisdom of continued U.S. support for relief efforts in Europe; the Republicans wanted to cut the president's budget wherever possible. Thus, the meeting in the oval office took place in an atmosphere of confrontation. President Truman's opening remarks were unimpressive and were received in chilly silence by the congressmen. Acheson whispered to him a request to speak. He knew the members of Congress had no conception of the crisis they were facing: It was his task to bring it home to them. He later recalled saying that, during the past eighteen months,

> . . . Soviet pressure on the Straits, on Iran, and on northern Greece had brought the Balkans to the point where a highly possible Soviet breakthrough might open three continents to Soviet penetration. Like apples in a barrel infected by one rotten one, the corruption of Greece would infect Iran and all to the east. It would also carry infection to Africa through Asia Minor and Egypt, and to Europe through Italy and France, already threatened by the strongest domestic Communist parties in Western Europe. The Soviet Union was playing one of the greatest gambles in history at minimal cost. It did not need to win all the possibilities. Even one or two offered immense gains. We and we alone were in a position to break up the play. These were the stakes that British withdrawal from the eastern Mediterranean offered to an eager and ruthless opponent.[9]

A long silence followed Acheson's statement. Then Senator Arthur Vandenberg, chairman of the Foreign Relations Committee, said, "Mr. President, if you will say that to the Congress and the country, I will support you and I believe that most of its members will do the same."

General Marshall departed for Moscow a few days later, leaving

[9] Dean Acheson, *Present at the Creation: My Years in the State Department* (New York: Norton, 1969), p. 219.

Acheson in charge of efforts to draw up a plan and to gain Congressional support. He told Acheson to disregard the possible effects of these efforts on the foreign ministers' meeting; this was now less important than saving the pivotal position occupied by Greece and Turkey.

There was considerable controversy over the drafting of President Truman's message to Congress. George Kennan approved the objective of trying to save Greece and Turkey, but he thought the wording of the text supplied by the State Department committed the United States too broadly.[10] On the other hand, Clark Clifford (a young counsel to the president) thought the text needed strenghtening; Acheson persuaded him to withdraw his suggestions. On March 12, President Truman delivered his speech to a joint session of Congress. The crucial passage was

> I believe that it must be the policy of the United States to support free peoples who are resisting attempted subjugation by armed minorities or by outside pressures.
> I believe that we must assist free peoples to work out their own destinies in their own way.
> I believe that our help should be primarily through economic and financial aid which is essential to economic stability and orderly political processes.

This concept became known as the Truman Doctrine. By later standards, the amounts requested were not vast. But the ideas expressed were to have the broadest possible implications for U.S. postwar policy. The president asked Congress to provide $250 million in aid to Greece and $150 million for Turkey. He also sought authority to send U.S. civilian and military personnel to both countries to assist in reconstruction and military training.

Although the president received a standing ovation from congressmen of both parties at the end of his speech, Acheson saw this as a "tribute to a brave man rather than unanimous acceptance of his policy." However, it took only the relatively brief period of two months for Congress to reverse its initial

[10] See Kennan, *Memoirs: 1925–1950,* pp. 330–341 and 382–387.

stand against foreign aid and approve this new foreign policy by almost two to one majorities in both houses. In the committee hearings, Acheson tried to dispel any impression that the Truman Doctrine was a blank check to shaky governments everywhere.

The Marshall Plan

Although it rejected a U.S. role of universal policeman, the Truman administration was studying the much broader European economic crisis during the months that Congress debated aid to Greece and Turkey. Conditions in many parts of Europe during this bitter cold winter were in some respects worse than during wartime. Food was extremely scarce because the cities had neither goods nor sound currency to exchange; farmers produced mainly for their own consumption. War-damaged factories and transportation systems remained unrepaired. Unemployment rose to record heights as industrial production almost ceased for lack of coal, raw materials, and spare parts. Those who were lucky enough to have homes had little or no fuel to heat them. Under these conditions, class conflict and political antagonisms became vicious.

Among those who played prominent roles in shaping the U.S. government's response to this situation were Assistant Secretary of State Will Clayton, George Kennan (head of the new Policy Planning Staff), Dean Acheson, and General Marshall. Clayton, who was in charge of economic affairs, analyzed the problem and prodded the administration to take action. Kennan tried to forecast the Soviets' reaction to a major European recovery program. (It was agreed to invite them to take part—and let them bear the onus for dividing Europe if they refused.) Acheson served as coordinator of the administration's plans and political strategy. Marshall, who returned from Moscow on April 28, brought impressions of the Soviet leaders' current aims.

It was Marshall who first announced to the world the basic concept of the plan that eventually bore his name. In his brief speech at the Harvard Commencement of June 1947, he first described the existing conditions in Europe. Then he discussed how the concept related to Soviet-American relations. He explained that U.S. policy was directed "not against any country or doctrine, but against hunger, poverty, desperation, and chaos." Thus

> Any government that is willing to assist in the task of recovery will find full cooperation, I am sure, on the part of the United States Government. Any government which maneuvers to block the recovery of other countries cannot expect help from us. Furthermore, governments, political parties, or groups which seek to perpetuate human misery in order to profit therefrom politically or otherwise will encounter the opposition of the United States.

The actual plan proposed by Marshall was so brief and general that it was almost impossible for anyone to take exception to it. As Acheson later paraphrased his statement, "If the Europeans, all or some of them, could get together on a plan of what was needed to get them out of the dreadful situation . . . we would take a look at their plan and see what aid we might practically give." [11]

Marshall's speech evoked a rapid response in Europe. The British foreign minister, Ernest Bevin, immediately got in touch with his French counterpart, Georges Bidault. Two weeks later, they met in Paris with Molotov to discuss drawing up a plan, as General Marshall had suggested. However, Molotov was soon called home. As Bevin commented, his withdrawal "made operations much more simple." Shortly afterward, twenty-two European governments responded to a joint Bevin-Bidault invitation and began drawing up a plan. No East European nations attended; Czech and Polish leaders had hoped to come but were not allowed to by the Soviets. President Truman appointed Averell Harriman to head a nonpartisan U.S. committee to consult with the European planners and advise on coordinating U.S. resources to meet their needs.

By September 1947, the West European nations had formed a plan to achieve economic self-sufficiency by 1951. They esti-

[11] Acheson, *Present at the Creation*, p. 234.

mated they would need $19.3 billion in U.S. support over that period. When President Truman presented their proposal to Congress, he requested $6.8 billion for the first fifteen months and $10.2 billion over the next ten years. Congress cut the initial appropriation down to $3 billion. The program began in July 1948, continued for three years, and cost the American taxpayer $10.2 billion. By the early 1950s, it had clearly achieved its objectives of reviving the economic life of Western Europe and promoting economic integration within the region.

Two Germanys Emerge

Germany was not initially invited by the United States or by the other European nations to take part in the Marshall Plan, because it was not a self-governing state. However, in the spring of 1948, the three Western occupying powers met with representatives of Belgium, the Netherlands, and Luxembourg (Benelux) and agreed on the creation of a West German state. To prevent German rearmament, the Ruhr industrial region would be internationally administered by the six nations plus the new German republic. The people in the American, British, and French zones of Germany were allowed to elect a constituent assembly, which drew up a constitution for a federal state.

In September 1949, the German Federal Republic was established with Konrad Adenauer as chancellor. His government had control of the country's internal affairs and limited control over its foreign policy. Western occupation forces remained, although military government had ended in the Federal Republic and Germany was not initially allowed to rearm. Under firm but democratic leadership, inflation was checked, the morale of the German people revived, and their country was made eligible for Marshall Plan aid. West Germany later played a central role in the European economic revival.[12]

The Soviet Union reacted to the Marshall Plan and to the

---

[12] As described in the next chapter, Japan regained its sovereignty in 1951 (after signing peace and mutual security treaties with the United States). As in Germany, a period of rapid economic growth followed in the 1950s and 1960s.

establishment of the Federal Republic of Germany by tightening its control over the states of Eastern Europe. The U.S.S.R. held a meeting in Warsaw to condemn the Marshall Plan (which Poland had wanted to join). Communist-led strikes in France and Italy followed. The Soviets held another meeting in Yugoslavia to organize the Communist Information Bureau, which, ironically, Tito left in 1948. Moscow also signed new defense treaties with Bulgaria, Finland, Hungary, and Rumania. The most aggressive Soviet move was its support of a coup which overthrew the relatively independent Czech government in February 1948 and replaced it with a puppet regime.

In April 1948, the Soviet Union began to restrict surface travel from West Germany to Berlin, which was entirely surrounded by the Soviet zone but under joint Allied administration. In June 1948, the Soviet Union's "Berlin blockade" was in full swing, and the Western powers began to organize an airlift of food and fuel. By September, they were bringing in four thousand tons of cargo a day. This test of wills continued throughout the winter and was ended only by negotiations in May 1949. A month after the founding of the Federal Republic of Germany (in September 1949), the Soviet Union announced the transformation of its occupation zone into the German Democratic Republic.

The North Atlantic Treaty Organization

Meanwhile, the Truman administration, mindful of the great inferiority of Western conventional military forces compared with those at Moscow's command, decided to lay the groundwork for a military alliance linking the countries of Western Europe and North America. In March 1948, President Truman asked Congress to authorize U.S. support for a mutual defense treaty that had just been signed by Britain, France, and the Benelux countries. Truman also asked Congress to adopt the principle of universal peacetime military training and to revive the draft temporarily.

In June 1948, the same month that Congress appropriated the first Marshall Plan funds, the Senate adopted the Vandenberg resolution. The resolution declared that the United States should associate itself "by constitutional process, with such regional and other collective arrangements as are based on continuous and effective self-help and mutual aid, and as affect its national security."

With this authorization, the Truman administration proceeded to negotiate the North Atlantic alliance, which came into being in the summer of 1949. The heart of the treaty was the statement that an attack on any one of the members in Europe or North America would be considered an attack on all; each member would assist the party attacked by "such means as it deems necessary, including the use of armed force."

Looking back on his government's great decisions (in which he had played no small part) to support the reconstruction of Western Europe and the containment of Soviet influence, George Kennan wrote these proud and hopeful words in 1948:

> Recovery is progressing rapidly in the West. New hope exists. People see the possibility of a better future. The Communist position in France has been deeply shaken. The Western nations have found a common political language. They are learning to lean on each other, and to help each other.[13]

There were many, both in Europe and in the United States, who agreed with Kennan and considered the work done in 1947 and 1948 the finest achievement of American foreign policy.

Suggested Reading

ACHESON, DEAN. *Present at the Creation: My Years at the State Department.* New York: Norton, 1969.

CLAY, LUCIUS D. *Decision in Germany.* Garden City, N.Y.: Doubleday, 1950.

FERRELL, ROBERT H. *George C. Marshall.* New York: Cooper Square, 1966.

GARDNER, LLOYD C. *Architects of Illusion: Men and Ideas in American Foreign Policy, 1941–1949.* Chicago: Quadrangle, 1970.

---

[13] Kennan, *Memoirs (1925–1950)*, p. 382.

HARRIMAN, W. AVERELL. *America and Russia in a Changing World.* Garden City, N.Y.: Doubleday, 1971.

JONES, JOSEPH M. *The Fifteen Weeks (February 21–June 5, 1947).* New York: Viking, 1955.

KENNAN, GEORGE F. *Memoirs.* Vol. 1, *1925–1950.* Vol. 2, *1950–1963.* Boston: Atlantic Monthly Press, 1967, 1972.

SHULMAN, MARSHALL D. *Beyond the Cold War.* New Haven, Conn.: Yale University Press, 1966.

SMITH, GADDIS. *Dean Acheson.* New York: Cooper Square, 1972.

ULAM, ADAM B. *Expansion and Coexistence: Soviet Foreign Policy, 1917–73.* 2d ed. New York: Praeger, 1974.

VANDENBERG, ARTHUR H., JR. (ed.). *The Private Papers of Senator Vandenberg.* Boston: Houghton, Mifflin, 1952.

10

Confrontation in Asia

The Truman administration's main achievement in Asia was to reconstruct Japan as a sovereign, democratic nation, linked to the United States by ties of mutual interest. In developing its policy toward China from 1949 on, the administration was handicapped by earlier decisions—particularly the failure to dissociate the United States from Chiang Kai-shek's regime. American influence in China was never as great as most Americans believed; in fact, by 1946 it was almost nil. Yet the U.S. political system proved strangely sensitive to China's revolutionary upheaval.

Embittered by the Democrats' unexpected victory in 1948, a right-wing coalition in Congress launched a smear campaign against leading administration figures and career foreign service officers, charging that they were Communist or pro-Communist. The apparent aim of this completely unjustified attack was to wrench control of U.S. foreign policy from the hands of the moderate coalition of Democrats and Republicans who had reshaped America's position since the early days of World War II. What sort of policies could the administration pursue in the face of these baffling pressures? Were its leaders forced to adopt the views of their right-wing critics to prevent a paralysis of government? Or did the administration manage to keep the initiative in foreign policy throughout the years 1949 to 1952?

America's "Special Relationship" with China

The lavish hopes fostered by the Roosevelt administration for a Chinese postwar role as a major power turned out to be completely unrealistic. Nationalist and Communist armies resumed their civil war, and large areas of the country lapsed into chaos and misery. Yet Americans continued to feel that it was in their country's power to shape China's destiny.

Americans generally assumed that the Chinese were grateful for the work of American missionaries, for the remission of the Boxer indemnity, and for U.S. support of the "open door" and China's territorial integrity. In fact, these pious deeds made little imprint on the history of modern China. Educated Chinese were more likely to recall the fact that Americans had demanded all the economic privileges that Britain and France had gained by force. This attitude was held by Chinese Nationalist leaders (no less than the Communists) until their great need for U.S. aid in the late 1930s caused them to pay lip service to the American concept of a "special relationship."

During and immediately after World War II, some Americans in China, particularly those of missionary background, idealized the Nationalists and their leader, Chiang Kai-shek, whom they saw as embodying the best Chinese and Western values, including unshakable loyalty to American interests in Asia. Other Americans in China tended to romanticize the Chinese Communists as basically "agrarian reformers," interested mainly in defeating Japan and giving the Chinese peasant his first taste of honest government. Both groups of Americans tended to exaggerate the identity of interests between China and the United States and the American government's power to influence developments in China. This power reached its zenith shortly before U.S. forces were committed against Japan—and had all but vanished by the start of General Marshall's mediation effort in 1946.[1] Under the strain of renewed civil war, popular support

[1] General George Marshall spent the year in China as President Truman's special representative trying to arrange a cease-fire and coalition government. This effort, which ultimately proved fruitless, was in part a political holding action by the Truman administration, which had already been stung by right-wing charges that it was "abandoning" China.

for Chiang Kai-shek's corrupt and ineffectual regime dwindled.

State Department officials urged General Marshall, after he became secretary of state in 1947, to explain publicly why U.S. policy in China had reached a dead end. Marshall agreed that disengaging from China would be in the U.S. interest, but he chose to delay taking action. He did not want it said that the United States gave Chiang Kai-shek's regime the final push over the precipice. He knew that disengagement would provoke a great debate on Capitol Hill just when the administration needed all the votes it could muster for the reconstruction of Western Europe. Moreover, many people believed that President Truman would be defeated in the 1948 election. Thus, his successor could be allowed to cope with the U.S. public's reaction to Communist victory in China. In retrospect, the decision to delay disengagement was one of the most disastrous political gambles of the postwar years.

President Truman's unexpected victory in the 1948 election coincided with major reverses for the Chinese Nationalists. As their morale sagged, whole armies deserted. Half a million Nationalist troops melted away after the great battle of Hwai-Hai in January 1949. At the end of the month, Peking fell with its 250,000 Nationalist defenders. Chiang Kai-shek relinquished his title of president in the hope of getting peace talks started, but Mao Tse-tung insisted on unconditional surrender. In April, Mao's forces crossed the Yangtze River, occupied Nanking, and trapped another 300,000 Nationalist soldiers in Shanghai.

Diplomatic Relations with Whom?

Dean Acheson was sworn in as secretary of state the day after President Truman's inauguration. A month later, he met with thirty congressmen who had written to President Truman protesting his "inaction" in China. Acheson told the congressmen that he could not predict what the administration's next move would be "until some of the dust and smoke of the disaster clears away." This phrase (often shortened to "waiting for the dust to settle") focused the attention of the administration's critics on Acheson personally.[2]

Senator Joseph McCarthy, who emerged in 1950 as the most violent and demagogic critic, was preceded in 1949 by a large group of right-wing Republicans (and some Democrats) who released their bitterness at Truman's victory and the resumption of Democratic control of Congress through wild charges of State Department collusion in the "loss" of China. This had the intended effect of placing the administration on the defensive; most of its time was spent refuting such charges rather than adjusting American policy to the changing reality in China.

Acheson's "wait for the dust to settle" phrase indicated a desire to keep all options open. However, key political decisions would probably have to be made in response to the rapidly changing situation. Should the United States recognize Peking if the Communists gained control of the country? In the meantime, what could the United States do to prevent the defeat of the Nationalists? The administration's critics professed to believe that the State Department was planning to "dump" Chiang and recognize Mao Tse-tung's regime without consulting Congress.

There is little doubt that during most of 1949 the administration was groping toward disengagement from the Nationalists. The State Department's Office of Chinese Affairs was given the task of preparing a "white paper," which was to be a detailed record of U.S.-Chinese relations in the immediately preceding years.[3] The aim was to demonstrate that Chiang's impending

[2] The State Department's China specialists had been under sporadic attack by a right-wing coalition in Congress since late 1945, when Ambassador Patrick Hurley suddenly resigned his post in China and publicly accused a group of foreign service officers who had been detailed to General Stilwell's staff of pro-Communist sympathies. Hurley, an Oklahoma politician who never developed much rapport with the State Department, easily generalized his criticism to apply to the State Department as a whole and to liberals in the administration. Although Acheson as undersecretary was often involved in China policy from 1945 to 1947, he did not become a target for personal attack until he became secretary of state in 1949.

[3] See *United States Relations with China, with Special Reference to the Period 1944–1949*, 2 vols. (Stanford: Stanford University Press, 1968).

defeat was caused by his regime's shortcomings and was not the result of anything the United States did or left undone. The white paper, when issued in mid-1949, failed to halt the decline in public support for administration policy toward China. Critics of the exercise on both the left and right tended to agree that the tone set by Secretary Acheson's covering letter (the most widely read portion of the document) made the white paper seem like a self-serving justification of U.S. policy, which had not been conspicuously successful in mediating the civil war or in restoring stability in East Asia.

Also in the first half of 1949, the administration began to study the question of recognizing the Chinese Communists, in the likely event that they should win the civil war and form a national government. Available evidence indicates that the Truman administration initially planned to decide this question according to the traditional Jeffersonian formula.[4] However, under pressure from members of Congress who regarded recognition, in Wilsonian terms, as a form of approval, Acheson promised in June 1949 that the administration would consult Congress before any decision was made on recognition.

Meanwhile, unknown to his critics, Secretary Acheson began to explore ways of achieving a goal he shared with them—stopping the spread of Communism—without adopting the purely military approach which they seemed to favor (although they preferred not to specify any concrete course of action). Acheson appointed a special three-man committee to study possible U.S. policy options based on the assumption that "it is a fundamental decision of American policy that the United States does not intend to permit further extension of Communist domination on the continent of Asia or in the Southeast Asia area." According to one well-informed source, Acheson was contemplating "no

[4] Jefferson held that the United States should recognize any government once it was firmly in control of its national territory and once it could be said to represent "the will of the people substantially declared." According to Jefferson's concept, recognition did not imply approval; it merely provided for an exchange of diplomatic and consular representatives, enabling both governments to safeguard their national interests more effectively. In October, Acheson added to Jefferson's criteria the requirement that the country in question "meet its international obligations."

more than possible economic or military aid to China's neighbors." In other words, he was not thinking of the use of American combat forces.[5]

In October, the State Department convened a special meeting of academic specialists on China and leaders in business and other fields. According to the minutes (made public two years later), a "prevailing group" favored recognizing Peking. But former Secretary of State Marshall pointed out that neither Congress nor the American people would support recognition of Peking at that stage.

Over the next few months, the Chinese Communist government accelerated its campaign of abuse against remaining U.S. officials in China and deliberately destroyed American consular property. On October 24, 1949, it jailed the American consul general in Mukden, Angus Ward, for allegedly assaulting a Chinese employee. The *New York World-Telegram* demanded Ward's release "alive—or else," and the American Legion and various other groups added to the uproar. Ward was freed and deported a month later. In January 1950, American consular property in Peking was destroyed. Acheson reacted to these and similar Chinese acts by stating publicly that Peking apparently did not want American recognition. James Reston of the *New York Times* reported that Acheson and the State Department still abided by the Jeffersonian formula, but did not consider recognition of China feasible until Congress adopted a less menacing attitude.

Believing (rightly or wrongly) that they had scored a tactical victory on the question of recognizing Peking, the critics of the Truman administration now launched a vigorous campaign to commit the United States to Chiang Kai-shek's support. The Nationalist government and armed forces had just taken refuge on the island of Formosa. General MacArthur adopted the view that keeping Formosa out of Communist hands was vital to American security in the western Pacific, reversing his previous position that Formosa lay outside the American defense perim-

[5] See Foster Rhea Dulles, *American Foreign Policy Toward Communist China, 1949–1969* (New York: T. Y. Crowell, 1972), pp. 45 and 66.

eter.[6] Former President Hoover and several Republican senators called for various types of U.S. intervention, ranging from "nonmilitary" occupation of Formosa to naval action in the Formosa Strait.

The Joint Chiefs of Staff opposed U.S. defense of Formosa against a Communist attack (for which Peking was already massing its forces). In spite of strong pressure from Defense Secretary Louis Johnson, the Joint Chiefs held their ground against further American intervention in the civil war. At a meeting of the National Security Council, on December 29, 1949, President Truman decided to give no new military support to the Nationalists, although they were allowed to use some unexpended funds from previous aid allotments. If the Communists launched their expected assault on Taipei, the United States would adopt a hands-off attitude toward the fate of the island and the Nationalists.

Also on December 29, the State Department sent a secret message to all U.S. missions abroad describing the administration's policy on Formosa and providing guidance for any public statements the missions might make on China policy. Formosa, the message, said, was "politically, geographically and strategically" part of China. If it should fall under Peking's control, the United States government would take the position that this event had not seriously damaged U.S. interests or those of any other free world countries. Thus, any move to establish U.S. bases on Formosa or to furnish military aid to the Nationalists would accomplish no particular good for China; subject the United States to charges of militarism, imperialism, and interference in other countries' affairs; and play into the hands of the Soviet Union.

This message was promptly leaked to the press by someone in General MacArthur's Tokyo headquarters, creating a furor on the part of critics of the administration in Washington.

[6] On March 2, 1949, the *New York Times* quoted MacArthur as saying the line the United States should defend "starts from the Philippines and continues through the Ryukyu Archipelago, which includes its main bastion Okinawa. Then it bends back through Japan and the Aleutian chain to Alaska."

As a result, President Truman issued a statement on January 5, 1950, which said plainly that

> The United States has no desire to obtain special rights or privileges or to establish military bases on Formosa at this time. Nor does it have any intention of utilizing its armed forces to interfere in the present situation. The United States government will not pursue a course which will lead to involvement in the civil conflict in China.
>
> Similarly, the United States Government will not provide military aid or advice to Chinese forces on Formosa. In the view of the United States Government, the resources on Formosa are adequate to enable them to obtain the items which they might consider necessary for the defense of the Island. The United States Government proposes to continue under existing legislative authority the present ECA program of economic assistance.[7]

On January 12, 1950, Acheson delivered a speech at the National Press Club in which he described the American defense perimeter in precisely the same terms MacArthur had used the previous March. He was attacked vigorously by his right-wing critics for failing to provide U.S. military guarantees for Formosa. The same omission of guarantees for South Korea went unnoticed at the time, although Acheson's critics concluded five months later that this had encouraged North Korea's invasion. Acheson's response was:

> If the Russians were watching the United States for signs of our intentions in the Far East, they would have been more impressed by the two years' agitation for withdrawal of combat forces from Korea, the defeat in Congress of a minor aid bill for it, and the increasing discussion of a peace treaty with Japan.[8]

---

[7] In responding to reporters' questions about the statement the same day, Acheson said that the phrase "at this time" in the sentence quoted above did not modify the president's statement; it simply reserved his freedom of action in the unlikely event that U.S. forces in the Far East should be attacked.

[8] Acheson, *Present at the Creation*, p. 358. With a declining defense budget during the early postwar years, the Pentagon had recommended withdrawing U.S. occupation forces from Korea, where living conditions were harsh and the occupation had been marked by a series of unpleasant inci-

Acheson's view, quoted above, has found increasing support from historians.[9] The whole history of U.S. actions toward South Korea from 1945 may have given the impression that the U.S. government would not respond if a lightning North Korean attack drove all the way to the southern tip of the peninsula. If the United States failed to support South Korea, Japan would not necessarily have fallen into Stalin's hands. But the effect in Japan could only have been to weaken and demoralize those leaders, such as Prime Minister Yoshida, who were seeking a liberal peace treaty and mutual security agreement with the United States.

Japan as Free World Ally

By early 1950, Acheson and his colleagues at the State Department realized that converting Japan from former enemy to ally would bolster the free world position in Asia and might also improve the administration's position at home; they decided to move ahead with a peace treaty in spite of Pentagon opposition. The occupation, masterfully directed by General MacArthur, had long since accomplished its main objectives. It had produced a transformation of Japanese society that was even more dramatic than changes wrought by U.S. influence in Europe. (MacArthur's reform edicts were given substance by Japan's own liberal tradition and were skillfully carried out by Japanese officials, but this only redounded to MacArthur's and his country's credit.) Responsible parliamentary government

---

dents of theft and violence. Both U.S. and Soviet occupation forces were withdrawn by mid-1949, although some 500 U.S. advisers remained in South Korea to complete the equipping of the Korean Republic's army.

[9] For example, in a June 1970 interview with the author, George Kennan pointed out that internal political pressures in the Soviet Union may have tempted Stalin to launch a diversionary proxy war in 1950. According to Kennan, there was extensive Soviet press commentary on the subject of a U.S.-Japanese security treaty during the first half of 1950—indicating that this subject was being given close attention by Stalin. Although Kennan was succeeded as director of policy planning by Paul Nitze on January 1, 1950, he remained as counselor of the State Department until late summer of that year, dissenting strongly from the administration's decision to send U.N. forces into North Korea.

had replaced the prewar system, in which often corrupt party politicians vied for limited power while military and civilian bureaucrats ran the country. As the new constitution gained legitimacy in the eyes of the people, the prestige and power of party politicians gradually became greater than that of the bureaucracy.

The armed forces and service ministries were abolished; under the new constitution, Japan relinquished the power to make war. Other major reforms included improvement in the status of women, encouragement of a free press and labor unions, land reform, and decentralization of control over the police and education (later partly recentralized). The breaking up of large industrial combines was also partly reversed after Japan's economic recovery became an important occupation goal. The net result of these reforms and the purge of most senior officials was to create a more pluralistic and dynamic society.

With the completion of these programs, however, the occupation was viewed by General MacArthur himself and by the Japanese people as unnecessary and a potential source of friction. The fact that the Truman administration almost completed the normalization of West Germany's status before it began to tackle this problem in Japan plainly revealed its regional priorities. But American experience in Germany provided useful insights that could be applied to Japan. For example, tight controls and supervision (especially by an occupying power) did not end economic stagnation or inflation. It seemed clear to men like Acheson that the way to revive a great industrial society was to give it its freedom, give it access to world trade, relieve it of the burden of military expenditures (which would also reassure its neighbors), and harness the resulting dynamism to the tasks of regional economic and political integration.

Secretary Acheson made John Foster Dulles his special assistant and gave him responsibility for negotiating the Japanese peace treaty and security treaty.[10] Dulles was assisted by John Allison,

[10] Senator Vandenberg reportedly pressed for the appointment of Dulles in order to make the administration's policies more acceptable to Republican

a foreign service officer with long experience in Asian affairs, who later served as ambassador to Japan.

For the next year and a half, Dulles and Allison engaged in marathon negotiations on three separate levels: with Japanese leaders, with governments that had been at war with Japan (and still technically were), and with the U.S. Pentagon and Congress. Most of the former allied nations sought U.S. support in gaining reparations from Japan—both to insure Japan's continued military weakness and to help develop their own economies. The United States had precisely opposite goals. It wanted Japan to be strong enough economically to resist Communist subversion; eventually, the United States hoped Japan would take the lead in promoting political stability through economic aid to its Asian neighbors.

After the start of the Korean war, the administration began to think of rearming Japan for regional defense. President Truman authorized Dulles to offer American military and economic support to some of the former allied powers in return for their acceptance of a lenient peace treaty—one that contained no promises of reparations. With the understanding that the United States planned to remain a leading power in the Pacific, most of the former allied nations gradually decided that they could accept a nonpunitive peace treaty. Many of them welcomed the fact that a U.S.-Japanese security treaty would take effect at the same time as the peace treaty.

The main dissenter was the Soviet Union, which claimed a role in peace-making because of its brief (and highly profitable) participation in the Pacific war against Japan. Moscow had no desire to see Japan linked to the United States in a security treaty. Yet this was the only arrangement that was acceptable to the United States (and to many of the former allied powers, who saw the security treaty as insurance against Japan's re-

---

internationalists in Congress. Dulles's views were not far removed from those of Truman or Acheson at this stage; for example, he had just published a book, *War or Peace*, in which he advocated admitting Communist China into the United Nations if that country met its international obligations. See Townsend Hoopes, *The Devil and John Foster Dulles* (Boston: Little, Brown, 1973), pp. 85–88.

militarization). Because the Soviet Union objected strongly to the security treaty, it refused to sign the peace treaty.[11]

In negotiating with the government of Japan, Dulles obviously had the upper hand. However, Prime Minister Yoshida was an extremely shrewd and stubborn professional diplomat; he had given more thought than Dulles had to the way he wanted U.S.-Japanese relations to develop. Yoshida pointed out that, under the democratic constitution imposed by the United States, the Japanese people could reject an unfair treaty, and they could replace him with someone much less friendly to the United States.

The main issue between Dulles and Yoshida was over Japan's future military role. Dulles argued that Japan should gradually rearm and assume the role of the leading free world power in the western Pacific; until Japan did so, it could not be regarded as a fully sovereign major power. Yoshida replied that the United States had imposed a constitution in which Japan renounced war; its people had no wish to rearm and no intention of doing so. They would give valuable military assistance to the free world by assuming full responsibility for their internal defense and by providing the United States with forward bases in times of emergency. Yoshida argued that this was enough of a contribution to entitle Japan to the status of a fully sovereign equal partner of the United States. Interestingly, General MacArthur supported Yoshida's position in favor of a small internal self-defense force. However, the agreement that was finally reached clearly placed Japan in the role of a junior partner, almost a protectorate of the United States. (In 1960, it was formally revised to give Japan the full equality Yoshida had sought.) [12]

Perhaps the most difficult negotiations involving the Japanese peace treaty were those conducted by Acheson with the Defense Department and by Dulles with Republicans in the Senate. The Pentagon resisted ending the U.S. occupation of Japan because

[11] As of 1974, the Soviet and Japanese governments had not eliminated certain territorial and other disputes arising from World War II, although they had ended the state of war existing between their two countries.

[12] See Martin Weinstein, *Japan's Postwar Defense Policy, 1947–1968* (New York: Columbia University Press, 1971).

this would mean sacrificing an enormous range of military rights, privileges, and prerogatives. By 1949, the State Department was concerned that further delay might produce intolerable political pressures in Japan. Acheson moved cautiously, however, fearing that an open split within the administration would doom the chances of getting a reasonable treaty through the Senate. To the basic concept of a conciliatory peace treaty, worked out within the State Department, was added MacArthur's suggestion of coupling it with a U.S.-Japanese security treaty. Acheson then outflanked the Pentagon by demonstrating that all legitimate U.S. security interests in the Pacific could be met.

Dulles began his negotiating marathon with exploratory talks on Capitol Hill, and he briefed the senators constantly between trips abroad. After the treaty had been signed and forwarded to the Senate for ratification fifty-six senators announced they would block the treaty unless Japan gave prior assurances that it would recognize Chiang's regime and not Peking. Dulles had allowed the British government, which recognized Peking, to believe that Washington would not seek to influence Japan's China policy until after the treaty was ratified. Nevertheless, he proceeded to extract a public commitment from Prime Minister Yoshida that he would follow America's China policy and not Britain's. The Senate then ratified the treaty—but British officials remembered the incident and never fully trusted Dulles when he became secretary of state.[13]

The Korean War and China Policy

The invasion of South Korea by its northern rival in June 1950 helped precipitate a new U.S. policy of military containment. On June 26 (two days after the attack began), President Truman took four important steps: (1) U.S. air and naval units

[13] See Hoopes, *The Devil and John Foster Dulles*, pp. 111–113. Acheson's relations with the British were always excellent. Although he publicly supported Dulles in this matter, he believed the British deserved some private warning before the Japanese commitment was made public.

were ordered to support the South Korean forces; (2) the Seventh Fleet was sent to the Formosa Strait to prevent the Chinese Communists from attacking the Chinese Nationalists (or vice versa); (3) U.S. bases in the Philippines were strengthened and aid to the Philippine armed forces was accelerated; and (4) U.S. aid to Indochina was increased.[14]

In announcing these actions the following day, President Truman justified his movement of the Seventh Fleet on grounds of national security. He said that an attack on Formosa under these circumstances would be a direct threat to the Pacific area and to American forces performing their lawful and necessary functions there. While few people have questioned the legality of defending South Korea,[15] Truman apparently sent the fleet to the Formosa Strait mainly in order to rally Republican political support for his foreign policy. (Senator Taft and former President Hoover had suggested U.S. naval protection of Formosa six months earlier. President Truman had responded promptly and firmly by renouncing any further involvement in China's civil war. Ironically, Acheson had criticized Taft and Hoover at the time for their "amateur military strategy.")

The idea of naval protection may have been revived in June 1950 by Assistant Secretary of State Dean Rusk, who played a key role in shaping the initial U.S. response to North Korea's June 24 attack. Others were thinking along similar lines, however. Defense Secretary Johnson, who had recently visited MacArthur in Tokyo, brought a memo by the general on Formosa's strategic

[14] This posture of military containment was later reinforced when President Truman authorized Dulles to negotiate mutual security agreements with the Philippines. Australia, and New Zealand in order to obtain their acceptance of a lenient peace treaty with Japan.

[15] The legality of U.S. action in South Korea did not rest on the fact that the U.S. government chose to seek a resolution approving its position by the U.N. Security Council. The United States had gained a responsibility under international law to protect South Korea when it conquered and occupied that country in 1945. People have questioned the constitutionality, and also the political wisdom, of President Truman's decision not to seek a Congressional resolution in support of his use of American military forces in Korea. For Secretary Acheson's comments on this point, see *Present at the Creation*, pp. 414–415.

importance to a meeting of senior advisers with President Truman on June 25. This irritated Acheson (like almost everything Johnson did), but at the same meeting Acheson proposed that Truman send the Seventh Fleet to the Formosa Strait.[16]

The buildup of U.N. (mainly American) troops in South Korea seemed agonizingly slow. But in September 1950, General MacArthur's amphibious landing at Inchon forced the North Koreans to retreat across the 38th parallel. Relief and exhilaration greeted this news in most non-Communist nations, where people had feared that South Korea would be swallowed up and that general war might follow. After the Inchon landings, the U.S. and allied governments seemed to abandon all caution. Worried warnings (from neutrals, such as India) about the dangers of provoking China were disregarded; the Truman administration decided to send American and South Korean forces across the 38th parallel to complete the destruction of North Korea's army.

As before, the United States sought U.N. support for its move. The British Labour government gave the idea its backing, as did the U.N. Secretary-General, Trygve Lie (little realizing that it would provoke China's entry into the war). On October 7, the General Assembly voted forty-seven to five (with seven abstentions) for "all appropriate steps . . . to ensure conditions of stability throughout Korea." This vague language could be interpreted to mean not just destruction of North Korea's striking power but unification of Korea under U.S. occupation. The day before the vote was taken, Premier Chou En-lai warned the Indian ambassador in Peking that China would be forced to enter the Korean war if U.S. forces actually crossed the 38th parallel. Earlier, he had announced that "the Chinese people will not tolerate foreign aggression, nor will they supinely tolerate seeing their neighbors savagely invaded." [17]

---

[16] Truman agreed, but he did not decide what orders to give the fleet until it reached its destination. See Acheson, *Present at the Creation,* pp. 402–406.

[17] This evidently applied to U.S. action in the Formosa Strait as well as to possible action in North Korea. After the U.N. resolution was passed, Chou again warned that the Chinese people "cannot stand idly by."

The Truman-MacArthur Conflict

During the summer of 1950, MacArthur issued frequent public statements, first hinting at, and then openly advocating, U.S. occupation of Formosa. Undoubtedly, this caused great concern in Peking—perhaps even more so than the signs that U.S. forces would enter North Korea. Both the Truman administration and General MacArthur grossly underestimated China's reaction to their moves and its ability to strike back. However, administration leaders (and the Joint Chiefs of Staff) were consistently more cautious than MacArthur. They ordered that only South Korean forces be used near the Chinese and Russian borders; ground and air attacks across these borders were prohibited. As for the general, his increasingly blatant attacks on administration policy suggested that his mind was on the 1952 elections.

In July 1950, Ambassador Harriman (Truman's special assistant for national security affairs) went to Tokyo and obtained MacArthur's promise not to exceed his authority. However, MacArthur soon began issuing statements again about the importance of Formosa to the United States. On October 11, President Truman met with him on Wake Island and tried to gain his support for established policy. This meeting hardly enhanced Truman's stature, since it had the character of a "summit" meeting with one of his own generals. However, MacArthur again promised to toe the line; he also reassured the president on the ease with which he would destroy Chinese Communist forces if they entered North Korea.

By the last week in October, as American troops approached the Yalu River (which separates North Korea from Manchuria), there were reports from war correspondents of sporadic contact with Chinese Communist units. These reports were ridiculed by U.S. military press spokesmen. In reports to Washington, MacArthur confidently predicted that Peking could support no more than sixty thousand troops in North Korea. He complained bitterly about orders restraining him from bombing base areas in China.

On November 28, MacArthur cabled Washington, "We face

an entirely new war." His offensive, launched November 24, turned into a 400-mile retreat—to the extreme southern tip of Korea—after the U.N. forces encountered two hundred thousand Chinese "volunteers" in North Korea. Confidence in American leadership at home and abroad fell drastically as the posture of military containment seemed to be leading rapidly toward general war.

Although China's entry into the conflict was a deeply embittering shock to the American people, administration leaders avoided the extremes of overreaction or retreat under fire. A more limited aim was set of restoring South Korea's hold over its former territory; and by April, General Matthew Ridgway, U.N. field commander in Korea, had pushed the battle line north to a point just above the 38th parallel. When General MacArthur persisted in airing publicly his disagreement with this "no-win" policy, he was relieved of all his commands by President Truman in the same month.

China Branded an Aggressor

Meanwhile, events in the United Nations were adding another dimension to the Korean crisis. India had proposed, in September 1950, admitting Communist China to the United Nations. The Soviet Union, having ended its boycott, urged that Nationalist China be expelled. With the United States strongly opposed, India's resolution was defeated thirty-three to sixteen (ten abstentions); Russia lost by thirty-eight votes to ten (eight abstentions). Subsequently, the Soviet Union sponsored a resolution in the Security Council calling on the United States to withdraw from Formosa immediately and inviting Peking to take part in the debate on the subject. Initial U.S. opposition was eventually modified, and the resolution passed eight to two (Nationalist China and Cuba opposed). By the same majority, Peking was invited to take part in the debate on Korea. The main allies of the United States were extremely nervous during the Korean crisis about the possibility of its leading to a general atomic war. It was to try to calm their fears that the United States voted for a Chinese Communist role in the debates—producing an entirely predictable storm of criticism from the right-wing bloc in Congress.

General Wu Hsiu-chuan, the Chinese Communist representative, arrived in New York on November 24 (the day MacArthur began his offensive). General Wu addressed the Security Council on November 27—without departing from his prepared text to make even the slightest reference to China's spectacular counter-offensive. U.S. Ambassador Austin responded to Wu's statement by arguing that China's entry into the war represented "aggression, open and notorious." Wu's speech, which heaped abuse on U.S. "imperialism," failed to draw away many supporters of American policy. The vote against the U.S.S.R.'s resolution, which amplified General Wu's charges of U.S. "imperialism," was nine to one. The Soviets then vetoed an American resolution calling for Communist China's withdrawal from Korea.

In January 1951, the United States voted in favor of a British-Indian-Canadian resolution for cease-fire, phased withdrawals of foreign troops, and political negotiations by the major powers. As Acheson had expected, this resolution was approved by the General Assembly (fifty to seven), but it was ignored by Peking, whose forces still held the initiative in Korea. With U.S. representatives exerting maximum effort, the United Nations then considered a resolution stating that the People's Republic of China "has itself engaged in aggression in Korea." The resolution was passed on February 1, 1951, by a vote of forty-four to seven (with eight abstentions); it called on U.N. members to consider additional measures to repel aggression (a clear threat of economic sanctions).

Did the Truman administration foreclose all search for accommodation with China out of conviction or political expediency? Many foreign governments that voted to brand China an aggressor under strong U.S. pressure believed the latter was the true motive. They thought it might still have been possible to find some form of working relationship with the People's Republic. They concluded that the Truman administration secretly shared their view—but that it decided to yield to its Congressional critics on China policy in the hope of gaining cooperation on other matters.

Is this a fair assessment of the Truman administration's position during its final two years in office? No one can say for certain. But it should be noted that Truman administration officials such as Dean Rusk have denied that they acted out of expediency. They argue that there was never any time when the executive branch of government was forced by Congress to maintain a rigid policy toward China. They stress their belief that it was the external situation—China's implacable hostility, the Soviet Union's growing nuclear strength, the instability of most third world nations, and the frail status of even the NATO powers—that was the basis for their decisions. Interestingly, their explanation of the administration's motives is upheld by some of its most vehement critics, whose views on China became official policy during the decade of the 1950s and most of the 1960s. They concede that the Truman administration was influenced more by its own assessment of the external Communist threat than by domestic politics.

Suggested Reading

ACHESON, DEAN. *Present at the Creation: My Years at the State Department*. New York: Norton, 1969.

BARNETT, A. DOAK. *Communist China and Asia: Challenge to American Policy*. New York: Harper & Row, 1960.

DULLES, FOSTER RHEA. *American Policy Toward Communist China, 1949–1969*. New York: Crowell, 1972.

DUNN, FREDERICK S. *Peace-Making and the Settlement with Japan*. Princeton, N.J.: Princeton University Press, 1963.

KAWAI, KAZUO. *Japan's American Interlude*. Chicago: University of Chicago Press, 1960.

REISCHAUER, EDWIN O. *The United States and Japan*. Cambridge, Mass.: Harvard University Press, 1965.

ROVERE, RICHARD H., and ARTHUR M. SCHLESINGER, JR. *The MacArthur Controversy and American Foreign Policy*. New York: Farrar, Straus & Giroux, 1965.

SPANIER, JOHN W. *The Truman-MacArthur Controversy and the Korean War*. Cambridge, Mass.: Harvard University Press, 1959.

TSOU, TANG. *America's Failure in China, 1941–1950*. Chicago: University of Chicago Press, 1963.

United States Relations with China, with Special Reference to the

Period 1944–1949. Department of State Publication 3573. Washington: Department of State, 1949. Stanford, Calif.: Stanford University Press, 1967.

YOSHIDA, SHIGERU. *The Yoshida Memoirs: The Story of Japan in Crisis.* Boston: Houghton, Mifflin, 1962.

YOUNG, KENNETH T. *Negotiating with the Chinese Communists: The United States Experience, 1953–1967*. New York: McGraw-Hill, 1968.

11

The Eisenhower-Dulles Era

Truman selected Eisenhower as the first NATO commander, and Acheson chose Dulles to help make peace with Japan. It was typical of Truman and Acheson that, when they met in retirement, they could joke about having advanced the careers of their successors. There was less informality in relations between the new president and secretary of state, and no senior Democrats were asked to serve in the Eisenhower administration. However, U.S. policy in the middle and late 1950s was marked by rigid adherence to positions established during the Truman era. Only rather small adjustments were made to a rapidly changing world situation.

When he left the Truman administration in 1951, Dulles's views as a liberal internationalist were widely known.[1] However, during the 1952 election campaign, his position seemed to undergo a striking change. He began to place greater emphasis on unilateral American action in Asia, less on cooperative efforts in Western Europe. In the past, he had upheld the policy of containment; now he began to advocate "liberation" of countries under Communist control (though he implied this could be done mainly by propaganda). To American and foreign diplomats,

[1] He had accompanied his uncle, Secretary of State Robert Lansing, to the Versailles peace conference in 1919, and had gone on to become a leading international lawyer. As one of the main Republican supporters of bipartisanship during the 1940s, he had helped gain his party's backing for the United Nations, the Marshall Plan, and NATO. His major achievement in foreign affairs—negotiation of the Japanese peace treaty—came a year before his nomination as secretary of state.

180

it was never clear whether Dulles's statements should be taken at face value or discounted as political rhetoric.

As president, Eisenhower retained the views he had held before 1953. Close cooperation with the NATO allies formed the bedrock of his position. Containment was to be pursued in Europe and Asia, but with minimum risk of further U.S. involvement in land wars. Eisenhower also tried to reduce military spending because he was afraid it would bankrupt the country. He seemed to feel that Dulles shared these basic views but that he adopted hard-line attitudes in public to avoid alienating conservatives in Congress.

Although Eisenhower believed the nuclear balance should lead to better Soviet-American relations, he did not pursue a systematic policy of détente. He relied almost completely on Dulles for the day-to-day conduct of foreign affairs. This allowed the secretary to discourage speculation that Soviet-American relations were about to improve rapidly in the mid-1950s (e.g., because Washington might consider accepting the division of Germany). Eisenhower overruled Dulles mainly on questions such as U.S. intervention in Indochina, where there seemed to be an obvious and unnecessary risk of involving the United States in war.

Dulles was so determined to make his personal imprint on American policy that he often bypassed the State Department and U.S. missions overseas. He traveled hundreds of thousands of miles, dealing personally with crises of great or little importance. He alone knew which apparent U.S. commitments abroad were real and which were based on bluff or rhetoric. Only he could make all the pieces of his policy fit together. When this man of iron will and boundless energy succumbed to death by cancer, American foreign policy lost much of the coherence he had given it.

Massive Retaliation and Liberation

In early 1952, the moderate internationalist wing of the Republican party supported General Dwight Eisenhower for the presidency while the more conservative and isolationist wing favored Senator Taft. Dulles, who was seeking the post of secretary of state, visited Eisenhower at his NATO headquarters in May 1952 and showed him an article which he was about to publish in *Life* magazine.[2] His thesis was that the Truman administration's strategy of containment called only for continuous, costly reaction to Soviet initiatives. It was not designed to reduce or eliminate the Communist threat to the free world; it merely aimed at making it possible to live with the threat. Dulles argued that containment required "gigantic military expenditures [which] unbalance our budget and require taxes so heavy that they discourage incentive." Besides, "this concentration on military matters . . . transfers from the civilian to the military decisions which profoundly affect our domestic life and our foreign relations."

But how could the United States reduced its defense budget and at the same time gain greater security? Dulles proposed a new strategy that seemed to rely almost entirely on the willingness to use nuclear weapons wherever U.S. interests were threatened:

> There is one solution and only one: that is for the free world to develop the will and organize the means to retaliate instantly against open aggression by Red armies, so that, if it occurred anywhere, we could and would strike back where it hurts by means of our choosing.

Dulles did not stop at hinting at nuclear retaliation against any and all Soviet offensive moves. He also urged the United States to roll back the Russian gains in Eastern Europe. Soviet leaders had trampled on the "moral or natural law," he said; "for that violation they can and should be made to pay." The United States must let it be known that "it wants and expects liberation to occur," for that would give hope to captive peoples and "put heavy new burdens on the jailers." He insisted that this was not a call for "a series of bloody uprisings and reprisals." But he did not specify how liberation should be

[2] See John Foster Dulles, "A Policy of Boldness," *Life*, May 19, 1952, Vol 32, pp. 146–160. The article summarized the strategy which would characterize Dulles's six-year tenure as secretary of state.

achieved—except to urge that the Voice of America and Radio Free Europe concentrate their programs on this theme.

General Eisenhower wrote Dulles, shortly after his visit to NATO headquarters, thanking him for his article and saying he was "as deeply impressed as ever with the directness and simplicity of your approach to complex problems." This comment may have been slightly tongue-in-cheek. To his old friend General Lucius Clay, Eisenhower wrote that he agreed with the idea of retaliation where a vital U.S. interest such as Berlin was at stake. But

> . . . what should we do if Soviet *political* aggression . . . successively chips away exposed portions of the free world? So far as our resulting economic situation is concerned, such an eventuality would be just as bad for us as if the area had been captured by force. To my mind, this is a case where the theory of "retaliation" falls down.[3]

Dulles performed the difficult task of writing the foreign policy planks for the 1952 Republican platform; these had to be acceptable to both the Taft and Eisenhower wings of the party, whose views were often diametrically opposed. Dulles's planks resolved this problem by attacking the Democrats for abandoning the peoples of Eastern Europe to Soviet domination. The GOP platform promised to repudiate the Yalta agreements and any others which "aid Communist enslavements." The platform pledged that "we shall again make liberty into a beacon light of hope that will . . . mark the end of the negative, futile, and immoral policy of 'containment.' "

"Liberation" was the theme of Dulles's campaign speeches on behalf of General Eisenhower. Although Eisenhower himself had reservations about using this theme, it probably helped to draw together the two main wings of the Republican party. After Eisenhower's landslide election, Taft and other conservatives supported Dulles's nomination as secretary of state.

[3] See Townsend Hoopes, *The Devil and John Foster Dulles* (Boston: Little, Brown, 1973), pp. 128–129.

Ending the Korean War

General Eisenhower promised during the campaign to go to Korea if he were elected. In December 1952, he redeemed the pledge and then issued a brief statement urging the opposing side to accept an honorable settlement. In Eisenhower's view, they would do so only if they were convinced the United States was prepared to use more force to achieve this result. Therefore, shortly after his inauguration, he sent more U.S. aircraft to South Korea, made public a plan to enlarge the South Korean Army, and placed nuclear missiles on Okinawa. He also "unleashed" Chiang Kai-shek's forces by canceling orders to the Seventh Fleet to prevent their return to the mainland of China.

It is, of course, impossible to know just what effect these moves produced on Chinese and North Korean leaders. In any case, American pressure was probably reinforced by Soviet advice. Stalin died in March 1953, and his place was taken by a group of younger leaders. Some of them could see the obvious advantage to Russia of "peaceful coexistence" with the West, and they appear to have helped persuade their North Korean and Chinese comrades to accept a truce. The Chinese government agreed to an exchange of sick and wounded prisoners on March 28, and China then announced that prisoners unwilling to return to their native land could be handed over to a neutral state. (The negotiations had long been stalled by the problem of how to deal with thousands of Chinese and North Korean prisoners who did not want to go home.)

However, South Korean President Syngman Rhee refused to sign a truce without an American pledge to resume the war unless Korea were unified in ninety days. President Eisenhower rejected this condition as wholly unjustified and unrealistic. Attempts to console the Korean leader with offers of a U.S. security treaty, economic aid, and diplomatic support all failed. After the United States signed a prisoner exchange agreement, Rhee freed twenty-seven thousand North Korean prisoners who refused repatriation. The time had come for the Eisenhower administration to deal firmly with its Asian ally.

Assistant Secretary of State Walter Robertson was sent to

Seoul to make Rhee listen to reason. For two weeks, he allowed the autocratic Korean nationalist to blow off steam; then he gently but firmly persuaded him to cease sabotaging the negotiations, trust Eisenhower and Dulles, and allow the armistice to go into effect. Next, Robertson, Dulles, and Eisenhower all applied themselves to the task of persuading members of the China bloc in Congress that the armistice agreement was in the U.S. interest.[4] To mollify potential critics, the United States issued a warning (in the name of all U.N. members with troops in South Korea) that renewed aggression in Korea might lead to retaliatory action beyond that country's borders.

The 1954 Geneva Conference on Indochina

The Korean truce released the French government from its pledge to continue the war in Indochina as long as American forces were fighting in Korea.[5] Secretary Dulles deplored the speed with which French leaders made contact with Ho Chi Minh and tried to open negotiations. However, in February 1954, the Big Four foreign ministers agreed (over Dulles's initial objection) to convene a meeting of all the parties to the Indochina and Korean wars, including Peking. This was the first major international conference to which the People's Republic of China was invited.

Meanwhile, the French and Viet Minh forces each planned to stage a climactic battle to bolster their negotiating position. By the end of March 1954, it was obvious that the French had placed their forces in an untenable position—a town called Dien Bien Phu that was surrounded by hills in which the Viet Minh hid its artillery. After eight weeks of intensive fighting, with thousands of killed and wounded on both sides, the French garrison was overrun by the Viet Minh on the eve of the Geneva conference on Indochina.

Dulles sought repeatedly to stave off what he considered a

[4] Dulles had put Robertson (a conservative Democrat who had served in China) in charge of Far Eastern affairs at the suggestion of pro-China members on the Congressional "China bloc," with whom Dulles wanted to maintain good relations.

[5] For the background of this arrangement, see Chapter 13.

disastrous defeat for the free world by organizing a joint Anglo-American-French commitment to defend Inchochina.[6] Four out of five of the U.S. Joint Chiefs of Staff opposed American intervention in Indochina. (Only Admiral Radford stood with Dulles.) President Eisenhower ruled that the United States would not intervene without a Congressional declaration of war—and then only if Britain would join the effort and if France would grant its Indochinese colonies full independence. France seemed willing to meet the final condition, but neither Congress nor the British government was willing to support Dulles's policy of "united action."

Dulles distinguished himself at Geneva by a public display of rudeness to China's Premier Chou En-lai (with whom he refused to shake hands) and by a generally obstructive attitude, even after there emerged the outline of an agreement that limited the area of Vietnamese Communist control to North Vietnam and two provinces of Laos. (Historians have continued to speculate on the motives of Molotov and Chou En-lai in forcing their Viet Minh allies to relinquish other parts of Indochina that their forces controlled.)

Foreign Minister Eden became greatly upset by Dulles's resistance to any compromise. The secretary of state seemed more concerned with playing up to the China bloc in Congress than with helping France extricate itself from a hopeless colonial war. Finally, Eden, Churchill, Eisenhower, and Dulles met in Washington and it was arranged that Dulles's deputy, Bedell Smith, would attend the last session of the Geneva conference. Thus, at the final meeting, Undersecretary Smith announced that the United States would not use force to upset the agreements that had been reached.

The Offshore Islands

The Geneva conference on Indochina was followed by the first of a series of crises over two small islands, Quemoy and Matsu, located only a few miles from the China mainland. They were

---

[6] At one stage, Dulles and Admiral Radford, Chairman of the Joint Chiefs of Staff, proposed a U.S. bombing attack against Viet Minh bases near Dien Bien Phu.

occupied by Chinese Nationalist forces and subjected to periodic artillery barrages by the Chinese Communists. Peking evidently sought to test Soviet and American willingness to intervene militarily in the western Pacific. Chiang Kai-shek professed to need the islands for his planned reconquest of China.

The situation offered a wide range of possibilities. Most of Amercia's allies hoped that Eisenhower would see the futility of giving Chiang further support and that he would opt for normal relations with Peking. Conversely, there was the possibility of war between Chinese Communist and American forces if the United States went to extremes in backing the Nationalist position. Dulles's influence was probably crucial in preventing disengagement from the Nationalists. However, Eisenhower decided that the United States would not risk war by using force to protect the offshore islands.

This condition was spelled out in a December 1954 defense agreement between the Chinese Nationalist and American governments. The agreement was supplemented by an exchange of notes in which the Nationalists renounced the right to use force (clearly meaning against the China mainland) without U.S. concurrence. For the next fifteen years, Sino-American relations remained static, although U.S. relations with Russia improved gradually and Sino-Soviet friendship turned to bitter rivalry.

Germany and NATO

America's Western European allies were continually bothered by Dulles's preoccupation with Asian affairs, because he seemed to risk overextending American power with new politico-military commitments. Western Europe signaled its recovery from the war by increasing its independence from the United States. America still had the greatest influence on matters affecting the Atlantic alliance, but conflicting viewpoints were being more and more emphatically expressed. A good example was the question of rearming West Germany and linking its forces with NATO. The U.S. government was convinced that this was the only way to make NATO a viable military force. Other allies saw the problem differently.

French leaders regarded German rearmament with extreme distaste, although they realized that American insistence made it inevitable. They therefore proposed a European Defense Community—a supranational European army made up of army corps, each composed of several nationalities. West Germany would contribute half a million troops to the European Defense Community, which would be under the supreme command of NATO.

For West Germany, this limited right to rearm and take part in the making of European defense policy would be a major step toward regaining full sovereignty. The Western occupying powers would be transformed into allies of West Germany, but they would retain the right to station troops in Germany (for the common defense); they would also continue to govern West Berlin, and they (not West Germany) would have the right to negotiate with Moscow on the issue of German reunification.

The European Defense Community treaty was signed in May 1952. When Eisenhower and Dulles took office, nearly a year later, it had still not been ratified. Although EDC had been proposed by the French (to make the best of the U.S. demand for German rearmament), strong resistance to the idea had developed within the French National Assembly. Some French leftists opposed further military alignment with the West; rightist deputies strongly resented the loss of national control over French armed forces. Faced with this opposition, French leaders tended to stall by offering amendments that would dilute the EDC concept and delay its realization.

During the first two years of the Eisenhower administration, Secretary Dulles maintained constant pressure on the French to ratify the treaty. If this chance to link West Germany with NATO were lost, Dulles believed, the Bonn government (under a less pro-Western chancellor than Konrad Adenauer) might seek to reunify Germany on terms favorable to Moscow. Adenauer shared Dulles's fears—and staked his political prestige on EDC. In January 1954, Dulles warned that failure to ratify the EDC treaty could lead to an "agonizing reappraisal" of U.S. policy toward Western Europe. This was strong language, and it created no little resentment in allied circles.

Shortly after the Geneva agreements on Indochina were signed, Premier Mendès-France submitted the EDC treaty to the French National Assembly without recommending that it be ratified. It was summarily rejected.[7] Dulles, who had gotten out of step with his main allies both at Geneva and on EDC, declared that rejection of the EDC treaty had produced a "crisis of almost terrifying proportions." He himself set to work forming the Southeast Asia Treaty Organization, a project which the British had, with great difficulty, prevailed on him to delay so as not to wreck the Geneva conference.[8]

Meanwhile, Foreign Minister Eden applied his diplomatic skills to creating a substitute for EDC that France would accept. Eden and Prime Minister Churchill agreed with Dulles that it was necessary to rearm West Germany and link its forces to NATO. But the British leaders did not share Dulles's alarmist view of the possibility of West Germany falling under Communist influence if EDC failed.

Eden's approach was to bring West Germany and Italy into the Brussels treaty of 1948 (which linked Britain, France, and the Benelux countries). The treaty, renamed the Western European Union, was then amended to regulate the armament of its members on the continent of Europe. Germany accepted limits on the size of its forces, and Britain pledged to maintain ground and air units on the Continent indefinitely. Both commitments reassured France. Thus, in barely a month of intensive negotiations, Eden achieved a solution to the problem of rearming Germany that satisfied all the Western powers. Having threatened an "agonizing reappraisal" if EDC were rejected, Dulles had little choice except to let Eden play the primary role in salvaging the situation. Cooperation between these two oddly contrasting

[7] Some writers believe that Mendès-France felt obliged to let the treaty be killed in return for Soviet support at the Geneva conference; others point out that Mendès-France had no strong feelings for or against the treaty but knew his government would fall if he staked his prestige on ratification.

[8] SEATO linked Britain, France, Thailand, Pakistan, the Philippines, Australia, New Zealand, and the United States against Communist subversion and aggression in Southeast Asia. The treaty was not used by the United States or any other power as the basis for its military role in Laos or Vietnam.

statesmen probably reached an all-time high during the WEU negotiations.

The main difference between EDC and the Western European Union (WEU) was that the latter treaty merely bound the West European states to a common set of defense principles. Their national forces retained their individual identities, although most were under the NATO command structure.

Détente with the U.S.S.R.?

The broadest foreign policy challenge faced by the Eisenhower administration was Khrushchev's campaign for "peaceful co-existence" with the West. Coinciding with evidence of rapid Soviet military and economic progress, it raised uncomfortable doubts about the belief that Russia was basically weak and morally rotten. A great many Americans had shared this perception of Stalinist Russia. They had debated whether the United States should "liberate" areas under Russian control or merely "contain" Soviet expansion, but few Americans questioned the basic premise that their country was stronger than Russia because of its system of participatory democracy and free enterprise.

Many Americans in the early postwar years also assumed that newly independent nations would choose to follow the American political and economic model because it proved that political freedom and economic progress were closely related. They believed that America's traditional anticolonialism, its vast resources of capital and technology, and the moral superiority of the principles on which its society was based could not help but place their country in a position of world leadership.

Dulles's perception of the Soviet system under Stalin (based on reading and contact with Soviet diplomats and others who had lived in Russia) was not far different from Kennan's.[9]

[9] George Kennan's famous "long telegram" of February 22, 1946, had emphasized the point that the struggle between the Soviet Union and the free world was largely a test of the moral fiber of two social systems. In Kennan's view, Stalinist Russia would emerge from the war far weaker in every way than the Western world. But Kennan, unlike Dulles, favored recognizing a Soviet sphere of influence in Eastern Europe and pursuing containment by largely nonmilitary means. See Kennan, Memoirs, pp. 380–385 and 596.

However, Dulles refused to believe that the Soviet system might be evolving under Khrushchev's leadership in the mid-1950s. His moralizing approach to foreign policy led him to discount the new leader's achievements in the domestic sphere (e.g., the elimination of police terror from the political process and the partial success in rationalizing agriculture). To have acknowledged that conditions were improving in the U.S.S.R. would have meant conceding that the moral gap between Russia and the United States was narrowing.

Although the Soviet government used its growing affluence to attain a rough strategic balance with the United States, Eisenhower and other liberal statesmen of the free world tended to view this as a potentially hopeful development, since it made nuclear war unthinkable. Dulles and a few conservative political and military leaders continued to speak as if the strategic balance had not yet been attained and it was still possible to use America's nuclear arsenal to "roll back" Communist territorial gains. Moreover, when Khrushchev began to imitate the American programs of military and economic foreign aid, Dulles condemned as "immoral" those neutralist leaders who accepted aid from both superpowers.

However, Khrushchev had his problems too. His denunciation of Stalin and his modifications of Stalin's domestic and foreign policy led to serious tensions within the Communist world by the end of 1956. Soviet leaders had to cope with dissident students, accept a new Polish government of less certain loyalty to Moscow, and send tanks to suppress a major rebellion in Hungary. (The United States made no move to support the Hungarians, thus demonstrating that Dulles's talk of "liberation" was mere rhetoric.)

Chinese leaders saw in Khrushchev's policy of "peaceful coexistence" with the West a likelihood of reduced Soviet political and military support for China. Peking's fears were soon translated into charges of Soviet backsliding and "revisionism." Meanwhile, Khrushchev managed to gain the upper hand over other Soviet leaders who sought to take advantage of these tensions to unseat him. Russian hegemony in Eastern Europe was also placed on a more secure footing than in Stalin's day.

But Sino-Soviet relations continued to deteriorate. The more Khrushchev moved toward a pragmatic, nonviolent approach to foreign affairs, the more loudly Peking's leaders condemned his revisionism and abandonment of revolutionary struggle. It was not long, therefore, before Maoism was being proclaimed as the orthodox branch of Leninism, and Moscow and Peking were in open competition for political influence in many Asian and African countries.

Secretary Dulles persisted in viewing the Communist world as monolithic. He saw no evidence that Sino-Soviet relations were moving from cooperation to competition. Thus, he saw little value in the United States trying to improve its relations with either Communist power. Eisenhower's instinct was to be far more optimistic than Dulles about the prospects for Soviet-American détente. He probably sensed that the U.S. government would forfeit much of its remaining world influence unless it explored the possibilities for reducing East-West tensions.

The 1955 Geneva Summit Conference

Among the Western powers, Britain's Tory government took the lead in urging a summit conference with the new Soviet leaders to permit the West to gauge their aims and abilities. The French premier, Mendès-France, suggested holding the conference before he submitted the Western European Union (WEU) treaty for ratification. But the British insisted that ratification of the treaty precede a summit meeting, and they managed to win their point. Eisenhower agreed to attend the East-West summit in part to help the Tories (and their new leader, Anthony Eden) win the May 1955 election.

Dulles's reluctance to have the United States attend a summit meeting was hardly surprising. Any major agreement with the Soviets would have to involve Western acceptance of the division of Germany, and Dulles was unalterably opposed to this, on the grounds that it would make Adenauer's political position untenable. Dulles believed it was vital for Germany to be reunified as a democratic, pro-Western state while Adenauer (whom he trusted) was still chancellor.[10] However, Dulles knew the Soviets would not allow this to happen. Hence, he concluded that an East-West summit could only serve to foster the illusion of Soviet political and moral equality with the United States. This would repudiate Dulles's most cherished convictions about the nature of relations between the two states.

In briefing memoranda prior to the summit, Dulles warned Eisenhower that one of the main reasons the Soviets wanted the meeting was to project the "appearance that the West concedes the Soviet rulers a moral and social equality which will help maintain their satellite rule by disheartening potential resistance." Fraternization with the Soviet leaders at Geneva would encourage neutralism abroad, Dulles feared, by "spreading the impression that only 'power' rivalries, and not basic principles, create present tensions." Dulles urged the president to avoid social meetings at Geneva where he would be photographed with the Soviet leaders and to maintain "an austere countenance on occasions where photographing is inevitable." [11]

In spite of these warnings, Eisenhower allowed his basic optimism to shine through in public statements immediately prior to the summit. The purpose of the meeting, he announced, was "to change the spirit that has characterized the intergovernmental relationships of the world during the past ten years." This was what most people wanted to hear. In the United States and allied countries, in the Soviet Union, Eastern Europe, and China, and in the emerging nations of Asia and Africa, people recognized that the world would be a safer place if the United States and Soviet Union each accepted the fact that the strategic weapons balance made major war unthinkable.[12]

[10] Or else Adenauer's successor might seek reunification on Soviet terms. In fact, the Bonn government made considerable progress in normalizing relations with the (East) German Democratic Republic by 1974 (and followed the U.S. lead in seeking détente with Moscow). The United States recognized the German Democratic Republic in 1974.

[11] Dulles's memorandum to Eisenhower, June 18, 1955 (contained in the Dulles papers at the Princeton University Library), cited in Hoopes, *The Devil and John Foster Dulles,* p. 295.

[12] Dulles himself reflected the natural impulse to look for some easing of world tensions; at the public celebration of the Austrian peace treaty in May

The Big Four summit conference at Geneva in July 1955 was the first East-West meeting of the heads of government since the start of the cold war. The agenda items were: German re-unification and European security, disarmament, and develop-ment of East-West contacts. As expected, no important issues were resolved, but the meeting was widely hailed as marking the emergence of Eisenhower and Khrushchev as major statesmen who accepted the balance of power and hoped to reduce world tensions. President Eisenhower surprised his colleagues by his "open skies" proposal (for an exchange of data on military in-stallations by the major powers). The idea was not pursued at the time, in part because none of the delegations had the neces-sary technical specialists.

Informal meetings provided some opportunities for the dele-gation leaders to size each other up. The British and French were the most skilled and active practitioners of this informal diplomacy. The Soviets brought along Marshal Zhukov, who had known Eisenhower during the war, but the president seemed to be following Dulles's advice by limiting his social contacts.

Khrushchev had rarely been abroad before and had never at-tended a major diplomatic conference. In a book alleged to be his memoirs, he records his impressions of the meeting.[13] Of all the delegates, Khrushchev got on best with Premier Faure, but he considered this of marginal value because French govern-ments changed so frequently. Prime Minister Eden seemed "more flexible and receptive to reasonable arguments" than the Ameri-cans, although "naturally" he followed "the same general line." Eden invited Khrushchev to visit Britain, and the Soviet leader

---

1955, he repeatedly shook hands with Molotov and even embraced him and professed to see in the withdrawal of Soviet occupation troops from Austria "something contagious."

[13] See *Khrushchev Remembers*, with an Introduction, Commentary, and Notes by Edward Crankshaw, translated and edited by Strobe Talbott (Bos-ton: Little, Brown, 1970), pp. 392–400. Khrushchev noted that Nelson Rocke-feller, a member of the U.S. delegation, was "dressed fairly democratically." (Khrushchev was self-conscious about his own baggy suit.) When introduced to the archcapitalist, Khrushchev said "So this is Mr. Rockefeller himself!" and poked him in the ribs. Rockefeller laughed and poked him back.

accepted, regarding the invitation as proof of his diplomatic success at Geneva.

Khrushchev recorded his impression that Eisenhower had "something soft about his character" and was "too dependent on his advisors." He was shocked to see that Dulles constantly supplied Eisenhower with written notes, which the president read before deciding what to say on any point. It seemed to the Soviet leader that Eisenhower found his duties a "great burden." Dulles was always "prowling around . . . snapping at him if he got out of line." Khrushchev thought Dulles "a very dry character" with little or no small talk when they were seated together at dinner. The Soviet leader was naturally aware of Dulles's position on "liberating" Eastern Europe. However, in his memoirs he noted that "Dulles knew how far he could push us, and he never pushed us too far."

On his way home from Geneva, Khrushchev stopped off in East Germany, where he was surprised by the friendly public reception he received from a people recently in open rebellion against Soviet rule. Perhaps some of the friendliness was due to his relaxed comment that "Neither side wants war," a very different line than Stalin had used to describe capitalist intentions. In his memoirs, Khrushchev called Geneva "an important breakthrough for us on the diplomatic front. We had established ourselves as able to hold our own in the international arena."

In their public comments, Eisenhower, Eden, and Faure each struck a positive note, claiming that all the major powers now saw that nuclear war was inconceivable. Only Dulles seemed to concentrate on dampening the euphoria. At a press conference, he said it was "premature" to talk about an "era of good feelings" between East and West. And in a secret cable to American ambassadors abroad he acknowledged that Geneva had created certain problems for the free world, which had been held together for the past eight years "largely by a cement compounded of fear and a sense of moral superiority." He called the Soviets' peace offensive a tactical maneuver forced upon them by their comparatively weak economic and military position. Although he expressed hope that this Soviet tactic might "assume the force of an irreversible trend," he pointed out that the U.S. government "does not acquiesce in the present power position of the Soviet Union in Europe."

The Suez Crisis

Ironically, just one year later, Dulles's own maneuvering through the maze of Middle Eastern interests and rivalries placed the United States and the Soviet Union side by side in opposition to Britain, France, and Israel. The 1956 Suez crisis emphasized several points, none of them reassuring from the American standpoint. First, the interests of the United States and those of its major allies were not always the same or easily reconciled. Second, the Soviet Union could and would use military aid (a familiar American device) to extend its influence into strategically important third world countries. Third, neutralist leaders such as Nasser saw nothing "immoral" about accepting Soviet aid, and they believed they could do so without opening their countries to Soviet subversion.

The fact that British and American interests in the Middle East had diverged by the mid-1950s does not seem to have been clearly recognized on either side of the Atlantic. During and after World War II, the United States had often deferred to Britain on Middle Eastern issues on the theory that both countries had an interest in the Suez Canal, Arab oil, and stability of the region generally. Britain's interest was recognized to be greater, and its political, military, and economic leverage in the area was far stronger than that of the United States. However, Britain's role as arbiter of the region was steadily undermined by the Arab-Israeli conflict, by complex Arab rivalries and ambitions (which made anticolonialism the only bond between Arab leaders), and by Soviet efforts to gain influence in the region.

In 1954, Britain entered into a transitional accord with Egypt by which the British military presence at Suez would gradually be phased out. Eden then looked to Iraq (Egypt's traditional rival in the Arab world) as the new focal point of British influence in the region. In 1955, Britain, Turkey, Iraq, Iran, and

Pakistan formed an alliance (known as the Baghdad Pact until Iraq withdrew in 1958) to try to block the spread of Soviet influence in the Middle East. Meanwhile, the Eisenhower administration sought to enhance U.S. relations with Arab nationalist leaders by encouraging the withdrawal of British colonial influence from Egypt, by taking a less pro-Israeli position in the Arab-Israeli conflict, and by hedging its support for the Baghdad Pact.

However, none of this temporizing altered the fact that Israel's military strength was far greater than that of its Arab neighbors. In early 1956, Nasser tried to seize the lead in dealing with this basic Arab concern by asking each of the major powers for military aid. All except Russia either stalled or refused him outright. A Soviet-Egyptian arms agreement was then reached, naming Czechoslovakia as the official supplier. (Nasser hoped this device would make the agreement seem less provocative to the West.)

On July 19, 1956, the United States reacted to Nasser's closer ties with Russia by withdrawing an earlier pledge to help finance the Aswan dam, Egypt's major economic development project. Nasser had hinted that the Soviets were willing to finance the whole Aswan project and that he would accept the Soviet offer unless the United States and Great Britain increased their contributions. Secretary Dulles believed the Soviets would be unable to make good on this offer. By withdrawing the American pledge to finance any part of Aswan, Dulles thought that he was calling Moscow's bluff. At the same time, he meant to show neutralist leaders everywhere—and governments that avoided ties with Russia—that the latter group of "free world" states had first claim on U.S. aid funds.

Nasser responded by nationalizing the Suez Canal, which had been run by an international company. His right to do so was firmly based on international law, provided he allowed all powers equal access to the waterway. (He would have strong incentive to do so, because he now planned to finance the Aswan dam out of toll receipts.) However, British, French, and Israeli leaders did not trust the Egyptian leader. They secretly planned an attack aimed at wresting the canal from his hands and overthrowing him. Britain saw this as the key to its continued influence in the region; France believed Nasser's support was keeping alive the Algerian insurrection; Israel sought to cut Egypt's military aid links with Russia. Dulles, unaware of the planned intervention, tried to mediate the Suez Canal dispute, but he found it difficult to conceal his own distrust of Nasser, which undermined whatever credibility his mediation might have had.

In October, Israeli, British, and French forces attacked but failed to seize the canal before the Egyptians blocked it by sinking a number of ships. The United States then intervened and threatened to forbid exports of oil to Britain unless it withdrew its forces. Because the British were temporarily dependent on oil imports from America (to replace Middle Eastern sources that were closed to them), the U.S. action was decisive in ending the short war. However, the U.S. gained little political credit to offset this severe blow to three important allies. Khrushchev reaped the main propaganda victory in Afro-Asian countries by threatening Britain, France, and Israel with rocket attacks unless they withdrew their forces—after they had already decided to do so.

Deepening Leadership Crisis

The Suez fiasco was symptomatic of America's weakening foreign policy leadership in the late 1950s. Stalin's ruthlessness had made him the ideal enemy against whom to mobilize the free world. The U.S. foreign policy establishment found it extremely difficult to adapt to the more subtle challenge of his successors. When Khrushchev spoke of the peaceful victory of Communism over capitalism, the new Afro-Asian states took heart—and began to look to the superpowers as competing sources of aid funds. Even China began to set up aid programs to compete with the United States and Russia, although its leaders criticized the Soviets for an alleged loss of revolutionary fervor.

In retrospect, the Eisenhower administration's most creative step in the conduct of foreign policy may have been its participation in the 1955 Geneva conference; this opened the way to further relaxation of cold war tensions. However, President Eisenhower suffered his first heart attack in September 1955; after he recovered, he was inclined to leave the day-to-day conduct of foreign affairs to others. Dulles served as the active manager of U.S. foreign policy until shortly before his death from cancer in May 1959. (He suffered his first attack of cancer, and was partially cured, shortly after the Suez crisis in 1956.) During these years, he exercised his gift for tactical maneuver, improvising a series of separate responses to crises but seldom seizing the initiative or setting in motion any long-range policies. More and more, his purpose seemed to be to maintain close relations with America's allies and client states that ringed the Sino-Soviet bloc. Dulles ignored the increasing groundswell of criticism, at home and abroad, of his hostile attitude toward China and Russia. In the eyes of a growing number of people, the onus for continuing cold war tensions lay mainly with the United States.

Dulles had two main strengths as a diplomat: He exercised close control over the whole range of U.S. agencies engaged in foreign affairs; and he sometimes displayed great skill at hedging his commitments—not in the case of Suez, but in Indochina, where he was more astute (as discussed in Chapter 13). After Dulles's death, no one asserted the same type of control over U.S. foreign policy for about three years, until the Kennedy administration began to develop a sense of direction.

From 1959 to the early 1960s, U.S. officials in many countries openly competed with each other for the major role in shaping U.S. policy. (One of the most absurd cases was in Laos, where the State Department supported one Laotian faction while the CIA and Pentagon backed another.) The sense that U.S. policy was rudderless and being buffeted by events helped John F. Kennedy and the Democrats gain control of the White House. But it did not provide them with any easy answers to the problem of making U.S. policy more effective.

Suggested Reading

EDEN, SIR ANTHONY. *The Memoirs of Anthony Eden: Full Circle.* Boston: Houghton, Mifflin, 1960.

EISENHOWER, DWIGHT D. *The White House Years.* 2 vols. Garden City, N.Y.: Doubleday, 1963, 1965.

FINER, HERMAN. *Dulles over Suez: The Theory and Practice of His Diplomacy.* Chicago: Quadrangle, 1964.

GERSON, LOUIS L. *John Foster Dulles.* New York: Cooper Square, 1967.

HOOPES, TOWNSEND. *The Devil and John Foster Dulles.* Boston: Little, Brown, 1973.

KHOURI, FRED J. *The Arab-Israeli Dilemma.* Syracuse, N.Y.: Syracuse University Press, 1968.

LAQUER, WALTER. *The Struggle for the Middle East: The Soviet Union in the Mediterranean, 1958–1968.* New York: Macmillan, 1969.

SAFRAN, NADAV. *From War to War: The Arab-Israeli Confrontation, 1948–1967.* New York: Pegasus, 1969.

SPANIER, JOHN. *American Foreign Policy Since World War II.* 6th ed. New York: Praeger, 1974.

12

Kennedy and Khrushchev

It would be hard to conceive of two statesmen who were less similar personally than John F. Kennedy—rich, young, Catholic, urbane—and Nikita Khrushchev, the stocky, professional Communist leader of earthy tastes and peasant origin. Yet each was highly intelligent and proved to have an unusual capacity to grow and mature in office. They came to share the belief that the proper arena for superpower competition was in aiding the development of "third world" countries of Asia, Africa, and Latin America. They engaged in the most nerve-wracking confrontation of the cold war, the Cuban missile crisis of 1962. But this ordeal enhanced their respect for one another, and they went on to negotiate a treaty banning nuclear tests in the atmosphere. Thus, these two men deserve substantial credit for easing cold war tensions, and their aims and actions deserve careful attention.

1961: Kennedy's on-the-Job Training

At their Vienna summit meeting in June 1961, Khrushchev joked that he had given Kennedy the half million votes he needed to beat Nixon by not releasing the captured U-2 pilot, Francis Gary Powers, until after the U.S. elections. (Had he freed Powers sooner, Nixon might have claimed it as proof of Republican skill in dealing with the Russians.) In fact, it was television, not Khrushchev, that won the 1960 election for Kennedy, although the question of who was best qualified to deal with Khrushchev was certainly an issue of major importance. Kennedy erased Nixon's advantage as the more "experienced" candidate in their series of four television debates, in which he demonstrated that he was at least as mature and well-informed as the vice-president.[1]

As president-elect, Kennedy faced an enormous task in selecting the foreign policy priorities of his administration and in organizing a team that could generate original ideas and translate them into action. A grueling two-year quest for the presidency had left him little time or energy to devote to foreign affairs, but he began with some general convictions. He was determined that his administration should pursue an active policy, and that it should try to shape events rather than react to them. More specifically, he sensed a need to orient U.S. policy toward the new, emerging nations. One of his first decisions was to call for a political solution to the struggle in Laos and to indicate that the United States would support a truly neutral government there, if one could be formed. He asked Averell Harriman, one of the most respected men in American public life, to take charge of the task. No longer was neutrality considered "immoral."

President Kennedy also decided, very early in his administration, to make the State Department the main instrument of his foreign policy. This decision was surprising because most activist American presidents who have tried to reshape the international system (such as Wilson and Franklin Roosevelt) have bypassed the State Department. They have usually found it too slow, too cautious, and too set in its ways to respond to their initiatives. (There seem always to be a few entrenched bureaucrats in the State Department who feel that any new administra-

---

[1] Studies show that 50 to 75 million people watched the TV debates, and some 3 million voters claimed to have decided how to vote mainly on that basis. Probably a substantial majority of these people voted for Kennedy; at least he was rated higher than Nixon in terms of "image" by the people polled (though Nixon received the highest rating for dealing with issues). A majority of the people polled thought the debates "were more effective in presenting the candidates than the issues." See Earl Mazov et al., *The Great Debates* (Santa Barbara, Calif.: Center for the Study of Democratic Institutions, 1962), pp. 4–5; see also Sidney Kraus, ed., *The Great Debates* (Bloomington, Ind.: Indiana University Press, 1962).

tion should be "protected from its first impulses" in foreign affairs.)

As the youngest president in history, with a very thin electoral margin and no prior experience as governor or cabinet officer, Kennedy faced a problem in finding people with enough stature to take charge of key posts who would also respond to his leadership. Dean Rusk, whom he chose as secretary of state, was one of the people recommended by Dean Acheson and several other senior members of the foreign affairs establishment.[2] As a former deputy undersecretary and assistant secretary of state, Rusk had demonstrated great diplomatic and managerial skill, particularly during the Korean war. He had no independent political base, and he sought none. He was older than most of Kennedy's associates and would add a note of dignity and solidity to the young administration.

Four Democratic ex-governors (who were also leading contenders for the post of secretary of state) agreed to serve in subordinate roles: Averell Harriman became ambassador-at-large (and then assistant secretary for East Asian affairs); Chester Bowles became undersecretary of state; Adlai Stevenson was named ambassador to the United Nations; and G. Mennen Williams was appointed assistant secretary for African affairs.[3]

The regional assistant secretaries of state were given much more prominent roles than in previous administrations. In fact, their responsibilties were far greater than those of most secretaries of state in the years before America became a world power. They were expected to orchestrate the various U.S. aims and activities within the regions covered by their bureaus. Secretary Rusk told Averell Harriman (and perhaps other assistant secretaries) to make any decisions he felt "comfortable" about making.

[2] The term is used here to refer to the most senior active and retired officials of cabinet rank, some senior military officers, and a few well-known journalists, academics, and other commentators on foreign affairs.

[3] Williams was promised this post months before Rusk was named secretary of state, in part because he delivered Michigan's votes to Kennedy at the Democratic convention but also because he was interested in African nationalism.

The State Department's five regional bureaus are: African Affairs, East Asian and Pacific Affairs, European Affairs, Inter-American Affairs, and Near Eastern and South Asian Affairs.

When the assistant secretaries did not feel they could decide a matter, they enjoyed ready access to Secretary Rusk and to President Kennedy. In addition, the president often telephoned them to ask questions about matters in which he was interested.

The National Security Council (NSC) was created in 1947 to coordinate the views of the State and Defense departments. During the early 1960s its staff, directed by McGeorge Bundy, Kennedy's adviser on national security affairs, was much smaller and more compact than Eisenhower's NSC staff. Its members were drawn from the State and Defense departments, the universities, and from other sources. They worked closely with the State Department's country desk officers and were sometimes shifted from the White House to the State Department in the hope of embuing that bureaucracy with more of the administration's activist spirit.

It took a year to establish close working relations between the Kennedy White House and the State Department. This was remarkably fast work, however, considering that the link was never achieved at all during most twentieth-century administrations. By late 1961, the State Department's influence on specific issues began to increase while that of the Defense Department diminished. However, because of the president's preoccupation with the need for a defense establishment large enough and flexible enough to meet any Communist challenge, the Pentagon continued to have a pervasive influence in foreign affairs.

The CIA probably reached the apogee of its power in the years directly after Secretary Dulles's death, when its station chiefs played a more active role than many American ambassadors in representing the United States abroad. During the early 1960s, the CIA suffered a more noticeable decline in influence than did the Pentagon. The abortive invasion of Cuba at the Bay of Pigs in April 1961, which was planned and directed by CIA personnel, was a profound embarrassment to President Kennedy, who authorized the venture and took full responsibility when it failed. That the president and his top advisers could have been persuaded to approve such an absurd venture without even submitting it for thorough review by the State and Defense

Departments indicates the naïveté of the new administration and the initially powerful position occupied by CIA Director Allen Dulles.[4]

Vienna and Berlin

When Kennedy and Khrushchev met in June 1961 in Vienna, Kennedy was fresh from a hero's welcome by the people of Paris. But President de Gaulle and Chairman Khrushchev both considered him young and untried as a statesman. His electoral mandate was thin (Khrushchev could not help reminding him). His honeymoon with Congress had ended, and he was already encountering opposition on certain major issues such as foreign aid. The Bay of Pigs fiasco and his decision to seek the neutralization of Laos were the main distinguishing marks of his foreign policy. Thus, Kennedy was not surprised when Khrushchev adopted an aggressive, almost bullying manner at this encounter.[5]

The meeting was notable for the almost complete disagreement between the two leaders on every issue except Laos. Their joint communiqué expressed support for a neutral Laos and the need for an effective cease-fire there. They disagreed most sharply on Berlin. Reviving an earlier ultimatum, Khrushchev threatened to sign a separate peace treaty with East Germany and terminate the Western powers' rights in Berlin unless the Western powers would agree to sign a peace treaty (greatly reducing these rights) within six months.[6]

[4] Allen Dulles, younger brother of John Foster Dulles, had been active in foreign affairs since the 1920s and CIA director since 1953. One of Kennedy's first moves after his election was to announce his intention of retaining Allen Dulles and FBI Director J. Edgar Hoover. Dulles was replaced by John McCone, a conservative industrialist, some months after the Bay of Pigs invasion.

[5] See Khrushchev's alleged memoirs, *Khrushchev Remembers,* with an Introduction, Commentary, and Notes by Edward Crankshaw, translated and edited by Strobe Talbott (Boston: Little, Brown, 1970), p. 458.

[6] Khrushchev adopted a similar stand in November 1958; then, faced by the Western powers' strong and unified assertion of their rights, he relaxed the time limit. Several lengthy meetings of the Big Four foreign ministers produced no agreement on Berlin. Khrushchev then met with President Eisenhower at Camp David, Maryland. They agreed that the matter should

Kennedy responded firmly, telling Khrushchev that it looked like a long, cold winter ahead in Germany. As in 1958, the United States, Britain, and France then sent similar notes to Moscow denying that the Soviet Union had any right to alter their position in Berlin, which was based on their common victory over Germany. They asserted their "fundamental political and moral obligation" to "maintain the freedom of over two million people in West Berlin." President Kennedy next asked Congress for a $3.25 billion increase in the defense budget to augment conventional U.S. military forces in order "to have a wider choice than humiliation or all-out nuclear action." Congress agreed, and 45,000 additional U.S. troops were sent to Europe. The Soviet Union countered by announcing a substantial increase in its own defense budget.

Meanwhile, in August 1961, East German and Soviet troops began constructing a wall along the boundary between East and West Berlin to halt the previously unchecked flow of people moving westward in search of better jobs and living conditions. (Prior to the building of the wall, the exodus out of East Berlin had been at a rate of 10,000 people per week, and the effect on East Germany's economy had been disastrous.) Although there were some tense confrontations between Soviet and American forces on both sides of the border, the United States limited its response to a strong protest. The Soviets then announced the resumption of nuclear tests in the atmosphere, ending an informal moratorium that had lasted four years. The American and British governments also resumed atmospheric testing. However, by March 1962, Khrushchev had once again removed his time limit for a German settlement and tensions on that front began to ease.

---

be settled by negotiations with no fixed time limit, and they rejected the use of force to settle "outstanding international questions."

However, the following May of 1960, when it appeared certain that no agreement on the status of Berlin or Germany as a whole was in sight, Khrushchev torpedoed a four-power summit meeting in Paris and revoked his invitation to Eisenhower to visit Moscow. More than likely, these moves were influenced by Peking's mounting criticism of Moscow's peaceful coexistence line.

The Cuban Missile Crisis

In 1962, the Soviets deployed long-range nuclear missiles to Cuba. As soon as this movement of arms was revealed by its U-2 overflights, the United States countered with a naval blockade and demanded their removal. For thirteen days, until Khrushchev agreed to the American demand, hundreds of millions of people lived in grave danger of being destroyed in the world's first nuclear exchange. In return for Khrushchev's withdrawal of all offensive weapons from Cuba, the United States agreed not to attack the island.

While much has been written about the motives behind each of these acts, there will probably always remain an air of mystery (and a "smell of burning," to use Khrushchev's phrase) about the crisis.[7] Why would Khrushchev and his colleagues create a situation that could so easily lead to devastating war— or at least to a major political defeat for their country? Were the Soviet missiles sufficiently threatening to the United States to justify the response President Kennedy chose? (He himself thought there was a 30 to 50 percent risk of nuclear war.) Assuming the Soviet missiles were that threatening, should the American response have been more cautious or more direct than it was? And how did the two sides reach agreement on the terms to end the crisis? What political process led to the key decisions in each capital?

On the question of the Soviet leaders' motives in placing long-range missiles on Cuba, Hilsman's account and the one attributed to Khrushchev are in substantial agreement.[8] Sometime in late 1961, the Soviet government had faced unexpected prob-

[7] For a lucid and informative account by an American who served at the time as director of Intelligence and Research at the State Department, see Roger Hilsman, *To Move a Nation* (New York: Doubleday, 1967), pp. 159–229; for Khrushchev's alleged statement of his aims and actions in the crisis, see *Khrushchev Remembers, op. cit.,* pp. 488–505; and for a sophisticated discussion of different ways of analyzing the above questions, see Graham Allison, *Essence of Decision* (Boston: Little, Brown, 1971). Allison's book lists many other contributions to the growing literature on the missile crisis.

[8] See peceding note. Of course, it is conceivable that Khrushchev's supposed "memoirs" were fabricated.

lems in closing the "missile gap" between itself and the United States. The Soviets encountered difficulties in deploying the giant rockets with which they had orbited their first space craft, *Sputnik*. Thus, Russian leaders found they lacked the resources to maintain their very costly missile and space programs, other military programs, a large foreign aid effort, and a greatly expanded production of consumer goods which they had promised their people.

The political costs of cutting back any of these programs would be very great—so great that Khrushchev and his colleagues were evidently tempted by the huge savings in the defense budget that could be achieved by placing intermediate range missiles (IRBMs) in Cuba. By doing this, they could greatly reduce America's lead in nuclear weapons. Once IRBMs were in place, the United States could not force the U.S.S.R to remove them. The Soviets might then feel safe in stretching out the period needed to build and deploy giant intercontinental ballistic missiles on Russian territory, enabling them to use more money for their other high priority programs. Thus, Soviet leaders gambled on getting the offensive missiles in place in Cuba before the United States learned what they were doing. They apparently believed that President Kennedy would not risk a nuclear war to remove the threat after he learned of it.

Since 1960, when Soviet arms began to arrive in Cuba in fairly large quantities, U.S. intelligence agencies had kept a close watch on Soviet shipping to Cuba and other activities on the island. The most effective means was the periodic overflights by U-2 spy planes, but the CIA also maintained agents on the island and questioned refugees who arrived in Florida. Because the subject was of vital interest to Congress and the American people, President Eisenhower and later President Kennedy followed a practice of making public the data gathered by these means—and warning Moscow in plain language that an offensive buildup would not be tolerated.

During the summer of 1962, large amounts of construction and communications equipment began to arrive along with about twenty-two thousand Soviet technicians and other personnel, including guards and laborers. There was still no evidence that the

Soviets were doing more than improving their air and coastal defense systems in Cuba (presumably to ward off a repeat of the Bay of Pigs invasion). American officials tended to doubt that the Soviets would be so irrational as to invite a confrontation with the United States by placing offensive weapons on the island. Senior Soviet officials gave repeated assurances that this would not happen.

Then, on October 15, a U-2 photo revealed erector-launchers, missile-carrying trailers, fuel trucks, and other unmistakable evidence that medium range ballistic missiles (MRBMs) with a range of about one thousand miles were being rapidly installed at San Cristobal on the western end of Cuba.[9]

Since the Soviets had not detected the U-2 overflights of Cuba, President Kennedy's first decision was to do everything possible to keep the fact of U.S. knowledge secret. Meanwhile, he and his advisers could evaluate the situation and decide on the best response. Once the Soviets knew or suspected that the U.S. government was aware of the missiles, they would probably speed the work of getting them ready to fire; they might also threaten U.S. interests in Berlin or elsewhere. The resulting crisis could all too easily mushroom into nuclear war.

During most of the first week after the discovery of the missiles, a small group of key officials explored alternative responses and began to reach a consensus.[10] Two responses were considered

[9] In all, the Soviets deployed to Cuba some 40 or 42 medium range ballistic missiles (MRBMs). They also prepared sites for (but did not actually deploy) 24 to 32 intermediate range ballistic missiles (IRBMs), capable of hitting targets almost anywhere in the continental United States. The IRBMs were evidently supposed to be operational by November 15, 1962, just after the U.S. elections (when it would be less upsetting to the Kennedy administrtion for Khrushchev to announce their presence) and just before a major Central Committee meeting of the Soviet Communist Party.

[10] The group came to be called "ExCom," for Executive Committee of the National Security Council. Its fifteen members were President Kennedy, Attorney General Robert Kennedy, Secretaries Rusk and McNamara, CIA Director McCone, Treasury Secretary Douglas Dillon, Special Assistant for National Security Affairs McGeorge Bundy, Special Counsel Theodore Sorensen, Undersecretary of State George Ball, Deputy Undersecretary of State U. Alexis Johnson, Assistant Secretary of State Edwin Martin, Soviet specialist Llewellyn Thompson, Deputy Defense Secretary Roswell Gilpatric, Assistant Secretary of Defense Paul Nitze, and Chairman of the Joint Chiefs of Staff Maxwell Taylor. Others joined them at some meetings.

and rejected fairly rapidly. The first was to do nothing; the second was to apply only nonmilitary pressures for removal of the missiles (e.g., at the United Nations or at the Organization of American States). These alternatives would make sense only if the emplacement of missiles in Cuba added little or nothing to the Soviet strategic threat to the United States. This simply was not so, however; the missile force being prepared in Cuba would roughly double the Soviet Union's destructive power aimed against the United States.[11]

Moreover, the missiles being installed in Cuba could be fired much more accurately than ICBMs placed on Soviet territory. In the case of a Soviet attack, the United States would have only two or three minutes' warning time, rather than fifteen minutes for intercontinental ballistic missiles launched from Russia. Moreover, if President Kennedy failed to take action to protect his own country by having the missiles removed—when he had said he would do so and when U.S. forces enjoyed the most favorable possible conditions for success—his word would cease to have very much value either at home or abroad.

Thus, the question was not whether but *how* to get the Soviets to remove their offensive weapons. The main alternatives debated were a naval blockade of Cuba and a swift U.S. military strike of some kind to seize or destroy the offensive missiles before they were ready for launching. (A quick strike could also *follow* a blockade if the latter failed to produce results.)

The blockade concept was attractive, because it would signal America's determination to stand up to the Soviets in the least threatening and provocative way possible. It would also provide time for Khrushchev and his colleagues to plan their next move carefully. President Kennedy was determined to do everything

[11] Even this would not have eliminated the U.S. lead over the Soviets in strategic missile production and deployment—nor would it have permitted the Soviets to close the gap in the immediate future. However, the Kennedy administration believed that the Soviets would reap great political advantage around the world, particularly in Latin America, if they were allowed to keep nuclear weapons in Cuba. The U.S. administration feared that the Soviets might thus be encouraged to take even bolder and riskier steps. President Kennedy decided not to surrender his country's superiority in nuclear weapons while working for their gradual control and for détente with Russia.

possible to prevent another major miscalculation by the Soviets. (They had already gambled on a U.S. retreat from nuclear confrontation, and they had not even camouflaged their IRBM sites or finished installing their antiaircraft missiles before setting up the MRBMs.)

The main objections to a blockade came from the Joint Chiefs of Staff. They probably argued that this weak form of pressure would not force the Soviets to remove their missiles; it might simply prolong the confrontation. An American blockade of Cuba could be countered by a Soviet blockade of West Berlin. This might buy the Soviets enough time to complete installation of their IRBMs—and might result only in each side calling off its blockade. Moreover, a blockade could be viewed as an illegal act, particularly by the Latin American states; this could add a new dimension to the problem.[12] The U.S. military chiefs probably also pointed out that U.S. conventional (nonnuclear) forces would enjoy an overwhelming advantage fighting so close to home.

Yet military action to seize or destroy the missiles also had very great disadvantages. It might lead to some hasty, ill-considered move by Khrushchev or by a subordinate Soviet field commander. With more than twenty thousand Soviet troops and technicians in Cuba, a U.S. invasion of the island would almost certainly lead to the deaths of Soviet and American soldiers, which could make it much more difficult to avoid a major war. Although the blockade plan also carried some risk, the potential danger was far less than in the case of direct military action against Cuba.

It appears likely that Robert Kennedy played a major role in marshaling support for a blockade rather than a surprise attack; he argued persuasively that the latter course would greatly damage the U.S. government's reputation, as Pearl Harbor damaged that of Japan. On October 20, President Kennedy decided to begin with a blockade, to be announced October 22

---

[12] The U.S. government had frequently taken the position that naval blockades were illegal. However, in this case the United States succeeded in persuading the Organization of American States to give its unanimous support to the course of action that President Kennedy finally adopted.

along with the fact that the United States knew about the presence of the missiles. At the same time, there would be no effort to conceal preparations for an air attack and an invasion. This would indicate to all concerned what the next move would be if the blockade failed to persuade Khrushchev to remove the missiles.

On Monday, Ooctober 22, the President announced the discovery of the missiles, called upon Khrushchev to remove them, and described the blockade (which he euphemistically called a "quarantine").[13] He also indicated that the United States would raise the matter before the Organization of American States and the U.N. Security Council.

Shortly before President Kennedy delivered his speech, he met with Congressional leaders and told them what he would say; he also briefed senior U.S. officials not in ExCom, the Soviet ambassador, and the ambassadors of forty-six allied nations. After the speech, other ambassadors and the press were briefed. Ambassador Stevenson presented the U.S. position at the United Nations.

President Kennedy chose to supervise all details of the blockade, because he wanted to avoid any Soviet misinterpretation of American aims. Thus, the first ship that was stopped and boarded was a Lebanese freighter chartered by the Soviet government; this was less upsetting than boarding a Soviet vessel. A number of Soviet freighters heading for Cuba stopped dead in the water; some had wide hatches (leading ExCom to suspect they carried missiles). These ships turned around and headed back toward Russia. On October 26, U.N. Secretary-General U Thant proposed that Soviet ships keep away from the quarantine zone and that the United States avoid intercepting them. Both Kennedy and Khrushchev agreed.

On the same day, the senior Soviet intelligence (KGB) officer in the United States, Alexander Fomin, asked an American television reporter, John Scali, to obtain the U.S. government's reaction to an outline of an agreement. The main points were that the Soviet government would remove the offensive missiles

---

[13] The term had been used by Franklin Roosevelt in 1938; it was meant to sound more like a defensive move than the term "blockade."

from Cuba, promise not to reintroduce them, and allow U.N. officers to inspect and verify the removal. The United States, in return, would publicly promise not to invade Cuba. This overture was reinforced by a long letter from Khrushchev to Kennedy, sent via the American embassy in Moscow, in which Chairman Khrushchev spoke in general terms of the dangers the world faced and their obligation to reach an agreement.

On the following day (Saturday, October 27), the Soviets seemed to adopt a harder position. They shot down a U-2 plane over Cuba, killing the pilot (Major Rudolph Anderson, Jr., who had taken the first photos of the missiles). Khrushchev also raised a new point by proposing that the United States remove its missiles from Turkey if the Soviets withdrew theirs from Cuba. President Kennedy had, on several occasions, prodded his subordinates to remove the obsolete and highly vulnerable U.S. missiles from Turkey. However, he rejected the implied link between U.S. missiles that had been placed in Turkey openly and Soviet missiles that had been sent to Cuba secretly, while Soviet leaders were denying any such scheme.

President Kennedy answered Khrushchev by the quickest means available, a public radio broadcast. He simply ignored the question of Turkey and expressed interest in the terms of the agreement Fomin had mentioned to Scali (as if these terms had been included in Khrushchev's more general message). Robert Kennedy then took the text of his brother's response to Soviet Ambassador Dobrynin, to whom he stressed the urgency of removing the missiles from Cuba. In carrying out this assignment, Robert Kennedy said that failure to remove them would bring "strong and overwhelming retaliatory actions." It is highly probable that this threat influenced the Soviet decision to withdraw the missiles, which was announced by radio at 9:00 the following morning in these words:

> In order to eliminate as rapidly as possible the conflict which endangers the cause of peace . . . the Soviet Government . . . has given a new order to dismantle the arms which you described as offensive, and to crate and return them to the Soviet Union.

President Kennedy then released a statement for the Voice

of America confirming the agreement and promising not to authorize an invasion of Cuba. This allowed Khrushchev, who came under strong political attack in his own country after the Cuban crisis, to claim that he had achieved his main goal without resort to war. President Kennedy and his top advisers avoided public expressions of triumph to make it as easy as possible for the Soviets to withdraw their missiles. The MRBMs and related equipment were soon removed; the Soviets allowed inspection of the ships from the air. Most of their military personnel were out of Cuba by the following March.

Nuclear Test Ban Treaty of 1963

In the aftermath of the Cuban missile crisis, President Kennedy and Chairman Khrushchev intensified their efforts to slow the arms race and reduce the risks of nuclear war. They began with two minor agreements: for the exchange of weather and other data from space satellites, and for a "hot line" teletype link to make possible quick, private communication between Moscow and Washington. However, they both believed that some form of nuclear test ban treaty would be a far more important achievement. It would also require considerable skill and courage on the part of both leaders.

Khrushchev was vulnerable to criticism, from Soviet rivals as well as from Peking, for recklessness in deploying the missiles to Cuba or for cowardice in removing them. (Some critics goaded him on both counts.) Kennedy's conduct during the crisis was also scrutinized by partisan opponents, but no serious attack was made on his administration's policy.[14] Paradoxically, his very success in dealing with the Soviets, during the missile crisis and in subsequent negotiations, created partisan jealousies that required mature and skillful managing on Kennedy's part.

President Kennedy had hoped since early 1961 to reach

[14] Some congressmen questioned the effectiveness of U.S. intelligence efforts before and during the crisis, and there were signs that this pressure might stimulate some backbiting between the State Department and the CIA. However, the general consensus was that the administration had made no serious errors and had come through the "Gettysburg of the cold war" with flying colors.

agreement with Chairman Khrushchev on a nuclear test ban treaty, but the long crises over Berlin and Cuba had barred the door to success. Another major stumbling block had been the question of on-site inspections; how many should each country allow the other powers to conduct? What was a safe minimum? Because of various technological achievements, the United States had gradually reduced its requirement to seven inspections a year. The Soviets had begun to recognize that total secrecy was no longer possible, perhaps because of the proven success of spy planes and satellites. Thus, Khrushchev let it be known, after the missile crisis, that he might allow as many as three annual inspections.

Neither Khrushchev nor Kennedy found it easy to apply to his own colleagues the necessary pressure to accept a compromise—at least not without a strong signal from the other side that agreement was possible. Both Kennedy and Khrushchev undoubtedly saw a test ban treaty as vitally important in slowing the arms race. However, the political stakes were much higher for Khrushchev, whose concept of peaceful coexistence was exposed to bitter criticism in the Communist world, particularly after the missile crisis. In May 1963, he sent word privately that he would welcome assurances from Kennedy that the latter seriously wanted a test ban treaty. At the same time, strong support developed in the U.S. Senate for a treaty banning tests above ground, which could be detected without on-site inspection.

President Kennedy and Prime Minister Macmillan responded to Khrushchev's request for a "signal" by proposing high-level talks in Moscow. Khrushchev's agreement to the meeting arrived just in time for Kennedy to announce it in a speech at American University on June 10, 1963. He used the same occasion to announce that the United States, once its current series of tests had ended, would not be the first to resume nuclear testing in the atmosphere.

By this time, President Kennedy had decided that a treaty banning underground nuclear tests (requiring on-site inspection) could not be approved: It was impossible to bridge the existing gap between the Soviet and American positions. But Kennedy believed that a partial test ban, covering tests above ground, would be a major step, both substantively and symbolically.[15] The president visited Europe during the next few weeks, and reassured America's allies (particularly West German Chancellor Adenauer) that such a treaty would not be made at their expense. On his way back to Washington, he received word that Khrushchev had endorsed the concept of a treaty banning atmospheric tests in a speech in East Berlin.

President Kennedy appointed Undersecretary of State Averell Harriman to head the American delegation to the Moscow talks. Kennedy himself kept in close touch with the negotiations, which lasted ten days. The resulting treaty was initialed by the British, Soviet, and American negotiators on July 25, 1963.

There remained for President Kennedy the task of maximizing support for the treaty in the U.S. Senate. Earlier votes had shown that a bare two-thirds majority needed to ratify the treaty could probably be obtained. But Kennedy wanted to build momentum for a realistic, bipartisan policy of détente with Russia. He and his aides therefore conducted a major campaign of education. Improperly managed (as was Wilson's campaign for the Versailles treaty), such an effort could easily have backfired and brought together those in Congress and in the executive branch who would have liked to deny Kennedy credit for a major diplomatic breakthrough in East-West relations.[16]

In a moving speech given one day after the treaty was initialed in Moscow, President Kennedy began his campaign by addressing the American people:

> I speak to you tonight in a spirit of hope. [Since] the advent of nuclear weapons, all mankind has been struggling to escape from the darkening prospect of mass destruction on earth. . . . Yesterday a shaft of light cut into the darkness. . . .

[15] His intuition proved correct. In September 1974, Fred Ikle, Director of the Arms Control and Disarmament Agency, announced the discovery that atmospheric tests could destroy the earth's ozone layer, which filters the sun's deadlier rays.

[16] For an excellent account of the Kennedy administration's substantive aims and political tactics on the test ban treaty and on other issues, by President Kennedy's special counsel and speech writer, see Theodore C. Sorensen, *Kennedy* (New York: Harper & Row, 1965), especially pp. 719–740.

This treaty is not the millennium. . . . But it is an important first step—a step toward peace, a step toward reason, a step away from war. . . . This treaty is for all of us. It is particularly for our children and grandchildren, and they have no lobby here in Washington.

During two months of debate by the Senate, support for the treaty gathered steadily. In the roll-call vote on ratification, only nineteen senators voted no (eleven Democrats and eight Republicans); fifty-five Democrats and twenty-five Republicans joined in voting yes. As President Kennedy remarked, it was "a welcome culmination."

Even while the president spoke, however, the United States was drifting into its longest and most divisive foreign policy crisis of the century. This chapter has focused on Soviet-American relations in the early 1960s without reference to the war in Indochina. In fact, President Kennedy was forced to devote a considerable amount of time to managing the Indochina crisis. He did so reluctantly, resenting it as an unrewarding diversion from foreign and domestic issues that offered greater hope of positive accomplishment.

By late 1963, Kennedy's relations with Khrushchev were beginning to produce some momentum toward defusing the more dangerous aspects of the cold war. At the time of his assassination, in November 1963, President Kennedy's administration was also preparing a series of moves designed to end fourteen years of confrontation with the People's Republic of China.[17] It is hard to believe that Kennedy would have chosen to sidetrack these efforts in order to concentrate on trying to preserve the status quo in South Vietnam by military force.

Suggested Reading

ALLISON, GRAHAM. *Essence of Decision: Explaining the Cuban Missile Crisis.* Boston: Little, Brown, 1971.

HALBERSTAM, DAVID. *The Best and the Brightest.* New York: Random House, 1972.

[17] See Chapter 13.

HANSON, SIMON G. *Five Years of the Alliance for Progress*. Washington, D.C.: Inter-American Affairs Press, 1967.

HARRIMAN, W. AVERELL, with ELIE ABEL. *Ambassador Extraordinaire* (tentative title). New York: Random House, 1975.

HILSMAN, ROGER. *To Move a Nation: The Politics of Policy-Making in the Administration of John F. Kennedy*. Garden City, N.Y.: Doubleday, 1967.

KENNEDY, ROBERT F. *Thirteen Days: A Memoir of the Cuban Missile Crisis*. New York: Norton, 1969.

KRAFT, JOSEPH. *The Grand Design: From Common Market to Atlantic Partnership*. New York: Harper & Row, 1962.

SCHLESINGER, ARTHUR M., JR. *A Thousand Days: John F. Kennedy in the White House*. Boston: Houghton, Mifflin, 1965.

SORENSON, THEODORE C. *Kennedy*. New York: Harper & Row, 1965.

13

Indochina: From Truman to Johnson

Looking back on their nation's long involvement in Indochina, many Americans view it as one of the great tragedies of this century, both for the peoples of the area and for the United States. How did we become involved in this torturous episode? Was it an isolated series of blunders, or was it symptomatic of deep distortions in the U.S. foreign policy process? Above all, what can be done to prevent the same situation from recurring?

Some writers cite the Indochina war as proof that America's quest for a worldwide open door to trade turned it into an imperialist juggernaut, destroying whole countries in order to "save" them for commercial penetration. A more common (and less sweeping) view is that all U.S. actions can be traced back to binding commitments made in the early 1950s—and that these commitments were made by statesmen operating under extreme cold war pressures.

Both explanations absolve American leaders of the 1960s and 1970s from all responsibility for the Indochina policies they pursued. Under the theory of economic determinism, the presidents and their top advisers were mere puppets of Wall Street. (But was Wall Street so eager to exploit the markets of South Vietnam, Laos, or Cambodia?) Under the second concept, Indochina policy was a mechanical conveyor belt, forcing each president to carry out policies conceived by his predecessor.

I shall offer a third explanation for U.S. intervention in Indochina: Each administration, from the 1940s to the 1970s, had a relatively free hand in choosing the Indochina policy it actually pursued. Moreover, Presidents Truman through Nixon seem to have believed that their Indochina policies were generally on the right track. When occasionally they were assailed by doubts, they seem to have feared the unknown consequences of adopting different policies more than holding to a familiar, if somewhat dubious, course.[1]

Not until the late 1960s did either the American public or Congress make any real effort to limit the president's power in foreign affairs. And none of these attempts was more than marginally successful until the Watergate scandal began, in 1973, to produce an apparent gradual shift in the balance of power between the executive and legislative branches.

Truman's Reluctance Is Overcome

Franklin Roosevelt had wanted to free Indochina from French rule. This aim eluded him, and after his death it was quietly forgotten by the overburdened Truman administration. After mediating the Dutch-Indonesian war, Truman's advisers were far from anxious to play the role of middlemen again. Thus, Indochina hardly figured in Washington's world view during the late 1940s. American officials knew that Marshall Plan aid was making it easier for France to afford a costly colonial war. But the United States supported the French aim of recovering France's colonial empire. How else could the French regain their prewar prosperity and block the rising tide of French Communism?

Until 1949, French leaders tried not to admit they were losing the war in Indochina. American officials were equally reticent about indirect U.S. financing of a colonial war. But Mao Tse-

[1] This interpretation is presented more fully in Peter A. Poole, *The United States and Indochina from FDR to Nixon* (Hinsdale, Illinois: Dryden Press, 1973).

tung's 1949 victory brought strong Congressional pressure to bear on President Truman to adopt an anti-Communist policy in Asia. With the signing of the NATO agreement (also in 1949), France began to describe the Indochina war as "anti-Communist" and to seek stronger U.S. support on these dubious grounds.

At first, Secretary of State Acheson countered by urging France to grant self-determination to the Indochinese peoples. But as Acheson's Asian policy came under strong Congressional attack, the administration began to move toward a policy of radical anti-Communism in Asia.[2] One of its first moves in this direction was to accept at face value France's claim that its war was "anti-Communist" rather than a war of colonial conquest. Early in 1950, the United States granted diplomatic recognition to the French-occupied Associated States of Indochina and began a program of direct U.S. military support for the French war effort.

At the outbreak of the Korean war in June 1950, President Truman announced that American support of the French war effort would be increased. Before long, the Truman administration accepted the French thesis that Indochina and Korea were two fronts in the same war. And as French public support for the Indochina war waned, the U.S. government obtained a pledge from the French that they would not seek peace in Indochina while Americans were still fighting in Korea. By the end of the Truman administration, the United States was providing a major share of the matériel used by the French in Indochina.

Dulles and Indochina

John Foster Dulles's strengths and weaknesses as secretary of state were revealed by his Indochina policy. Dulles was master of the oratorical fireworks needed to mobilize the support of conservatives behind an unfamiliar posture of peacetime internationalism. Yet there was always the danger that some stray sparks (e.g., slogans such as "liberation" or "massive retaliation") might start a dangerous fire that could lead to World War III.[3]

[2] See Chapter 10.

[3] For a broader discussion of Dulles's diplomacy, see Chapter 11.

The Southeast Asia Treaty Organization, created by Dulles, may have deterred North Vietnamese expansionism for several years, because no one knew how strongly the United States would back its vaguely worded commitments in the regioin. Cambodia, Laos, and South Vietnam were placed under SEATO's protection although these countries were not members of the alliance. In a letter signed by President Eisenhower, Ngo Dinh Diem's regime in South Vietnam was given U.S. support—but qualified in such a way that it could be withdrawn at will.

Laos, a landlocked kingdom of sparsely settled mountains and valleys with a population generally lacking both the will and resources to defend its thousands of miles of borders, was declared an "anti-Communist bastion" by Dulles. Over the Pentagon's protests, he insisted on creating a Royal Lao Army useful only for provoking a North Vietnamese or Chinese invasion or for focusing Lao villagers' resentment against the Vientiane government.

Indochina was probably never as important in Dulles's world view as his speeches implied. How much importance he attached to his forward policy in Southeast Asia is hard to judge. It was typical of Dulles's diplomacy that he always tried to leave the United States maximum leeway to interpret its commitments. While he lived, Dulles exercised firm control over the various instruments and agencies of American foreign policy. Under these conditions, a diplomatic style featuring vague but sweeping pronouncements tended to keep one's enemies (but also one's friends) off balance.

When John Foster Dulles died in 1959, however, central control over U.S. foreign policy disappeared. Dozens of agencies and individuals pursued their own (often conflicting) policy lines, each claiming to be carrying out "commitments" voiced by Secretary Dulles. The worst confusion tended to arise in Indochina, where Dulles had taught Americans to expect continual crises threatening U.S. interests—and where his private sense of how far to go was buried beneath mountains of public rhetoric.

Kennedy: Caught in the Quagmire

Some members of the Kennedy administration believed that Dulles's rhetorical pronouncements had placed the United States in absurd or indefensible positions (for example, the policies toward China and Laos).[4] However the overriding concern of the White House was to avoid projecting an appearance of weakness to the Soviets. Thus, when President Kennedy entrusted Averell Harriman with the task of finding a compromise solution in Laos, it was almost axiomatic that the administration would take a tougher line in some adjacent area as compensation.

Ambassador Harriman skillfully worked out an accord on Laos in which all external powers interested in the country agreed that they were unwilling to fight a war there. Harriman then helped the three main Lao factions to reach an agreement on a coalition government. In late 1962, these accords went into effect. At the same time, the Kennedy administration began to hint publicly that increased Vietnamese Communist pressure in South Vietnam might call forth a much stronger U.S. response.

Frequent official visits to Saigon by senior American officials such as Secretary McNamara, General Maxwell Taylor, and Vice-President Johnson linked American prestige to the autocratic government of President Ngo Dinh Diem. Faced with Viet Cong pressure, Diem's regime was beginning to flounder in a morass of suspicion, political repression, and grandiose projects funded by the United States (such as "strategic hamlets" in which millions of peasants were supposed to live behind barbed wire).

During 1963, Diem's powerful Catholic family engaged in a bloody confrontation with the country's militant Buddhists. Televised scenes of police brutality and Buddhist suicides brought Diem's incompetence home to the American people, and the Kennedy administration came close to disowning him. Meanwhile, "noncombat" U.S. military units were sent to

---

[4] See Chapter 11.

Vietnam; the increasing Americanization of the war was signaled by highly optimistic statements by Secretary McNamara,, who sought to refute the growing evidence that Saigon's army could no longer cope with its enemy.

The indignant reaction of the American public and Congress to Diem's handling of the Buddhist crisis would have made it less difficult politically for the Kennedy administration to withdraw from South Vietnam, if it had decided that this was in the U.S. interest.[5] However, the administration was deeply divided over whether or not to follow such a course. The Diem family had its obvious faults and seemed to be riding for a fall, but without them the United States would have no legal façade behind which it could pursue its military intervention. For some members of the administration (including Rusk, McNamara, Taylor, and Vice-President Johnson) this was the main task and one that should not be jeopardized.

If any leading figures of the administration had understood the situation well enough to foresee the problems that lay ahead, they might have agreed with the State Department's chief specialist on Vietnam, Paul Kattenburg, that the time had come to get out.[6] However, none of the top officials was personally familiar with Indochinese affairs, and they could spare the region only a small part of their workday. Thus, they were continually making decisions about complex political and military questions on the basis of educated hunches. Given the keen sense of competition among the various departments and agencies for control of policy, an activist approach was likely to win approval.

Johnson Chooses to Make a Stand

The Kennedy administration lacked a clear consensus on whether to fight or cut its losses in South Vietnam, just as it

[5] When Diem refused to liberalize his policies, the United States began to make selective cuts in its aid to South Vietnam to show that it was in earnest.

[6] See Neil Sheehan, *The Pentagon Papers as Published by the New York Times* (New York: Bantam, 1971), p. 174.

was divided on the immediate problem of whether or not to back a coup. The murder of Diem and his brother Nhu in early November 1963 removed this dilemma but deepened the gulf between "hawks" and "doves" within the administration—and thus made it more difficult for them to resolve the main policy problem.

Just after President Kennedy was assassinated on November 22, 1963, Assistant Secretary of State Roger Hilsman raised the possibility of a more moderate U.S. policy in East Asia by delivering a speech that called for better relations with China. A few weeks later, Secretary Rusk, with President Johnson's concurrence, fired Hilsman and replaced him with William Bundy, who supported the Johnson administration's emerging policy. This could be summed up as no change in the China containment policy and no sharp acceleration of the U.S. war effort in Vietnam, which might upset the American public. However, U.S. military pressure in Vietnam would be maintained and, if necessary, gradually increased until Hanoi's leaders decide to accept the existence of a non-Communist South Vietnam.

Dean Rusk was President Johnson's closest official consultant throughout the five years of Johnson's presidency. They came from essentially the same nonaffluent, Southern, middle-class background and shared an instinctively conservative approach to foreign policy. They had such deep respect for each other that it was hard for anyone to tell who influenced whom on certain questions. Rusk was perhaps the only man in Washington who could and sometimes did persuade Johnson to change his Vietnam policy.

In addition to Dean Rusk and William Bundy (both of whom served throughout the Johnson administration), four other men played major roles in shaping Vietnam policy. These were Robert McNamara and Clark Clifford (who succeeded McNamara as secretary of defense in early 1968) and McGeorge Bundy and Walt Rostow, Johnson's two national security advisers. The CIA director, the undersecretaries of state and defense, the chairman of the Joint Chiefs of Staff, and the assistant secretaries of defense for National Security Affairs also played major roles.

Together, these individuals were known as the "Vietnam principals." For the most part, they all viewed themselves as loyal subordinates—the "President's men." This fact, plus the lack of consensus among them on the need to alter policy, made it unlikely that any of them would speak out against a particular decision. They knew that Johnson (whose foreign policy style somewhat resembled Woodrow Wilson's) valued personal loyalty above all else. If an adviser questioned a major premise of administration policy, he was less likely to retain easy access to the president. In the jargon of the period, he would "lose his effectiveness." Many Johnson administration officials became deeply opposed to the Vietnam war, but they tended to hold their tongues in order to retain their "effectiveness" as long as possible.

Because of Johnson's obsession with secrecy and his fear of information leaks to the press and Congress, Indochina specialists of the State and Defense departments and the CIA were seldom asked for advice on policy. Their job was to keep the assistant secretaries informed of current developments and sometimes to brief the other Vietnam principals. The president and his senior cabinet officers acted as desk officers for Indochina, and the assistant secretaries were kept busy taking notes at their meetings and drafting instructions to military commanders and ambassadors in the field.

Because the senior Vietnam principals had no time to become deeply informed on the detailed issues they decided—and since they tended to be isolated from any viewpoints that clashed with their own—it is hardly surprising that they maintained their policy of gradual "escalation" for four long and bloody years.[7]

---

[7] From 1965 through 1968, many Vietnam decisions (including matters of detail, such as the choice of bombing targets) were made at Tuesday luncheon meetings in the White House. These meetings were attended by the president, secretaries of state and defense, and the president's press secretary. The CIA director, chairman of the Joint Chiefs of Staff, and Assistant Secretary William Bundy also sometimes attended. Known as the "Tuesday luncheon group," these meetings epitomized the practice of presidential supervision of minutiae, which left little time for broad policy review.

When some of them began to doubt that this policy would succeed, they still found it next to impossible to re-examine their basic assumptions and to make any major policy changes.

From November 1963 to June 1964, the Vietnam principals analyzed the situation in Vietnam that followed Diem's assassination, found it exceedingly chaotic, and wrote a secret "contingency plan" for wholesale U.S. intervention if Saigon seemed about to lose the war. The Johnson administration seems to have tacitly decided to wait until after the 1964 presidential election to seek a Congressional resolution authorizing a massive intervention. However, on August 2, 1964, a U.S. destroyer patrolling the Tonkin Gulf was reportedly attacked (but not harmed) by North Vietnamese torpedo boats. President Johnson decided not to retaliate, but added another destroyer to the Tonkin Gulf patrol. On the pitch-black night of August 4, these ships reported another attack, although later analysis seemed to show that the "attack" could have been imagined by inexperienced sonarmen or highly nervous members of the watch. The firing of the ships' guns throughout the incident compounded the confusion.

The officer in charge of the patrol courageously reported his doubts about the second attack. But by the time he did so, President Johnson and his advisers had decided to launch a retaliatory bombing raid against North Vietnamese bases and to seek a Congressional resolution giving the president advance authority to do what he considered necessary in Southeast Asia. It was much easier for the Vietnam principals to find "proof" that the attack had really taken place than to cancel these far-reaching plans.

Having carried out the retaliatory strike and obtained the Tonkin Gulf resolution from Congress, President Johnson next faced an easy election campaign against Republican Barry Goldwater. Johnson promised not to "send American boys to fight Asian boys' wars" (a pledge reminiscent of Wilson's 1916 campaign and Franklin Roosevelt's in 1940). Johnson's landslide victory in November 1964 was seen by many as a vote for moderate leadership in foreign affairs. Goldwater frightened too many people by speaking off the top of his head about issues of war and peace. The election was also, no doubt, a vote of support for a man who had taken up the burdens of leadership with courage and dignity and scored a historic breakthrough on civil rights.

The Credibility Gap

The 1964 election proved once again that presidential campaigns seldom clarify foreign policy choices or bind the winner to a specific course. In 1964, as in most U.S. elections, foreign policy was not the main issue as defined by the candidates. Both men emphasized domestic affairs; when they spoke about foreign policy they seldom mentioned Indochina. There was, in fact, no "Indochina issue" because Goldwater promptly endorsed Johnson's action in the Tonkin Gulf incident. Johnson was also aided by Goldwater's offhand remarks implying a general willingness to risk nuclear war with the Soviet Union. Johnson's more "restrained" posture was assumed by much of the public to apply everywhere, including Southeast Asia.

Therefore, public debate over Indochina policy virtually ceased until March 1965; then Johnson ordered the first air strikes against North Vietnam that were not described as retaliation for a specific Communist attack. This produced a flood of questions about where the new policy was leading. But an administration bent on proving the "credibility" of American power would not be easily deterred from its chosen course.

The situation in South Vietnam was more than usually fluid during the months just before and just after the U.S. election. There were coups and countercoups of varying importance every few weeks, with different generals and occasionally a few civilians gaining and losing power. Buddhist activists tried to prod successive Saigon governments toward negotiations with the Viet Cong. Throughout this period, General Maxwell Taylor served as U.S. ambassador in Saigon; he tried to hold together the semblance of a legal government and to obtain its approval for large-scale U.S. intervention. In February 1965, real political power passed into the hands of a fairly stable army junta, and Taylor obtained the permission he sought.

Meanwhile the Vietnam principals became increasingly convinced that U.S. military intervention—and perhaps nothing else—could prevent the Vietnamese Communists from overrunning South Vietnam. In spite of all the historical evidence of recent decades, they persuaded themselves that an alien army, whose only advantage lay in superior firepower, could somehow defeat a well-established, indigenous politico-military organization that most of the people in the country regarded as nationalist first and Communist second.

The Vietnam principals also tended to believe that the Viet Cong's success was due only to military factors, such as the quantity and quality of weapons received from the Soviet Union and China. They therefore concluded that U.S. military prestige and "credibility" would be jeopardized if the United States failed to intervene and defeat the "insurgents."

These assumptions were not systematically presented to the American public or Congress, however. The Vietnam principals knew that offering such a radical case for full-scale intervention might well provoke a long and bitter debate. The Tonkin Gulf resolution and the 1964 election offered a means of avoiding this problem, since they could be construed as a mandate for action. Once the action began to produce results, no one would condemn the president or his advisers for high-handedness.

Secretary of State Rusk and Assistant Secretary Bundy were disturbed by the course of secrecy, which they considered a serious political error. They felt it would be better to explain the new policy to the American people in advance. Ironically, once open discussion of the Vietnam issue was rejected, it was Rusk who went before Congress and the television cameras and argued that no new policy was being considered.[8]

[8] The policy of gradual "escalation" of U.S. military pressure adopted by the Johnson administration did, in fact, somewhat resemble the improvised responses of the Kennedy years. It could perhaps even be argued that this type of intervention was envisaged by Secretary Dulles in the 1950s, although his "commitments" were always deliberately vague and flexible. Some (but by no means all) members of the Eisenhower and Kennedy administrations shared the underlying assumption of President Johnson and his advisers— that U.S. military power was uniquely suited to the task of halting Communist politico-military expansion in Asia.

The bombing of North Vietnam soon proved to yield none of the hoped-for effects on Hanoi's morale or policy. As when it was used against England, Germany, and Japan during World War II, bombing merely stiffened the population's will to resist. The Johnson administration decided, nevertheless, to continue the bombing because it would be a useful bargaining counter in eventual negotiations. At the same time, it decided to begin a massive build-up of American ground forces in South Vietnam. The mission of the U.S. troops was to keep the enemy's regular combat units away from densely populated areas of South Vietnam and, where possible, to destroy them.

In spite of growing U.S. firepower on the ground and in the air, the rate at which North Vietnamese troops and supplies entered the South increased steadily. The U.S. Joint Chiefs of Staff believed that a rapid build-up of U.S. forces in the country would get the job done with fewer casualties. They estimated privately that at least a million U.S. troops would be needed to defeat the main Vietnamese Communist divisions. However, the military chiefs accepted the political verdict that "escalation" would have to be a slow process. Under these circumstances, they knew they could give no meaningful estimate of the time needed to achieve victory.

Knowing that it would shock the American public (and perhaps even the Vietnam principals) to say these things bluntly, the Joint Chiefs sought only incremental additions of troops, approximately every six months. Their requests were invariably accompanied by optimistic assertions that victory was almost in sight. Secretary of Defense McNamara made this a condition for supporting their troop requests, and he reported their optimism to Congress and the U.S. public.[9]

To many Americans, these repeated forecasts of light at the end of the tunnel began to sound distinctly dubious. The weekly casualty figures, for Americans alone, rose into the hundreds; and for Vietnamese civilians and military on both sides the weekly

---

[9] Secretary McNamara began to have serious doubts about the administration's policy in mid-1966, after the failure of a highly-touted "strategic-bombing" program. However, he continued to support Johnson's policy publicly until he resigned, more than a year later.

death toll numbered in the thousands. Equally disturbing were signs that President Johnson was determined to avoid peace talks until the military situation became more favorable.

In February 1965, U.N. Secretary-General U Thant implied publicly that the United States had concealed from its people his earlier offer to try to arrange talks with North Vietnam. "As you know," he said, "in times of war and of hostilities the first casualty is truth." In December 1966, the Vietnam principals forgot they had authorized an air attack on Hanoi a few days before U.S. and Democratic Republic of Vietnam (DRV) representatives were scheduled to meet in Warsaw. North Vietnam canceled the meeting. In February 1967, Prime Minister Harold Wilson's mediation effort was nullified by a last-minute change of U.S. peace terms. Because of leaks to the press by frustrated American and foreign officials, such incidents became widely known even before publication of the *Pentagon Papers*.[10]

Support for the administration's policy declined steadily in the news media, universities, Congress, church groups, and business and labor organizations during 1966 and 1967. For the first time in American history, large numbers of middle-class young men avoided the draft—and the morale of U.S. forces in Indochina sank to such a degree that small-scale acts of mutiny became common. In late 1967, Senator Eugene McCarthy announced that he would seek the Democratic presidential nomination on a platform of peace. This was the first major political challenge to President Johnson's leadership from within his own party.

Johnson Changes Course

At the time of the Vietnamese New Year (*Tet*) in January 1968, the Vietnamese Communists launched a surprise offensive against South Vietnam's major towns and cities. Obviously timed

[10] See, for example, David Kraslow and Stuart H. Loory, *The Secret Search for Peace in Vietnam* (New York: Vintage, 1968). The *Pentagon Papers* was a lengthy, heavily documented history of American involvement in Indochina through 1968, compiled at Secretary McNamara's request under the editorship of Leslie Gelb. The most complete version has been published by Grove Press.

to influence the American election campaign, this dramatic assault demolished the Johnson administration's claim that victory was near. Militarily, the Tet offensive backfired, in that many of the best southern Viet Cong units were destroyed, and the Saigon regime's army emerged with new self-confidence. But TV shots of the American embassy under siege and weeks of street fighting in Saigon and Hué convinced most Americans that the end was nowhere in sight.

This erosion of public confidence was reflected in the New Hampshire presidential primary in March. Senator McCarthy, the peace candidate, came within a few hundred votes of defeating President Johnson, whose supporters conducted a well-organized campaign for write-in votes using radio commercials which warned that the Viet Cong were watching New Hampshire. Meanwhile, word had leaked to the press that General West-moreland in Saigon had asked for 210,000 more troops. In fact, the chairman of the Joint Chiefs of staff had urged him to do so to justify calling up the reserves. However, the news seemed to confirm the impression that Communist forces were overrunning South Vietnam. Secretary Rusk spent an uncomfortable few days answering questions before the Senate Foreign Relations Committee on live television.

A week or two later, Johnson met privately with a group of "elder statesmen" (retired cabinet members, generals, and ambassadors) to whom he had looked for reassurance in the past. They told him bluntly that the country no longer believed his war of attrition strategy would bring victory in South Vietnam, except possibly with unlimited application of U.S. military force over an unlimited period of time. This private vote of "no confidence" impressed Johnson far more deeply than the New Hampshire primary, because the "elder states-men" had been given the same briefings Johnson received.

In his memoirs, Johnson says that Dean Rusk's counsel led him to make his dramatic decision to cut back the bombing of North Vietnam and begin peace talks. There is every reason to believe this is so. However, the totally unexpected Tet offensive, like a bolt of lightning, finally revealed the numerous doubters in the administration to each other and turned them to purposeful action.

McNamara had just been replaced as defense secretary by Clark Clifford, one of the most powerful kingmakers in the Democratic party, whose incisive questions soon revealed the woeful inadequacy of administration policy. The New Hampshire primary alerted Clifford, Harriman, and other administration members to the fact that their party would be in deep trouble unless the president changed course. (Few Vietnam principals seem to have paid much attention to domestic political considerations between Johnson's 1964 landslide and the start of the 1968 campaign.)

President Johnson announced a bombing cut-back on April 1, 1968, along with his decision to send 13,000 more troops to Vietnam (instead of the 210,000 requested by the Joint Chiefs of Staff). He also announced that he would not seek re-election, but would devote his remaining year in office to the search for peace.[11] Peace talks between Ambassador Harriman and DRV Politburo member La Duc Tho got under way in Paris in May 1968. Within five months, there was tacit agreement between the two sides to decrease the level of violence in the war and to include representatives of the Saigon regime and Viet Cong in the Paris talks.

Throughout the 1968 election year, the threads of American domestic politics and the Indochina war were constantly intertwined. There was a heightened sense of tragedy and violence throughout the year—including the assassinations of Robert Kennedy and Martin Luther King, continued heavy casualties in Vietnam, racial violence in cities, disruption of academic life, and televised street riots during the Democratic convention in Chicago.

Undoubtedly, Hanoi achieved one of its major aims in the Tet offensive by undermining public confidence in Johnson's policy. It is also likely that Saigon delayed the start of four-party talks in Paris in order to aid Richard Nixon's chances

[11] This decision, which was partly related to his health, may have been reached long before he decided to change his Vietnam policy.

of election. Although Nixon claimed he had a plan to end the war with honor, he refused to reveal any details. Vice-President Humphrey, on the other hand, was encumbered by his association with an unpopular administration. When he spoke out against continued bombing and bloodshed, support for him began to rise in the weekly opinion polls, but the voters on election day opted for a complete change of administration. Thus, in January 1969, a deeply worried American public listened hopefully to their new president promise that an "era of negotiation" would replace the old "era of confrontation."

Suggested Reading

AUSTIN, ANTHONY. *The President's War*. Philadelphia: Lippincott, 1971.

FALL, BERNARD B. *Last Reflections on a War*. Garden City, N.Y.: Doubleday, 1967.

GRAVEL, MIKE (ed.). *The Pentagon Papers, The Defense Department History of United States Decisionmaking in Vietnam*. 4 vols. Boston: Beacon, 1971.

HILSMAN, ROGER. *To Move a Nation: The Politics of Policy-Making in the Administration of John F. Kennedy*. Garden City, N.Y.: Doubleday, 1967.

JOHNSON, LYNDON B. *The Vantage Point*. New York: Holt, Rinehart & Winston, 1971.

KAHIN, GEORGE McT., and JOHN W. LEWIS. *The United States in Vietnam*. New York: Delta, 1967.

OBERDORFER, DON. *Tet!* Garden City, N.Y.: Doubleday, 1971.

POOLE, PETER A. *The United States and Indochina: From FDR to Nixon*. Hinsdale, Ill.: Dryden Press, Holt, Rinehart & Winston, 1973.

SHEEHEN, NEIL, et al. *The Pentagon Papers as Published by the New York Times*. New York: Bantam, 1971.

United States Department of Defense. *United States–Vietnam Relations*. 12 vols. Washington, D.C.: Government Printing Office, 1971.

14

Kissinger and Nixon:
The Policy of Détente

During the five and a half years of Nixon's presidency, he and Henry Kissinger dominated American foreign policy. They sought to create a more stable balance of power by fostering *détente* (a relaxation of tensions) with the Soviet Union and China. They indicated their belief that Soviet leaders in particular, and perhaps also the Chinese, would develop a greater stake in world order, and start behaving accordingly, if the United States fostered a relationship of interdependence with them.

The timing of the Nixon-Kissinger approach was propitious. Sino-Soviet relations had become so bitter by 1969 that the leaders of both Communist powers welcomed détente with America, particularly if the latter were prepared to make most of the concessions. In seeking better relations with the Soviets, the Nixon administration more or less conceded three out of four of Moscow's expressed aims: (1) nuclear parity with the United States, (2) recognition of the status quo in Europe, and (3) diplomatic recognition of East Germany. Neither the Soviets nor the Chinese made any concessions of this magnitude to the United States.[1] However, the shattering of certain cold war myths about

[1] In the communiqué at the end of his 1972 visit to China, President Nixon affirmed that removing all U.S. forces and military installations from Taiwan was the United States's "ultimate objective," and that U.S. troops and military facilities would be progressively withdrawn from Taiwan "as the tension in the area diminishes." The P.R.C. made no visible concession in return. The impact of détente on the U.S. position in Indochina will be discussed later in this chapter.

Communist behavior, which was one of the main by-products of détente, could be cited as a useful gain.

A fourth long-term aim of the Soviets in dealing with the West was to obtain credits to buy Western goods and technology to bolster their sluggish economy. This subject was under serious consideration in Washington during 1974. At the heart of Secretary Kissinger's concept of détente was his belief that the Soviet Union needed trade, credits, and Western technology so badly that it would make major foreign policy concessions in return.[2] Whether or not this proved correct would depend, to some extent, on both sides' skill in bargaining.

However, some Western specialists on the Soviet economy doubted that a high degree of Soviet-American interdependence was likely to develop in the foreseeable future.[3] For a variety of reasons (including bureaucratic red tape and excessive secrecy about technological research), Soviet agriculture and many Soviet industries had long been less efficient than Western agriculture and industry. But the Soviet economy had been improving gradually without receiving large amounts of Western goods, credits, or technology. Thus, while the Soviets could probably modernize and expand their economy more rapidly and painlessly with Western help, they could continue to advance with their own resources if necessary.

The West would be glad to buy oil and timber from the U.S.S.R. but there was no great exportable surplus of such commodities in the Soviet Union. Thus, a large increase in Soviet-American trade would depend on America's willingness and ability to extend long-term credits to Russia.[4] No one

[2] A major statement by Secretary Kissinger on the policy of détente was summarized in the September 20, 1974, New York Times and Washington Post. Among other points, Kissinger repeated his well-known concern about overloading the structure of U.S.-Soviet relations with demands for internal Soviet reforms. He argued that the Soviet Union's international behavior was a more valid area for American pressure.

[3] See, for example, Alec Nove, "Can We Buy Détente?" New York Times Magazine, October 13, 1974, pp. 34ff.

[4] The New York Times, on October 17, 1974, estimated that, during the period 1976–80, from $2.9 billion to $3.1 billion in commercial bank loans and from $0.5 billion to $1.1 billion in Export-Import Bank credits would be available to finance U.S. exports to Russia. In order to finance $9 billion

could possibly say in advance what types of transactions would be good or bad for the United States; each will have to be examined on its merits. For example, will the sale of certain types of machinery only strengthen the Russian economy, or will it also create more jobs and prosperity in a temporarily depressed American industry? Will wheat sales reduce American stockpiles to the point where America's traditional customers cannot be supplied? Questions such as these must be answered before one can say that expanding trade with Russia is or is not in the U.S. interest.

The policy of détente was also criticized because Nixon and Kissinger seemed to neglect relations with America's major allies, the democratic, industrialized powers of Western Europe and Japan. They also paid little attention to the developing nations of Latin America, Asia, Africa, and the Middle East—unless a major crisis forced them to concentrate on one of these areas. Many critics pointed out that dealing with highly centralized totalitarian states was far easier for a "two-man foreign policy establishment" than dealing with free, pluralistic societies.

However, there was far more at stake in dealing with the democratic powers. The main result of several years of high-level contacts with China, for example, was an agreement to resume near-normal diplomatic relations. This was undoubtedly very important, but it seemed quite unnecessary that part of the price paid by the United States should have been a sharp decline in mutual trust and cooperation with Japan. In July 1971, Japanese leaders were placed in an extremely embarrassing position when they received no warning of the sudden reversal of America's China policy.[5] This was the first of the so-called Nixon shocks to U.S.-Japanese relations. It was followed by a 10

---

in exports to the U.S.S.R. over the five-year period (the U.S. government's target figure), $6 billion in credits would be needed. Thus, the shortfall in available credits was between $1.8 billion and $2.4 billion.

[5] Two months later, Japan sided with the United States (after strong American urging) in defending the right of the Taiwan regime to retain a seat in the United Nations. Nevertheless, the U.N. General Assembly voted to expel Taiwan and admit the People's Republic of China's representatives. Kissinger was in Peking at the time, dramatizing the fact that America was far ahead of Japan in normalizing its relations with China.

percent surcharge on American imports, two devaluations of the dollar, and an American soybean embargo. Some Japanese also held the United States indirectly responsible for the Arab oil embargo and oil price increases in 1973–74. The Western European powers, which are much more dependent on Middle Eastern oil than the United States, were also extremely bitter about America's failure to coordinate its strategy with them in dealing with the 1973–74 crisis.

Kissinger's Background

Henry Kissinger accepted the post of national security adviser to Nixon a few weeks after the latter's election in 1968. Before that, he had been a professor at Harvard, had run its prestigious International Seminar, and was highly regarded in the foreign affairs community as a specialist on defense policy. As a consultant to the Eisenhower administration, he had been among the first to advocate the tactical use of nuclear weapons. In 1961, he became a consultant to the Kennedy administration; changing his earlier position, he argued persuasively for a more flexible balance between conventional and nuclear forces. This concept, adopted by the administration, led to greatly increased defense spending, but it also gave the United States a much wider range of choices than nuclear retaliation or retreat from its forward positions.

During the Johnson administration, Kissinger agreed with the premise that America must not accept military defeat in Indochina. But after two visits to South Vietnam, he saw little hope of winning what was essentially a political struggle by military means. Therefore he argued the need for a negotiated settlement. On behalf of the State Department, he went to Paris in 1968 on a secret and unsuccessful mission to get peace talks started with the North Vietnamese.

During the 1960s, Kissinger often said that he considered Nixon unfit to be president; he supported Rockefeller's unsuccessful bid for the Republican nomination in 1968. Yet his desire to be at the center of power was strong, and he showed little hesitancy in accepting the post of national security adviser when Nixon offered it to him. Presidents Kennedy and Johnson had each assigned leading academics (McGeorge Bundy and Walt Rostow) to the post, and these men had made the National Security Council staff the most powerful foreign affairs bureaucracy in Washington (not least because it was kept small). Nixon and Kissinger found that they were in close agreement on many issues; Kissinger's intellect, drive, and skill at bureaucratic maneuver soon made him the president's main adviser and his chief link with the rest of the executive branch on all questions of defense and foreign policy.

From January 1969 to July 1971 (when he returned from his secret first visit to China), Kissinger's work in shaping policy and negotiating with foreign governments was largely hidden from public view. He usually told newsmen that his role was to make certain the president had the information and recommendations he needed from the departments in order to make decisions. He never expressed his own views unless asked by the president to do so, he said. He joked about having a "Dr. Strangelove" image because of his German accent and past writings on nuclear warfare. But this was actually one of the reasons why he did not conduct on-the-record press conferences or briefings until he returned from his second trip to China in October 1971.

Another reason was that no one in the White House wanted to risk having Kissinger upstage President Nixon. Kissinger himself was always careful on this point. He knew that his own power depended entirely on his relationship with the president, and he let nothing jeopardize that relationship. He was particularly careful after an atmosphere of intrigue and suspicion developed in the White House in response to massive public criticism of the May 1970 incursion into Cambodia.

As the Watergate political scandals cut away Nixon's popular support during 1973–74, Kissinger emerged as the main political asset of the administration. He was awarded the Nobel peace prize in 1972 and appointed secretary of state in 1973 (just in time to receive Vice-President Agnew's resignation). On August 6, 1974, when President Nixon's resignation was expected momentarily, the Senate Foreign Relations Committee gave Kissinger a special vote of confidence—in effect, stating that he had told the truth during his confirmation hearings concerning his own involvement in wiretapping and other objectionable procedures, and that he would have its support after Mr. Nixon resigned.

Kissinger and Indochina

When he took office in January 1969, President Nixon evidently believed that the Soviet Union held the key to American withdrawal from Indochina. Kissinger was perhaps less confident than his chief that Moscow had the necessary influence to persuade North Vietnam to grant the United States a face-saving exit. Nevertheless, obtaining Soviet diplomatic support for this purpose became a major aim of the administration; in September 1974, Kissinger made a somewhat qualified claim that détente had aided the Vietnam negotiations:

> The honorable termination of America's direct military involve-ment in Indochina and the substantial lowering of regional con-flict were made possible by many factors. But this achievement would have been much more difficult—if not impossible—in an era of Soviet and Chinese hostility toward the United States.[6]

The link between détente and the Paris agreement of January 1973 can be neither proved nor disproved. However, in my view, the main result of détente with China and the Soviet Union was not that it caused those powers to intercede with Hanoi. The real impact was on American attitudes. Détente removed the whole rationale for American involvement in Indo-china. The visits by Nixon and Kissinger to Peking and Moscow underlined the fact that the United States had far more important concerns than who would rule in South Vietnam. No longer would American leaders have to brood about being blamed by history for "losing" the Vietnam war. A greater victory had been won by daring to close the door firmly on two decades

[6] See the September 20, 1974, *New York Times* and *Washington Post* sum-maries of Kissinger's statement on Soviet-American relations. An analysis of the Paris agreement on Indochina will appear later in this chapter.

of myth-making about China's "aggressive threat" to its neighbors.

Détente was only one of several elements in the Nixon administration's original strategy for disengaging U.S. forces from Vietnam. There was, first of all, the public peace conference in Paris, which sometimes provided hints of the other side's position. Second, there were Kissinger's secret contacts with North Vietnamese officials in Paris, beginning in the summer of 1969.[7] Third, there was the process of "Vietnamization," training and equipping an expanded South Vietnamese Army to replace departing American units. Fourth, there was the "Nixon doctrine," in which the president indicated that the United States would avoid direct involvement in future land wars in Asia by concentrating U.S. support in the countries whose governments had shown themselves capable of surviving without the aid of American ground forces. This "doctrine" seemed in part designed to gain tacit consent from Congress for the continued presence of U.S. air and naval forces in the western Pacific.

During 1969, none of the various "tracks" of U.S. policy produced any signs that Hanoi would agree to terms that would permit a "decent interval" of relative stability in South Vietnam after the last U.S. forces left. According to President Nixon's November 1969 speech, the North Vietnamese adopted an intransigent position, insisting that the United States actually preside over the liquidation of the Thieu regime. Ho Chi Minh's death in 1969 may have caused his heirs to stiffen their demands while they took stock of their situation. "Vietnamization" may also have had the unintended effect of hardening North Vietnam's position. However, the withdrawal of about one-fifth of the American troops from Vietnam and the reduced rate of American casualties (as South Vietnamese troops took over the more dangerous missions) eased pressures in the United States for immediate disengagement.

In May 1970, President Nixon ordered American and South Vietnamese forces to pursue the Vietnamese Communists into Cambodia. He thereby deliberately jeopardized a nation of 7 million people for the sake of the appearance of an orderly

---

[7] These were a continuation of the contacts, noted earlier in this chapter, that he made in 1968 for President Johnson.

U.S. withdrawal from Vietnam. Of those in government who knew Nixon was considering intervention, only Secretary Rogers and a few career State Department officials argued against it. Nixon was apparently stunned by the massive protest his move provoked from almost every element of American society. After the incursion began, and the degree of dissent in America became known, some cabinet members and a large number of congressmen went on record against this widening of the war. The administration responded by a program of illegal surveillance of domestic political "enemies" that was unprecedented in American history.

On June 30, 1970, the day President Nixon set for withdrawing U.S. troops from Cambodia, the Senate passed a resolution forbidding the return of any American forces to that country and any further bombing raids. The Nixon administration generally observed the Senate's restriction on ground operations, but bombing raids were intensified, with the tacit consent of Congress. President Nixon was evidently unwilling to adopt a policy of outright support for General Lon Nol's Phnom Penh government, but he sought and obtained from Congress large appropriations of military and economic aid. Thus the Lon Nol regime, and four or five million people living under its protection, became completely dependent on U.S. support.

In November 1971, President Nixon described the Cambodian situation as the "purest example" of the Nixon doctrine in action. This can only be understood to mean that shifting the war into Cambodia had raised the morale of the South Vietnamese Army (which had long sought U.S. consent to invade Cambodia) and had given President Thieu a breathing space in which to consolidate his authoritarian regime.

Most of the major battles in Cambodia of 1970 and 1971 were fought by the Saigon army and its Vietnamese Communist opponents. However, both Vietnamese sides worked diligently at training the forces of their respective Cambodian allies. When the Vietnamese Communists launched an all-out offensive in South Vietnam in early 1972, most Vietnamese forces left Cambodia. From that time on, the war in Cambodia (in which an estimated 10 percent of the Khmer people had been killed or injured by mid-1974) was largely fought by Cambodian troops. The Lon Nol side was supplied by the United States and the other side by North Vietnam and China.

North Vietnam launched its 1972 Easter offensive against South Vietnam during the interval between Nixon's Peking and Moscow visits. Probably one aim of Hanoi's leaders was to make it difficult for China or Russia to press them for concessions to the United States. They may also have hoped to stimulate anti-war sentiment in the United States during an election year. Rather evidently, neither aim succeeded. President Nixon ordered the mining of Haiphong harbor, and Brezhnev did not even make an issue of it, though it endangered Soviet shipping.

Hanoi's offensive began to lose momentum by early summer, while Saigon's forces showed that they could fight on their own a great deal better than anyone had believed possible. North Vietnam was also experiencing very serious floods. And the two-year transfer of the war to Cambodian territory had enabled Thieu to strengthen his administration. Under these circumstances, the Soviets and Chinese may have helped persuade the North Vietnamese that they had nothing further to gain by delaying an agreement.

Thus, in October 1972, Kissinger and officials of the D.R.V. announced that they had reached an accord. Then unexplained difficulties were raised in Hanoi. President Nixon, who had just been re-elected by a large majority, ordered carpet bombing raids on North Vietnam through the Christmas holidays. (Kissinger was reported to have told friends he opposed this action as being both brutal and unnecessary.) Many governments allied with the United States were appalled and made their views known publicly.

In January 1973, a slightly modified version of the October agreement was signed in Paris. North Vietnam was specifically allowed to keep its forces in the South, and a coalition government was supposed to be formed soon after a cease-fire took effect (if it did). Meanwhile, U.S. prisoners of war would be returned and the last U.S. forces withdrawn. Most observers expected the war would resume immediately following U.S. disengagement, and that was precisely what happened. Although

Congress sharply reduced the aid Nixon requested, the United States continued through 1974 to provide military and economic assistance to South Vietnam and to the Lon Nol government in Cambodia. However, all foreign military aid to Laos (except, apparently, North Vietnam's aid) ceased as a result of the 1974 agreement between the main Lao factions.[8]

Strategic Arms Control

The Nixon administration's first series of strategic arms limitation talks (SALT I) led to a five-year agreement limiting antiballistic missile (ABM) defenses and freezing the level of ballistic missile forces on both sides. Kissinger called this "the essential first step toward a less volatile strategic environment." He pointed out that, if Side A built an extensive ABM system to defend its cities, Side B might conclude that A was preparing a strategy of striking first. (Therefore, the ABMs were to protect A from B's answering blow.) The result would be an accelerating arms race, with each side preparing both offensive and defensive strategies and weapons systems.

Some critics argued that the May 1972 (SALT I) agreement allowed the Soviets more land- and sea-based nuclear launchers than the United States had. Kissinger pointed out that the Soviets had entered the negotiations with several ongoing programs; the United States had very few. The Soviets had more intercontinental ballistic missiles (ICBMs) and they were almost on the point of surpassing the United States in nuclear submarines. The May 1972 agreement put a ceiling on the Soviets' ICBM and submarine-launched missile progams. No American programs were abandoned or curtailed; no restrictions were placed on MIRVs[9] or bombers. Therefore, Kissinger

---

[8] For a more detailed discussion of Nixon administration policy toward Indochina see the author's *The United States and Indochina from FDR to Nixon* (Hinsdale, Illinois: Dryden Press, 1973).

[9] Multiple independently targeted re-entry vehicles. The United States had the lead in these weapons, each of which fired a number of warheads at different targets. It also had the lead in manned bombers. Kissinger reportedly originally opposed developing MIRVs, but he later described them as a necessary bargaining chip.

argued, the SALT I agreement reduced the danger of nuclear war, gave both sides a greater interest in restraint, and laid the basis for further talks.

The Middle East War

When Egypt and Syria attacked Israel in October 1973, Kissinger had been secretary of state for only two weeks. Although it proved impossible for him to completely isolate his mediation effort from U.S. domestic politics, he succeeded in doing so to a surprising degree. If his mediation did not bring peace to the chronically unstable Middle East, he at least managed to persuade Brezhnev that the Soviet Union could not have détente with the United States and also support an Arab war to liquidate Israel.[10] In the course of his mediation, the United States reestablished diplomatic relations with most Arab states for the first time since the 1967 Arab-Israeli war. Thus, American prestige in the Middle East was considerably enhanced, but new problems arose in relations with Europe and Japan.[11]

Egypt and Syria began the war with large stocks of the most modern Soviet tanks, artillery, and antiaircraft missiles; a Soviet airlift kept the Arabs supplied throughout the war. Kissinger's first task was to redress the military balance so that Israel could hold its own (but not enough for Israel to defeat its opponents). He had to overcome vast inertia in the Pentagon, where fear of an oil embargo was uppermost in the minds of senior officials.

With the airlift to Israel finally organized, Kissinger accepted an invitation to confer with Brezhnev in Moscow two weeks after the war began. By this time, Israel had gained the initiative and was pushing toward Damascus on the northern front and toward

[10] For a detailed description of Kissinger's mediation effort, see Marvin Kalb and Bernard Kalb, *Kissinger* (Boston: Little, Brown, 1974), pp. 450–542.

[11] Some governments implied that the American airlift of military aid to Israel was partially responsible for the Arabs' oil embargo. A more serious complaint of the NATO allies was that they were not consulted or given advance warning about the U.S. military alert. Moreover, very slow progress was made in developing a common program on the part of Western industrial powers to cope with the greatly increased price of oil.

Suez in the west. Kissinger's aim in Moscow was to explore ways of ending the war and to salvage the policy of Soviet-American détente. In two days of intensive negotiations, he and Brezhnev agreed on the details of a cease-fire to be followed by direct Israeli-Egyptian talks. The cease-fire would benefit the Arabs, who were now on the defensive; direct talks had been an aim of Israeli foreign policy for many years. President Sadat of Egypt agreed to direct talks with Israel only after Brezhnev promised that Russia would guarantee the cease-fire, alone if necessary. Israeli leaders believed they had no alternative but to accept the plan because of their dependence on U.S. military aid.

While Kissinger was in Moscow, Nixon had fired Archibald Cox, the special prosecutor he had appointed to investigate the Watergate affair. This move led to the resignations of Attorney General Richardson and his deputy. Thus, the Washington Kissinger returned to on October 23 was seething with bitterness, and pressures were growing for Nixon's resignation or impeachment.

On October 24, President Sadat sent an urgent radio appeal to Brezhnev and Nixon requesting a joint Soviet-American peacekeeping force to halt the Israelis, who had trapped the Egyptian III Corps east of Suez and were exploiting their own bridgehead west of the canal. This was followed, later in the evening, by Soviet proposals for a joint Soviet-American peace-keeping force and by a very brusque and forceful message from Brezhnev to Nixon warning that Soviet troops might be sent unilaterally to stop the Israelis. Kissinger advised that a U.S. military alert might be needed to deter the Russians. Nixon concurred in this view and gave Kissinger power to take charge of the U.S. response. If there were any problems, Nixon said he could be reached immediately.

About an hour later, at 11:00 P.M., Kissinger presided at a meeting with five key officials in the White House: Defense Secretary Schlesinger, CIA Director Colby, Admiral Moorer (chairman of the Joint Chiefs of Staff), and White House Special Assistants Haig and Scowcroft. Kissinger told the others of intelligence estimates that the Soviets would probably make some unilateral move in the Middle East, possibly including the dispatch of Soviet airborne units, which had been placed on alert.

At 11:30 P.M., the group decided to order a worldwide alert of U.S. military forces, and Schlesinger issued the necessary orders. Kissinger then drafted a presidential reply to Brezhnev's message, cleared it with Schlesinger, with Haig, and (by phone) with Nixon, who remained upstairs in his quarters. The message warned of the dangerous situation that would result from sending Soviet or American forces to the Middle East during the current crisis, pointed to the higher need to preserve détente, and promised cooperation in U.N. efforts to establish a peace-keeping force composed of nonnuclear powers. Only then did Kissinger inform the British ambassador by phone and the other NATO allies by cable of the U.S. actions.

The following day, Kissinger held a press conference to explain the military alert, which had already become public knowledge. He was bombarded with questions which implied that the alert was designed to distract public attention from Watergate. His reply was

> . . . we are attempting to conduct the foreign policy of the United States with regard for what we owe not just to the electorate but to future generations. And it is a symptom of what is happening to our country that it could even be suggested that the United States would alert its forces for domestic reasons.

Kissinger had also used his October 25 press conference to warn the Russians once more not to send their forces into the Middle East and not to expect the United States to take part in a joint peace-keeping force. He pointed out that this would only "transplant the great-power rivalry to the Middle East" and that it could lead to a nuclear clash. He pointed to the obvious responsibility of the nuclear powers to avoid such a catastrophe. However, he concluded on a more hopeful note:

> We do not consider ourselves in a confrontation with the Soviet Union. We do not believe it necessary at this moment to have a

confrontation. . . . We are not talking of a missile crisis type situation. . . . If the Soviet Union and we can work cooperatively —first, towards establishing the cease-fire, and then towards promoting a durable settlement in the Middle East, then détente will have proved itself.

Almost as soon as Kissinger finished speaking, his words were relayed over the phone to Brezhnev by Soviet U.N. Ambassador Malik; Brezhnev instructed Malik to stop insisting that the nuclear powers take part in a U.N. peace-keeping operation. The Security Council then passed a resolution forming a U.N. emergency force composed of personnel from nonnuclear states.

The U.S. military alert was eased the following day, October 26. That night, President Nixon held a press conference to defend his firing of the special Watergate prosecutor, and he also presented a version of the Middle East crisis that differed considerably from Kissinger's remarks the previous day. Nixon painted a much more menacing picture of the Soviet threat: "We obtained information which led us to believe that the Soviet Union was planning to send a very substantial force into the Mideast—a military force." Nixon also called the events of the preceding two days "the most difficult crisis we had since the Cuban missile crisis of 1962," while Kissinger said there had been no "missile crisis type of situation." Emphasizing his own ability to lead the country in spite of the Watergate scandals, President Nixon said that he had been the "coolest man in the room" while the situation was being dealt with. (In his emotional clash with reporters, he seemed to forget momentarily he had not been in the room.)

The second phase of Kissinger's mediation in the Middle East began with the relatively modest aim of persuading the two sides to present their terms for a settlement. His growing prestige with the Arabs brought him invitations to visit the capitals of Morocco, Tunisia, Egypt, Jordan, and Saudi Arabia. His deputy, Joseph Sisco, visited Jerusalem. Kissinger at first felt it would be a grave mistake to present an "American plan," which both sides would probably attack. Instead, he tried to present "ideas" or "suggested elements" of a settlement. Before long, however, it became evident that the Egyptians (who seemed to hold the key to an agreement) found it easier to consider terms that he offered in his own name, even if these were the same as Israel's terms.

During December and January, Kissinger conducted "shuttle diplomacy" between Israel and Egypt, gradually reducing the area of disagreement between the two parties so that they might disengage their forces on the western front. Kissinger's role as a mediator was accepted by both sides. The agreement that was signed by Prime Minister Golda Meir of Israel and President Anwar Sadat of Egypt on January 18, 1974, opened the way to a similar mediation between Syria and Israel, in which Sadat supported Kissinger; this led to an agreement in May 1974 Kissinger's diplomacy also helped to end the Arab oil embargo, though oil prices remained at much higher levels than before the war.

Transition to the Ford Administration

In August 1974, Richard Nixon resigned the presidency, and former Vice-President Gerald Ford took office. Two of the new President's first decisions were to ask Henry Kissinger to remain as secretary of state and to affirm his support for the policy of détente. A few weeks later, Kissinger outlined the administration's approach to strategic arms control, the key aspect of détente. He listed the U.S. objectives in the following order: (1) to break the momentum of rising levels of armament; (2) to control certain qualitative aspects, particularly MIRVs; (3) to slow the pace of new development of missiles; and (4) ultimately to achieve reduction of force levels.

In pursuing these goals in the SALT talks, the United States would seek a ten-year agreement. This time frame was chosen, Kissinger said, because it was "long enough to cover all current and planned forces but not so long as to invite hedges that would defeat the purposes of an arms control agreement." The main technical problem that Secretary Kissinger foresaw was working out a way of comparing and balancing the capabilities of different weapons systems (for example, U.S. bombers and Soviet ICBMs). The resumed SALT talks would aim at slowing the pace at which both sides deployed new weapons, particularly third generation Soviet ICBMs and submarine-launched missiles and the American B-1 bomber and Trident submarine.[12]

On other major issues, the new administration seemed to stress continuity with President Nixon's foreign policy, though there were changes in matters of detail. For example, both Ford and Kissinger seemed intent on demonstrating to Japan that the United States placed very high value on the Pacific alliance. Thus, President Ford's first state visit abroad while in office was to Japan. Some preliminary steps were also taken, in the fall of 1974, to work out an agreement among the Western industrial powers to assist each other when oil reserves dropped below a certain point. And in his first speech before the United Nations, President Ford intimated that he might seek to force a reduction in world oil prices by using the leverage of America's leading position as a food producer. In vetoing a Congressionally amended foreign aid bill, President Ford also served notice that he would resist pressures in Congress to revise drastically the principles under which U.S. foreign aid had been distributed for the past two decades.

Suggested Reading

BERNSTEIN, CARL, and BOB WOODWARD. *All the President's Men*. New York: Simon & Schuster, 1974.

DORNBERG, JOHN. *Brezhnev: The Masks of Power*. New York: Basic Books, 1974.

GRAUBARD, STEPHEN R. *Kissinger: Portrait of a Mind*. New York: Norton, 1973.

HSIAO, GENE T. (ed.). *Sino-American Détente and Its Policy Implications*. New York: Praeger, 1974.

KALB, MARVIN, and BERNARD KALB. *Kissinger*. Boston: Little, Brown, 1974.

KOHLER, FOY D.; LEON GOURÉ; and MOSE L. HARVEY. *The Soviet Union*

[12] See the summary of Kissinger's statement on Soviet-American relations in the September 20, 1974, *New York Times* and *Washington Post*.

and the October 1973 Middle East War: The Implications for Détente. Washington, D.C.: Center for Advanced International Studies, and University of Miami, 1974.

MORTON, HENRY W., and RUDOLF L. TÖKÉS (eds.). *Soviet Politics and Society in the 1970s.* New York: Free Press, 1974.

OKAZAKI, HISAHIKO. *A Japanese View of Détente.* Lexington, Mass.: Lexington Books (for the Atlantic Council of the U.S.), 1974.

15

Foreign Policy
Problems Today

The last quarter of the twentieth century has brought global economic interdependence. The only major powers that are comparatively isolated from the world economy are the Soviet Union and China. This fact should cause American policy-makers to discard any unrealistic hopes they may have for a concept of world order based mainly on growing trade with the Communist powers. The search for ways to foster détente, particularly through strategic arms control, should by all means continue. However, the United States must give its main attention to the vast problems and opportunities resulting from its extensive economic, social, and political ties with Western Europe, Japan, and the Third World.

Agenda for an Interdependent World

The world's main economic problems tend to be interrelated. The rising costs of oil and other sources of energy and the dwindling of North American grain reserves have accelerated worldwide inflation. The latter problem was already acute before the food and energy crises because of years of reckless spending on armaments by many nations. There are no magic solutions to problems such as these, though solving one may help to ease the rest. A way must be found to recycle the oil producers' huge profits into development that aids poor nations. Many of the least developed countries must also reduce their very high birth rates if they are to have any hope of raising living standards. Until the food deficit countries can expand their production, the United States and other major food producers must be prepared to meet many urgent nutritional needs. The United States, which is also the world's foremost arms merchant, must take the lead in slowing the highly inflationary global arms race. And finally, as the world's richest and most technologically advanced nation, America must strive to promote global cooperation to protect the environment.

This list of world problems seems almost overwhelming. Yet the American people do not stand alone in facing them. Two great achievements, for which America deserves substantial credit —the revival of Western Europe and Japan and the reduction of tensions with Russia and China—have laid the groundwork for a broad-based creative effort to improve the quality of human existence everywhere.

Limits to Détente?

In the preceding chapter, it was predicted that neither the Soviet Union nor China would quickly expand its share of total world trade or begin to participate very actively in solving global economic problems (such as the oil crisis). Neither of the major Communist powers has a large surplus of goods for which there is strong demand on the world market. Moreover, neither has been willing to open its society to broad contact with free nations. If this analysis proves correct, it will force adjustments in current American attitudes about détente.

The most optimistic group of Americans, led by Secretary Kissinger, have believed that Soviet-American trade should be encouraged because economic interdependence would result and this would tend to reduce Soviet-American political friction. A less optimistic group, led by such men as Senator Henry Jackson, has felt that the Soviets were simply taking advantage of new opportunities to trade with the West to strengthen their totalitarian society and increase their worldwide influence at America's expense. This group has concluded that America should force the Soviets to liberalize their society a step at a time in return for Western trade concessions. Finally, a third group of Americans has argued that there is no way for the United States to extract either political or economic advantages from trade with the Soviet Union. This rather pessimistic group believes that détente will end as soon as Moscow and Peking patch up their differences and no longer need to frighten each other by consorting with the United States.

If it is true that the United States cannot "buy" détente because the Soviets and Chinese are unable and unwilling to become interdependent with the West, then plainly the United States should not pin much hope on relations with the Communist powers. The United States lacks the leverage to transform their foreign or domestic policies. If American leaders want the Soviets and Chinese to help promote world peace and stability, they will have to use persuasion, not economic bribes or coercion. It would also make sense to follow normal diplomatic practice and not press for drastic changes in Soviet internal policy, because this can only raise cruelly unrealistic hopes (as Dulles's "liberation" slogan did). It may even cause the Soviets to react by reducing their people's freedom.

However, if Americans cannot realistically hope to transform Soviet or Chinese policy by expanding trade with these countries, this is no reason to predict a return of the cold war. One result of détente has been that Americans have managed to shed some of their misconceptions about the behavior of Communist powers (and Communist leaders may have adopted more realistic attitudes about the West). Both the Soviet and the Chinese leaders have generally been cautious in their dealings with the outside world. They probe continually for openings to expand their influence, and when they find them they move ahead. But when faced with firm resistance, they almost invariably retreat. Meanwhile, there have been signs of very gradual erosion of revolutionary ideological fervor in the Soviet Union and China as one generation replaces another. The worst mistake the West can make in dealing with these two Communist powers is to assume that their interests and ours are identical. But the second worst mistake would be to assume that there is no similarity between Western interests and those of China and Russia.

Foreign Affairs Procedures

Almost every administration in this century has carried out some reorganization of the foreign affairs bureaucracy. Since the start of World War II, the tendency has been to increase the size of traditional foreign affairs agencies, such as the State Department, and to add whole new bureaucracies as well. Yet the more complicated the bureaucratic machinery becomes, the less likely a president is to make use of it. The vast concentration of power in the hands of Presidents Johnson and Nixon seems to have produced a consensus among the American people and Congress that foreign affairs should be brought back into "normal" operating patterns. Three basic procedural changes have been widely discussed, and in my view should be implemented: (1) The number of political appointees in the foreign affairs establishment, both at home and abroad, should be reduced; (2) the size of the official American presence in most countries should also be cut; and (3) the Central Intelligence Agency should be placed under the control of the State Department.

The practice of awarding ambassadorial posts to campaign contributors continued as late as 1974. Hopefully, it will be curbed by legislation enacted that year limiting personal and corporate campaign contributions and permitting the use of public funds to finance presidential campaigns. However, limits still need to be imposed on the practice of appointing political associates of the President to a very wide range of senior positions in the State and Defense departments and other foreign affairs agencies. Not only does this disrupt the conduct of foreign affairs by placing unqualified people in key positions, it also demoralizes able career officials by reducing the number of top positions for which they can compete.

One of the most important and difficult reforms needed is to reduce the size of official American establishments abroad. Even in a small country such as Burma, where there are very few official U.S. programs, as many as about a hundred people have been employed by the American embassy. In countries in which the official American presence runs into the thousands, the conglomeration of agencies, of which the embassy forms only one (not necessarily dominant) element, is usually known as the "U.S. Mission." There are many countries, particularly in the Third World, in which the number of Americans assigned exceeds the number of officials in the entire national government. Wherever regional organizations are being formed and trained local specialists are available, it makes sense to shift from bilateral aid programs (conceived and staffed by Americans) to support of regional development programs, which are planned and staffed by the people of the region.

A third, and related, problem is the independent status of the Central Intelligence Agency. As described in Chapter 11, there was a time in the late 1950s, just after Secretary Dulles's death, when CIA station chiefs tended to wield more power and influence than American ambassadors in many countries. The Kennedy administration tried, with some success, to change this situation after the Bay of Pigs fiasco. However, the CIA is still widely believed to be answerable only to itself, and its agents are considered far too prone to use money and other forms of pressure for ruthless political ends. However deserved or undeserved this reputation, it clearly does not promote confidence in the motives and methods of the U.S. government as a whole.

It would greatly enhance U.S. prestige (and also eliminate some costly duplication of effort) if Congress were to vest the present responsibilities of the director of Central Intelligence in an undersecretary of state and merge the personnel and facilities of the State Department and the CIA. Congress could also direct that cloak-and-dagger operations be funded at a small fraction of their budget over the previous five-year period. This would not, of course, eliminate the need for continuing Congressional oversight in the area of intelligence. But it would help to clear the air and make a fresh start in a period in which there is broad consensus that the nation's intelligence needs have changed drastically since the cold war period.

Suggested Reading

FRANCK, THOMAS M., and EDWARD WEISBAND (eds.). *Secrecy and Foreign Policy*. New York: Oxford University Press, 1974.

FREEMAN, S. DAVID. *Energy: The New Era.* New York: Walker (for the Twentieth Century Fund), 1974.

HENDERSON, GREGORY; RICHARD NED LEBOW; JOHN G. STOESSINGER; et al. *Divided Nations in a Divided World.* New York: McKay, 1974.

HOWE, JAMES W., et al. *The U.S. and the Developing World: Agenda for Action.* New York: Praeger (for the Overseas Development Council), 1974.

KEMP, GEOFFREY; ROBERT L. PFALTZGRAFF, JR.; and URI RA'ANAN. *The Superpowers in a Multinuclear World.* Lexington, Mass.: Lexington Books, 1974.

KUZNETS, SIMON. *Population, Capital, and Growth: Selected Essays.* New York: Norton, 1973.

MCDERMOTT, GEOFFREY. *The New Diplomacy and Its Apparatus.* London: Plume Press/Ward Lock, 1973.

MARCHETTI, VICTOR, and JOHN D. MARKS. *The CIA and the Cult of Intelligence.* New York: Knopf, 1974.

MORLEY, JAMES WILLIAM (ed.). *Prologue of the Future: The United States and Japan in the Postindustrial Age.* Lexington, Mass.: Lexington Books, 1974.

Stockholm International Peace Research Institute. *Nuclear Proliferation Problems.* Cambridge, Mass.: MIT Press, 1974.

Index

Acheson, Dean, 136, 144–46, 150–55, 162–74, 178, 203

Adams, Henry, 6, 7, 8

Adenauer, Konrad, 192–93, 216

air war, U.S., in Indochina, 228, 230–34, 242–43

Allison, John M., 169–70

Anglo-Japanese alliance (*1902*), 28, 74, 75

Arcadia summit (*1942*), 105–6

Argentina summit (*1941*), 100

Arms Control and Disarmament Agency (ACDA), 216*n.*

Atlantic Charter, 101

atomic weapons; *see* nuclear and atomic weapons

Baghdad Pact, 196–97

Baruch, Bernard, 145

Berlin crises, 136, 157, 205–6

Bevin, Ernest, 155

Bidault, Georges, 155

Bliss, Tasker, 60–61

blockade, naval, 46–50, 210–12

Bowles, Chester, 203

Boxer Rebellion, 17–19

Brezhnev, Leonid, 243, 245–48

Bryan, William Jennings, 41, 43, 45, 48–49, 72

Bulgaria, 125, 145

Bundy, McGeorge, 225

Bundy, William, 225, 226*n.*, 229

Byrnes, James F., 141–43, 145–46, 148

Cairo summit (*1943*), 114–15

Cambodia, U.S. intervention in, 241–44

Central Intelligence Agency (CIA), 199, 204–5, 208–9, 214, 255–56

Chamberlain, Neville, 95

Chiang Kai-shek, 92–93, 112–14, 129–31, 146–47, 161–63, 184, 187

China: early U.S. relations with, 14–19; U.S. aid to, 112–13; U.S. policy toward, 112–15, 136–37, 160–78, 217; U.S. mediation in, 113, 146–47; Yalta agreement on, 129–31; White Paper on, 162–64

China bloc in U.S. Congress, 146–47, 160–67, 185

Chou En-lai, 174, 186

Churchill, Winston S.: at wartime summit conferences, 101, 105–11, 120, 124–32; and Morgenthau Plan, 118, 127; "iron curtain" speech by, 149; on Indochina, 186; on EDC, 189

Clemenceau, Georges, 51, 56, 63

Cleveland, Grover, 6, 8, 26

Clifford, Clark, 153, 233

Colombia, 24–25

Combined Chiefs of Staff, 106

containment policy, 136–37, 148–50, 164–78, 180–83

Coolidge, Calvin, 76–77, 79, 83

Cuba: and Spanish-American War, 8–11; Bay of Pigs invasion of, 204–5; and *1962* missile crisis, 207–14

Czechoslovakia and Soviet Union, 133, 147, 155, 157

de Gaulle, Charles, 116
Deane, John, 139
Defense Department, U.S., 199, 204–5, 209–14, 245–47
Democratic Party and foreign affairs, 6, 41, 46, 60, 66–69, 136–37, 160–72, 180–85, 233–34
depression, worldwide, 79–80
destroyers-for-bases deal, 98
détente, U.S.-Soviet, 190–99, 214–17, 235–36, 240–41, 244–50, 252–54
Dien Bien Phu, 185
diplomatic recognition: Wilson's criteria for, 43, 65; Jefferson's formula for, 164n.; Acheson's views on, 165
dollar diplomacy, 35–37
Dominican Republic, 26–27, 83
Dulles, Allen, 205
Dulles, John Foster, 150, 169–72, 180–83, 187–99, 221–22

Eden, Anthony, 123, 186, 189–90, 192, 194
Egypt, 196–98, 245–49
Eisenhower, Dwight D., 121–22, 136–37, 180–86, 192–95, 199
energy crisis, 245, 249–50, 252–53
Ethiopia, 89–90
European Advisory Commission, 117
European Defense Community (EDC), 187–90
Executive Committee (ExCom), 209
extraterritoriality, U.S., in China, 15n., 114

Finland, 133, 145
Fomin, Alexander, 212–13
food crisis, 250, 252–53
Ford, Gerald, 249–50
Formosa; see China; Taiwan, U.S. protection of
France: wartime relations of, with United States, 115–16; Indochina policy of, 185–86, 220–21; Middle East policy of, 196–98
Franco, Francisco, 91

Geneva agreements on Laos (1962), 223

Geneva conferences (1954), 185–86; (1955), 192–95
Germany (1898–1913), 23, 26, 28–32, 40–41; (1914–19), 44–52, 54–60, 63–65; (1920–32), 71, 79–80; (1933–41), 84, 86–91, 94–103; (1942–45), 108–12, 116–18, 120–29, 133–34; (1946–49), 147–48, 156–57; (1950–74), 187–90, 192–96, 205–6
Goldwater, Barry, 227–28
good neighbor policy, 83–84
Great Britain (1900–1920), 23–24, 45–52, 58–65; (1921–35), 74–78, 82; (1936–41), 88–92, 95–99, 101–2; (1942–45), 105–18, 120–34; (1946–48), 151, 155, 157–58; (1949–60), 177, 180–81, 185–90, 192, 194, 196–98; (1961–74), 215–16, 231, 247
Greece, 124–26; U.S. aid to, 150–53
Grew, Joseph, 83, 92, 99, 142–43
Grey, Edward, 50, 51
Guam, U.S. annexation of, 10

Haig, Alexander, 246–47
Harding, Warren, 83
Harriman, W. Averell, 124, 139–42, 155, 202–4, 216, 223, 233
Hawaii, U.S. annexation of, 4, 6, 10
Hay, John, 6, 7, 8, 13, 15–19, 23–24, 30n., 32
Hilsman, Roger, 207, 225
Hippisley, Alfred, 16
Hiroshima, 143–44
Hitler, Adolf, 87–91, 94–96, 102
Ho Chi Minh, 185, 241
Hoover, Herbert, 77–78, 82, 166, 173
House, Edward M., 42, 45–46, 49–51, 59, 60, 61, 63
Hughes, Charles Evans, 71, 74–76
Hull, Cordell, 84, 99–100, 116–18, 123, 124n.
Humphrey, Hubert H., 233–34
Hungary, 125, 145, 147
Hurley, Patrick, 163n.

Indochina, war casualties in, 230–32, 241–43
inflation, 250, 252–53
Inquiry, The, 42, 61–62
Iran, 150

isolationism, U.S., 3–5, 20, 65–69, 86, 88–92, 95, 98, 102
Israel, 196–98, 245–49
Italy, 64, 121–22, 125–26, 133–34, 145

Japan (*1898–1908*), 18–19, 28–31, 33–35; (*1909–30*), 37, 57–58, 64, 71–78; (*1931–45*), 81–83, 92–94, 97, 99–103, 111–15, 118–19, 129–31; (*1946–74*), 160, 167–72, 180n., 237–38, 250, 252–53
Johnson, Lyndon B., 136–37, 225–33
Joint Chiefs of Staff, U.S., 106, 186, 211, 225, 230

Kattenburg, Paul, 224
Kellogg, Frank B., 71, 77
Kellogg-Briand Pact (*1928*), 71, 77, 82, 96
Kennan, George F., 139–40, 145–46, 148–49, 151, 153, 154, 158, 168n., 190
Kennedy, John F., 136–37, 199, 201–17, 223–25
Kennedy, Robert F., 209, 211, 213, 233
Khrushchev, Nikita, 190–99, 201–17
Kissinger, Henry A., 137, 235–50
Korea, Republic of (South), U.S. policy toward, 167–68, 172–77

Lansing, Robert, 41, 45, 47–49, 52, 60–61, 72–73, 75, 180n.
Laos, 199, 205, 222, 223
League of Nations, 51, 54, 62–69, 88–90
Leahy, William D., 116, 119
Lend-Lease Act, 98–99
Lenin, Nikolai, 57
liberation of Eastern Europe, 180–83
Lilienthal, David E., 144–45
Lincoln Brigade, 91
Litvinov, Maxim, 95
Lloyd George, David, 51, 56, 63, 65
Lodge, Henry Cabot, 6–8, 10, 14, 19, 24, 56, 61, 67–69
Lusitania, 48

MacArthur, Douglas, 147, 165–66, 168–69, 172, 174–76

McCarthy, Eugene, 231–32
McCarthy, Joseph, 163
McCloy, John J., 144n.
McKinley, William, 7–15, 19, 21
Macmillan, Harold, 215
McNamara, Robert, 223, 225, 230, 233
Mahan, Alfred Thayer, 5, 6, 19, 23
Maine, U.S.S., 9
Manchurian crisis (*1931–32*), 81–83
Mao Tse-tung, 136, 162–63
Marshall, George C., 106, 142, 146–48, 151–55, 161–62
Marshall Plan, 154–58
massive retaliation, 181–83
Matsu, 186–87
Meir, Golda, 249
Molotov, Vyacheslav M., 95–96, 109, 123, 140–41, 155, 186
Monroe Doctrine, Theodore Roosevelt's "corollary" of, 26–28, 44, 83–84
Morgenthau, Henry, 117–18, 127
Moscow foreign ministers' conference (*1943*), 114, 117
Mussolini, Benito, 87, 89–91, 95, 121

Nagasaki, 143–44
Nasser, Gamal Abdel, 196–98
National Security Council (NSC), U.S., 204, 239
Navy, U.S., 5, 6, 35, 50, 55, 77, 83, 173, 250
neutral rights, U.S. policy on, 44–52, 91–94, 96–103
neutralism in Third World, U.S. response to, 197, 202
Neutrality Acts (*1935–39*), 86, 88–92, 102
New Hampshire, *1968* presidential primary in, 232
Ngo Dinh Diem, 223–25
Nicaragua, 24, 83–84
Nitze, Paul, 168n.
Nixon, Richard M., 137, 201–2, 233–35, 237–42, 246–50
Nixon Doctrine, 241–42
North Atlantic Treaty Organization (NATO), 157–58, 187–90

nuclear and atomic weapons, 143–45, 184, 207–17, 235, 238, 244–45, 249–50
nuclear test ban treaty (1963), 214–17

oil embargo (1973–74), 245, 249
Okinawa, 184
open door policy, 13–19, 73, 75, 81–83
Oppenheimer, J. Robert, 144n.
Organization of American States (OAS), 210–12

Page, Walter Hines, 41, 45
Panama Cañal, 23–26
Panay, U.S.S., 93–94
Paris peace talks (1968–73), 233–34, 238, 241, 243
Pearl Harbor, 103
Pentagon Papers, 231, 234
Pétain, Henri, 116
Philippines, U.S. annexation of, 8–14, 19
Platt amendment, 28
Poland, 65, 96, 120, 123–25, 133–35, 141, 155, 157
Potsdam conference (1945), 143
prisoners of war: North Korean, in South Korea, 184; U.S., in Indochina, 243
Puerto Rico, U.S. annexation of, 10

Quemoy, 186–87

recognition; see diplomatic recognition
reparations, German, 59, 63, 79–80, 111, 127, 128, 129, 147–48
Republican Party and foreign affairs, 6–8, 11–13, 21, 60, 61, 66–69, 71, 136–37, 150, 152, 160–72, 180–85, 234, 238–40, 249–50
Rhee, Syngman, 184–85
Richardson, Elliot, 246
Ridgway, Matthew, 176
Robertston, Walter S., 184–85
Rockefeller, Nelson, 194n., 238
Rockhill, William, 16–17, 19
Roosevelt, Franklin D., 83, 84, 86–135, 139–41

Roosevelt, Theodore, 6–10, 21–35, 37, 44, 60, 83–84
Root, Elihu, 23, 28, 32, 34
Rostow, Walt W., 225
Rumania, 125, 145
Rusk, Dean, 173, 203, 225, 229, 232

Sadat, Anwar, 246, 249
Santo Domingo; see Dominican Republic
Scali, John, 212
Schlesinger, James R., 246–47
Senate Foreign Relations Committee, 77, 95, 232, 239–40
Shidehara, Kijuro, 76, 83
Sino-Japanese War (1937–45), 92–94
Sino-Soviet relations, 191–92, 206n., 214–15, 235
Sisco, Joseph, 248
Smith, Walter Bedell, 186
social Darwinism, 5
Southeast Asia Treaty Organization (SEATO), 189, 222
Soviet Union: and Poland, 120, 123–25; and Germany, 126–29; and Czechoslovakia, 133, 147, 155, 157; Middle Eastern policy of, 196–98; economic relations of, with U.S., 236–37, and China, see Sino-Soviet relations
Spanish-American War, 8–14
Spring-Rice, Cecil, 6, 23
Sputnik (1957), 208
Stalin, Joseph: and World War II, 106–8, 110–12, 120–35; and Franklin Roosevelt, 120–35; and origins of cold war, 134–35; on "inevitable" war with capitalism, 149
State Department, U.S., 42, 92, 117–19, 151–55, 161–66, 181, 199, 202–5, 207, 209, 212, 214, 226, 255–56
Sternberg, Speck von, 23, 26
Stevenson, Adlai, 203, 212
Stilwell, Joseph, 113
Stimson, Henry L., 71, 77–78, 82–83, 107, 109, 140n., 142–44
Strategic Arms Limitation Talks (SALT), 244–45, 249–50
submarine warfare, 47–52, 59

Suez crisis (*1956*), 196–98
Syria, 245, 249

Taft, Robert, 173, 182–83
Taft, William H.: and agreement with Katsura, 33; and Theodore Roosevelt, 35, 37; and dollar diplomacy, 35–37
Taiwan, U.S. protection of, 165–67, 173–75, 184, 186–87, 235n.
Taylor, Maxwell, 223, 228
Teheran summit (*1943*), 115, 122–24
Teller amendment, 9
Tet offensive (*1968*), 231–33
Thant, U, 212, 231
Tonkin Gulf incident (*1964*), 227–29
Tripartite Pact (*1940*), 99
Trotsky, Leon, 56, 57
Truman, Harry S., 134–36, 140–46, 151–58, 160–63, 166–67, 170, 172–78, 220–21
Truman Doctrine, 153–54
Turkey, U.S. aid to, 150–53

U-2 spy planes, 201, 208–9, 213
unconditional surrender, 110–12, 143
United Nations, 114, 131–32, 140, 142, 145, 173n., 174, 176–77, 184, 210–12, 237n., 250

Vandenberg, Arthur, 150, 152, 157–58
Versailles peace conference (*1919*), 61–65
Versailles treaty, 64–69, 90, 111
Vienna summit meeting (*1961*), 201, 205–6
Vietnam principals, 225–27, 229–31
Vietnamization, 241–43
Vishinsky, Andrei, 122

Washington Naval Conference (*1921–22*), 74–76
Watergate scandal, 239, 242, 246–48
Western European Union (WEU), 187–90
Westmoreland, William, 232
White, Henry, 32, 60–61
Williams, G. Mennen, 203
Wilson, Harold, 231
Wilson, Woodrow, 22, 39–69

Yalta conference (*1945*): European questions at, 124–29; Asian questions at, 129–31; United Nations discussed at, 131–32; and Declaration on Liberated Europe, 133
Yoshida, Shigeru, 168, 171–72
Yugoslavia, 64, 125–26